TITANS & OTHERS

TITANS & OTHERS

The Rt Hon Malcolm MacDonald

COLLINS
ST JAMES'S PLACE
LONDON

William Collins Sons & Co Ltd
London · Glasgow · Sydney · Auckland
Toronto · Johannesburg

First published 1972

ISBN 0 00 221835 1

Set in Monotype Imprint
Made and Printed in Great Britain by
William Collins Sons & Co Ltd Glasgow

Contents

1 *Introduction* *page* 9
2 Ramsay MacDonald 13
3 Eamon De Valera 55
4 Winston Churchill 89
5 Achmad Sukarno 131
6 Prince Sihanouk 159
7 Jawaharlal Nehru 203
8 Jomo Kenyatta 239

Illustrations

Ramsay MacDonald	*Facing page* 13
Eamon De Valera	55
Winston Churchill	89
Achmad Sukarno (photo by John Stevens)	131
Prince Sihanouk	159
Jawaharlal Nehru	203
Jomo Kenyatta	239

Acknowledgments

I have drawn on two articles that I wrote for *The Observer* some years ago in my chapter about Ramsay MacDonald, on passages from my book *Angkor* (published by Jonathan Cape) in the chapter on Prince Sihanouk, and on a few paragraphs in my book *People and Places* (published by William Collins) in the chapter on Jawaharlal Nehru. For this I must express my thanks to the publishers.

I am particularly grateful to my friend Philip Ziegler for helping to curb my tendency towards verbosity.

To Audrey, with love

Introduction

ONE of the great privileges I have enjoyed is knowing fairly well a number of distinguished people in different fields of activity in various countries round the world. They displayed their high talents and asserted their often fascinating personalities as statesmen, men and women of letters, artists, theatrical stars, business tycoons, diplomats, or other interesting types. Some of them will live in history long after they are dead, almost as vividly as in their own lifetimes.

Among them I got to know certain grand public personages with whom I was associated for a while here or there in politics, diplomacy or government. A few of these were Titanic figures, and they especially will be remembered. Those of us who became familiar with them should record our memories in order to help make lively, accurate and complete the fuller pen portraits which will in due course be presented to posterity. In the following pages I therefore offer essays on several such individuals. I make no attempt to describe their whole lives with all the important details set down in proper perspective, or to pronounce a balanced appraisal of their over-all qualities. Those comprehensive appreciations will be composed by truly scholarly professional biographers – one of whose number I do not pretend to be. I merely write my recollections of periods and episodes in their lives when I was acquainted with them, and gained intimate glimpses of them at work and sometimes at play. Occasionally this involves describing policies which I myself pursued in co-operation with them. My comments on their characters and achievements spring from those scraps of experience. Naturally they reflect my personal impressions, with which other knowledgeable critics may sometimes disagree – for my judgments are inevitably influenced by my own viewpoints and prejudices, which have the frailties typical of any human being.

I should have liked to add to the company parading through this volume some other equally worthy statesmen, such as one of the great contemporary Chinese leaders; but in their cases it would be premature or inexpedient to present now a similar sketch. They can wait. The seven principals who do appear in these pages are a Scot, an Irishman, an Englishman, an Indonesian, a Cambodian, an Indian and a Kenyan. Incidentally, the fact that the skin hues of these great men ran the whole gamut from white through various shades of brown to black illustrates the most important lesson that I have learned during my decades of work among many different peoples scattered across the five continents and the seven seas – that men of all races are endowed with comparable abilities, sharing similar strengths and weaknesses, regardless of the colours of their skins. They are all brothers belonging to different ethnic branches of the same great family – the human family. Until that simple, vitally significant fact is much more widely recognised than it is today, many difficult inter-racial problems will endanger the peace, prosperity and happiness of Mankind.

Ramsay MacDonald

. . . his handsome appearance, richly melodious voice and compelling eloquence at public meetings.'

Ramsay MacDonald in conversation 'with his good friend Einstein.'

WHEN James Ramsay MacDonald died in 1937 he had a multitude of private friends, but few political allies and no public champions. The Labour leaders were naturally alienated from him when he formed the National Government in 1931, and neither the Conservative nor the Liberal chiefs felt any close accord with him because he would not join either of their Parliamentary teams after his expulsion from the Labour Party. He had no desire to be a member of any political organisation other than the Labour movement, since he always stayed faithful to his principles and remained a socialist to his dying day.

As a result of this political loneliness few commentators were interested in singing his praises at the time of his death. On the contrary, persisting Labour Party hostility made its leaders deliberately belittle his achievements, whilst the Tories' and Liberals' lack of sympathy with him caused their spokesmen to be half-hearted in their tributes. Nor have the prejudices of that period yet dissolved sufficiently to enable later observers to appreciate him at his true worth. The dusts of the various vehement political controversies which some of his actions stirred up have still hardly settled; unfortunately an authoritative biography of him based on his private papers as well as official documents has been delayed; and so a clear view of his real stature in the history of modern Britain is not at present possible.

Moreover, unprejudiced people's most recent memories of him when he died concerned his acts and speeches during his last few years, when his powers were seriously waning. His activities then were tamed not only by the tiredness of an elderly man worn out by decades of unusually energetic striving, but also by the persistent sadness that affected him ever after he felt it his duty to break with the Labour movement, to which he had devoted all his great creative abilities, passion and faith. For example, his previous eloquent and persuasive oratory had deteriorated into somewhat vague dissertations betraying old age. Again, his earlier aptitude for reaching firm decisions on problems was withering. Therefore many people had never known, and others had partly forgotten, his former fine qualities as a political leader; and critics were too apt to judge him by the defects of his declining years. This was to some extent inevitable, but unjust. It would be as unfair to assess another contemporary giant, Jawaharlal Nehru, by his performances during his last period of broken health and eroded capacities. Unlike most elder statesmen, both those men remained in high office long after their prime, and indeed until almost the moment of their deaths. Circumstances did not seem to permit them to retire to more leisurely positions where hectic governmental preoccupations would not tax unduly their dwindling energies, and their wisdom could express itself just now and then in sagacious counsel to their fellow men.

So MacDonald's remarkable, and in some ways almost unique, importance in the story of Britain during the first half of the present century has hitherto been under-estimated. Observers have been so concerned with the last six years of his life that they tended to ignore its previous sixty-five. This error is now beginning to be corrected, for a number of recent books by detached scholars on various aspects of affairs between 1900 and 1937 have accorded considerable, and in some cases surprised, praise to the parts he played in them. His resurrection as one of Britain's most significant statesmen in the twentieth century has begun.

*

I was one of his sons, so readers will no doubt bear in mind that I may be partially prejudiced by filial affection. But few people will deny that he was in many ways an attractive, heroic and brilliant figure. His career was a remarkable mixture of the orthodox and the unorthodox, with every now and then an astonishing element of the unexpected.

The first unorthodox event in his life occurred at its very start, when he was born. He was a love child – an illegitimate baby. His mother was a poor, unmarried girl. She was also pretty and intelligent; but after his birth she refused many suitors, and never did marry. I remember her well as she appeared more than forty years later when my brothers, sisters and I used to spend our summer holidays with her in her cottage in northern Scotland. She had then grown into a handsome, grey-haired old spinster in her sixties who was the most respected and popular inhabitant of the small fishing burgh called Lossiemouth, where her child had been born. And she was still known to all her neighbours as Miss Annie Ramsay – although her son had by then become the famous Member of Parliament at Westminster, James Ramsay MacDonald. 'Annie Ramsay' she remained to her dying day in 1910 – independent, gentle, witty and proud.

I do not know the story of her tragic romance, but I should not be surprised if a tale told me long afterwards by one of her fishwife friends was near the truth. Annie was a servant girl in a farmhouse in the countryside near Lossiemouth, and she fell in love with a ploughman named MacDonald. In due course they became engaged, and the banns of their marriage were about to be published in the local kirk – when they had an unhappy quarrel. She told him in no uncertain terms that their betrothal was cancelled, and that she would not become his wife.

He was astonished. 'But you're going to be the mither o' my bairn,' he said.

She replied that she was well aware of the fact, but that it made no difference.

She refused to change her mind, and went to live with her widowed mother in a cottage beside the Old Seatown in Lossiemouth. When her son was born he was christened James, and brought up by the two devoted women. Later he retained both his mother's and his father's surnames.

A different explanation of Annie's separation from her lover was given me later by another of her early acquaintances. This account stated that her mother objected to the proposed marriage because Annie's father (then dead) had been a baker, which gave him and his family a superior social position to that of a mere farm labourer; and that on this account she refused to consent to the proposed union. Annie could not defy her strong-willed parent, but remained in love with the ploughman in spite of their prompt parting, and afterwards refused all other proposals of marriage. I do not know which story is the more correct. The truth could be a mixture of the two.

This is not the place to write of MacDonald's early life – how as a child he walked miles to school every day, how he earned his first money picking potatoes during holidays, and how some years later the perceptive dominie in his classroom recognised him as a particularly promising student, and promoted him to being a pupil-teacher at a salary of seven pounds, ten shillings a year. . . . It is typical of the humble beginnings of many famous Scotsmen; and in due course he followed the example of similar ambitious young compatriots, and travelled the road south to England.

*

Another rather unorthodox event in his life was his marriage a dozen years later to a young lady born of a very different social class from his own. A daughter of an impeccably respectable, well-to-do and quite distinguished pair of Victorian worthies living in the fashionable West End of London, her maiden name was Margaret Ethel Gladstone. Her father was an eminent Fellow of the Royal Institution, her mother was closely related to the famous scientist Lord Kelvin, and the family were distantly connected with the Grand Old Man, William Ewart Gladstone. Nothing could be more proper than all that.

Margaret was of rather saintly and yet practical disposition, and in her late 'teens and early twenties did a lot of charitable work in various parts of London. In its course she came in touch with adherents of the Socialist movement, whose pioneers were then commencing their political campaigning in Britain. Attracted by its doctrine, she attended some of their meetings, and soon afterwards fell under the spell of the fine oratory and handsome looks of a youthful Scots propagandist for their cause called James Ramsay MacDonald. They met, and a deep affection grew between them. When she broke the news of her love for him to members of her family, many of them disapproved, especially as one fact touching his humble origin was in those days unmentionable in polite society. But her widowed father met the young man, liked him, and with great good sense agreed to the match in spite of his poverty, his radicalism and his bastardy.

They married in 1896, and for the next fifteen years lived in ideal happiness together, perfect partners not only in their private lives but also in their public activities – for she became the most influential and beloved leader of the women's organisation in the Labour movement, whilst he was a principal creator of its political party. Both by nature extremely hard workers, they dedicated themselves with enthusiasm to the promotion of better conditions of life for the masses of British workers.

*

I have many happy memories of our family life in their London home during my childhood. We lived in a flat at 3 Lincoln's Inn Fields, a rather modest apartment consisting of a living room, a study, three bedrooms and a kitchen, but no bathroom. We bathed in water poured from jugs into a tin tub on a bedroom floor, and our W.C. was situated on a higher landing, where other people in the building shared its use.

The tall bow windows of our sitting- and dining-room overlooked the trees, lawns and walks of the pleasant, spacious public garden which is the central feature of Lincoln's Inn Fields. The roadway encircling it was cobbled, and when a horse-drawn hansom-cab or open landau trotted into the precincts, their hooves and wheels made a noisy clatter on the stones. I can still hear that sound echoing nostalgically in my ears. Those vehicles were the customary means of private transport in London at the time. Only occasionally did a primitive motor-car appear, progressing slowly with much honking of its trumpet-like horn. Along neighbouring Kingsway horse-buses were the means of public travel. I liked to sit on a high front seat on the open-air upper deck of one of them, watching the driver manipulating his lengthy reins and flicking his whip to guide the pair of steeds.

Before falling asleep on summer evenings I enjoyed lying in bed listening to a military band in the Fields play the popular tunes of the day. Occasionally I crept out of bed to peep at the men and women dressed in prim Edwardian fashion strolling through the park. When the sun set men came with tall, torch-like implements to light the street lamps, which all burned gas flames.

My brothers, sisters and I (six of us by 1910) were brought up in somewhat strict Victorian style. We could not have been blessed with more affectionate parents, but they did not express their love for us in a lot of hugs and kisses and sentimental chatter. They talked instructive common sense to us, discussed helpfully our childish interests, and disciplined us with kindly but unfaltering firmness. However, they were both so constantly busy with their public work that much of the time we youngsters were left in charge of the domestic staff, consisting of a squint-eyed maidservant called Ada and a grey-haired, black-bonneted charlady named Mrs Gurling. They arrived early each morning and disappeared again in the late afternoons. Our parents taught us to have no sense of class distinction, and to be equal friends with people in all walks of life. Often we enjoyed the treat of going for supper with Mrs Gurling, her husband and their son Johnnie (who was about the same age as ourselves) in their garret in a working-class district, where we guzzled fish-and-chips picked from newspaper wrappings and winkles gouged from their boiled shells. No banquet that I have tasted since has given me more pleasure than those feasts.

When we reached an age to go to a kindergarten school we walked or bussed to it by ourselves. Our mother and father wished us to grow up with a sense of self-reliant independence, not seeking to impose ideas or customs on us against our wills. Nevertheless, their opinions on social, ethical and other matters of course greatly influenced our thoughts.

At Lincoln's Inn Fields they introduced us incidentally into the atmosphere of politics. They were extremely hospitable, their door being always open to friends, acquaintances and strangers. And regularly every few weeks they gave an evening 'At Home' in our flat to a crowd of guests, including many political and other public figures of the day. Prominent among them were men and women – eminent and humble alike – who were pioneer leaders or followers in the newly emerging socialist movement in Britain. We small children were never banished from the rooms on those occasions, but on the contrary helped to hand round food and drinks to the noisy, earnestly conversing company almost as close packed as sardines in a tin. So we became juvenile friends of many great personalities. Among them quite often were distinguished socialist leaders from abroad, for whenever those celebrities came to England they visited our parents for long discussions. So we youngsters became familiar with historic characters such as Jean Jaurès of France, Vandervelde of Belgium, Bebel of Germany and kindred spirits from all over Europe and beyond.

Nor did such visitors arrive only for sociable gatherings. Frequently groups of them came for business talks with our parents throughout mornings or afternoons. Indeed, when the Labour Representation Committee – the precursor of the Labour Party – was first formed in 1900 it could not afford an office of its own, and the study in our flat became its headquarters. Its meetings were held in our sitting-room. Again, we children were not dismissed from sight during those conferences: our mother would lay her latest infant on cushions on the floor at her side so as to keep a maternal eye on it throughout the meeting, and the rest of us were permitted to sit elsewhere in the room reading books, scribbling exercises or pursuing other silent occupations. As one attender at those gatherings wrote later, our flat was 'always full of blue-books and babies, pamphlets and pinafores'.

In those early days my father expressed his political beliefs not only in his talk but also in his dress. He always wore a flamboyant red tie. My mother was as convinced, quietly passionate and hard working a socialist as he, and one of the last acts of her all too short life was the founding, with a group of half-a-dozen like-minded females, of the Women's Labour League, which did an immense amount to spread their political message among working-class housewives. Nor did she champion only the political side of feminine causes, giving ceaseless active help also to various campaigns for the proper treatment of women in the nation's social and industrial life. She joined in the struggle to win women the vote in Parliamentary elections, although she never became a militant suffragette, disapproving of violent means of achieving aims. She believed in peaceful, constitutional methods of agitation. My first recollection of myself taking a part in politics was when, at about the age of five, I marched at her side through the streets of London in a procession carrying banners demanding 'Votes for Women'.

In 1906 my father was elected a Member of Parliament, and his and my mother's political activities took on new dimensions. The need for him to attend the House of Commons most evenings deprived them of much time which they used to spend together, and their great devotion to each other made them wish to escape periodically from the hurly-burly of public life in London to the quiet of a home where they could enjoy private, if none-the-less busy companionship together. This was impossible in our constantly invaded flat at Lincoln's Inn Fields; so they rented a cottage in the then quiet village of Chesham Bois in Buckinghamshire, and most Friday afternoons we all went there to spend a family week-end. During the next two days we looked after ourselves, my father making the Scots porridge for our breakfasts, and Mother cooking the other simple meals.

Always they had lots of routine political work to complete before returning to London on the Sunday evening, but they made leisure to be with us children. Each afternoon they took us for walks through the countryside, listening to our chatter as we strolled beside them, asking us questions about our lives in the previous week, and joining in the fun of our play-acting as Red Indians, pirates, gnomes and other such romantic characters. These games were inspired by tales in story books which our father read us each evening before we went to bed during those week-ends, with our mother sitting sewing at his side. Over the years he introduced us to all the children's classics written by such authors as Lewis Carroll, Rudyard Kipling, Walter Scott and Robert Louis Stevenson. He also stimulated our interest in less fictional romance by reading us books about natural history and the sciences, with periodic diversions into the realms of poetry. On Sundays, however, he laid aside those secular volumes, and read us Bible stories written for young people. Although our parents never went to church except during holidays in Lossiemouth – when they attended the Free Kirk with our Granny every Sabbath – they were deeply religious. They instructed us about the lives of Jesus and His disciples; we said grace before each meal; and every evening our mother came to hear us murmur our prayers in bed before kissing us goodnight. Late on Sunday afternoons we would return from the country to Lincoln's Inn Fields, and before bedtime our mother sat at a piano playing hymn tunes whilst our father and we stood around her chanting the words.

The furnishing of the cottage at Chesham Bois was simple, but a feature of it threw light on one of my father's favourite pieces of English history. On its walls hung engraved portraits of Oliver Cromwell, John Hampden, Henry Ireton and other leading figures in the Parliamentarians' struggle during the civil war. Those men were among his heroes. I remember that several years later, when I was chosen to champion the Puritan cause against apologists for King Charles I in a debate at my boarding-school, I wrote to him asking what arguments I could use, and he sent me a long hand-written reply summarising a formidable case. Alas! that letter was stolen by a thief a few decades later, and has not to my knowledge ever been seen since.

Every summer we children went to spend our holidays with our grandmother in her cottage in Lossiemouth. Usually our parents accompanied us for a while, for ties of deep affection united not only my father but also his wife to the old lady. However, when they could get free for some weeks from official work, their chief longing was to enjoy their own companionship *à deux*, and to achieve this they sometimes made long travels abroad. In any case their interest in international affairs was as intense as their concern with national problems, and they wished to gain first-hand knowledge of peoples and places round the globe. So they journeyed at different times in Canada, the United States of America, South Africa, Australia, New Zealand, India and other distant lands as well, of course as in many countries of Europe. Those expeditions were in fact not so much holidays as changes of environment and broadenings of horizons, for wherever they went they met the local political leaders, trades union chiefs, social workers and similar personalities, visited all sorts of public institutions as well as tourist sights, and studied local problems. The first-hand knowledge which they acquired was invaluable to their socialist colleagues in forming policies on foreign affairs when they returned to England; and it laid the foundations of my father's deep understanding of international relations.

On other occasions they made shorter travels to various European countries. Twice they took Alister and Ishbel (my elder brother and sister) and me with them. The first time was when they attended a conference of the Socialist International at The Hague, and led us afterwards on jaunts along the Dutch canals; and the second was when we went in 1910 to see the famous Passion Play at Oberammergau, and afterwards to glimpse the Rhineland. Incidentally, at Oberammergau we were lodged in the home of the peasant who acted the part of Judas

Iscariot in the great theatrical performance. He could not have been a more charming, innocent friend off the stage.

*

But that became a period of tragedy in my father's life. In 1910 my infant brother David died, a few weeks later our Granny passed away, and in the following year my mother also died at the early age of forty-one. Her death was partly due to overwork, for fatigue undermined her health and prevented her recovery from an attack of blood-poisoning. This was the supreme tragedy of my father's life. Throughout their partnership she had been his constant wise counsellor as well as devoted wife. One of the things she did for him was to break down a certain shy reserve which characterised him before their marriage. She had a genius for friendship with all kinds of people, and this helped to develop greatly a similar trait in him. My most precious memory of my childhood is the superlative affection which bound them together in good times and bad, in work and leisure, in sorrow and laughter. Naturally I regarded them then as elders; but later I realised how young they were, judged by Man's normal span of life, and what long years of promise and achievement apparently lay ahead of them both.

I can never forget the anguish which my father suffered at his beloved partner's death – the tears, the heartbreak, the awful loneliness. I do not think he ever really recovered from that disaster through the rest of his long, publicly crowded and yet privately rather solitary life.

In his desolation he nonetheless persevered as a champion of the human causes to which she and he had dedicated themselves.

*

There are several reasons why Ramsay MacDonald's ultimate place in history will be as one of the most important British statesmen of the present century. The first is that, more than anyone else, he was the moulder of the British Labour Party. His organising ability, political wisdom and popular appeal were distinctly instrumental in raising that fresh young force from obscurity to power, thus enabling it to make its vital contribution to the peaceful revolution in British society which has followed. From almost their very beginnings he was associated with the new stirrings of political thought in certain working-class and intellectual circles which preceded, and gradually prepared the way for, the formation of the party. When in the year 1884, as a poor youth aged eighteen, he migrated from Scotland to England to take a humble job in Bristol, he showed his already forming political beliefs by joining one of the small socialist groups that were being founded here and there in Britain. Two years later in London – where he then lived, often unemployed and at other times earning a small wage which he spent more on buying books for his self-education than on food for his nourishment – he became a member of the Fabian Society. Not long afterwards he sent a letter of support to Keir Hardie during his first contest for a Parliamentary seat in Mid-Lanark as a working-men's representative; and throughout the next decade he was a zealous propagandist for the socialist cause as journalist, speaker and active member of various organisations. His reputation grew so impressively among the early crusaders that when the Labour Representation Committee was founded in 1900 to strive for the election of Labour members separate from Liberals and Conservatives in the House of Commons, he was chosen as its first secretary – a post which he continued to fill for the next dozen formative years both before and after it became constituted as the Labour Party in 1906. In the General Election of that year twenty-nine Labour Members of Parliament were returned to Westminster, including himself.

He was, of course, only one in a remarkable team of pioneers of the Socialist movement in Britain. The most revered among them was Keir Hardie, the humble Scottish coal-miner who became the first working-class Member of Parliament, and whose physical appearance like an Old Testament prophet illustrated vividly the role he filled. I remember the awe that his gleaming-eyed, tousley-haired, grey-bearded figure inspired in me as a child, and the affection that his gentle and kindly as well as stubborn personality aroused. There were many other memorable characters in the youthful political and industrial Labour organisations. Eminent among them were the poetic ex-shepherd boy turned journalist, Bruce Glazier, with his vivacious wife Katherine; the physically crippled but intellectually potent Philip Snowden; the ponderously efficient Arthur Henderson; the almost girlishly young yet maturely capable Margaret Bondfield; the simple but immensely characterful Bob Smillie; the vast, laughing John Hodge; tiny but equally merry Will Crookes, and numerous others; whilst in more academic circles Annie Besant, George Bernard Shaw, Sidney and Beatrice Webb and similar rising celebrities did much to make converts to the socialist cause long before adherence to its creed became a fashion in Britain and other countries across the world.

Yet the dominant individual force in forming its organisation, strategy and policy as a political party was undoubtedly the young Scot from Lossiemouth who was then its secretary – just as later he became its most powerful platform orator, its most skilful Parliamentarian, and eventually its first Prime Minister. As Keir Hardie said of him, he was 'the biggest intellectual asset which the Socialist movement has in this country'. Apart from his outstanding ability as an organiser, in two fields of political thinking his contribution was vitally important. First, throughout the Labour Party's early years a great majority of its members (including most of the trade unionists) were radicals rather than socialists, and his consistent preaching of socialist ideas was influential in converting them, and persuading them in due course to adopt socialism as the party's official policy. Second, during the formative years at the end of the last century and beginning of this a controversy raged between rival socialist schools of thought as to whether their objective could be attained by gradual, peaceful processes or must be seized by sudden, violent means in the final battle of a class-war. He was the principal advocate of the former course. Indeed, more than any other individual he was the author of the British Labour Party's philosophy of 'evolutionary' as opposed to 'revolutionary' socialism.

As a result of the ceaseless efforts of its leaders – impelled in those times by a sort of religious fervour – the party steadily gained strength in industrial centres throughout Britain; and by the summer of 1914 its group of Members of Parliament numbered about forty. MacDonald had become their chosen leader in the House of Commons – a self-made man aged forty-seven with a future of great promise.

*

Then the First World War broke upon mankind, and as a result of his attitude towards it that promise seemed to be shattered. MacDonald could have become a Minister in the War Cabinet a few months later (as one of his colleagues did in his place) if he had been willing to do so; but instead he persisted in a policy which appeared to exclude him for ever from high office. Feeling opposed to Britain's entry into the war, and being in a small minority among his Labour colleagues on that all-important issue, he resigned from the Parliamentary party's leadership. The correctness of his policy will no doubt be a matter of controversy for countless years to come. On the one hand it might have been impracticable or wrong for Britain to keep out of the European conflict; on the other, if the leaders in this country and Europe had followed his advice either then or at any prudent time during the next four years – and so had achieved a politically negotiated instead of militarily imposed peace – many of the disasters which have afflicted Humanity since, including a second World War, could perhaps have been avoided. He and those few who agreed with him (including some of the most respected statesmen of the day like John Morley and John Burns, who resigned from Asquith's government on the question) foresaw far more clearly than their contemporaries the chronic and in some cases disastrous upheavals which would follow the initial world-wide Armageddon.

He persistently refused every tempting prospect of political reward if he would change his attitude, and not only resigned his Parliamentary leadership but also apparently renounced his promising future in public life. The tiny group of Labour and other personalities who opposed Britain's entry into the war knew that their decision would bring extremely unpleasant consequences on themselves, for the declaration of hostilities aroused a furore of patriotic enthusiasm among the population throughout the British Isles. Having taken their decision, they held a private meeting to discuss plans for pursuing their policy with all its attendant risks. Keir Hardie was one of the company, although he was now too old and frail to take a very active part in their virtually hopeless crusade.

MacDonald's attitude can be briefly though inadequately summarised as follows.* He thought that the British Government could probably have prevented the war if it had pursued a rather different policy in European affairs during the preceding years, and that, when fighting did break out, Britain should have remained a benevolent neutral instead of becoming a belligerent. Nevertheless, having got involved, he accepted that the nation must fight in a way which would bring victory, and he did nothing to prejudice this. But he urged passionately that the victory should not be simply and solely a military one; the declared war aims of the British Government and its conduct of diplomacy throughout the struggle should be such that at the end of hostilities the peace terms would be negotiated with the beaten enemy, not dictatorially imposed upon them. Only by this means would the political wounds of war be healed, and the European nations be able to live subsequently in harmony together. Otherwise the defeated Germans would emerge in bitterly discontented, frustrated mood, and bide their time for a later war of revenge. Indeed, MacDonald prophesied a great deal of what actually did happen through the next twenty years, culminating in the second world-wide conflict.

*For a fuller account see *The Life of James Ramsay MacDonald* by Lord Elton. (Collins, 1939).

Through the four war years he showed extraordinary fortitude in leading the splinter group of about half-a-dozen 'pacifist' M.P.s and their comparatively few followers in the country in a reasoned agitation for such a negotiated peace. He was denounced through the length and breadth of the British Isles as a traitor, a pro-German, and even an enemy agent in the Kaiser's pay. His public meetings were often broken-up by hostile crowds, and he was frequently stoned, and sometimes threatened with death. As a schoolboy I occasionally accompanied him to his meetings, and witnessed the terrible insults and dangers to which he was constantly exposed – an experience which, incidentally, was a good beginning to my own education in politics, especially as I did not feel sure that I agreed with his policy. Nevertheless, I then formed the only personal political ambition which I have ever held – that I should one day become the son of the Prime Minister of Great Britain. It seemed a hopeless aspiration!

For him the sole compensations in those dreadful years were the affectionate loyalty of his small band of followers, and his own conviction of the rightness of their cause. He probably assumed – as everyone else did – that his once bright career had collapsed in ruins.

*

Within a few years of the war's end that last assumption proved to be incorrect. Defeated in the 1918 general election for Parliament, he was supposed to disappear obediently into the political wilderness. Instead he turned his attention to the post-war national and international problems facing Britain, Europe and the world, and wrote and spoke about them with persuasive reason. In 1921 he attempted to re-enter the House of Commons in a by-election, but was again frustrated because the Conservative Party cleverly nominated as his opponent a gallant nonentity whose only claim to fame was that he had won a Victoria Cross on the recent battle-fields. Popular prejudice against the war-time 'pacifists' was still sufficiently strong to make this almost speechless hero the conqueror in the ballot-boxes. So MacDonald was forced to retire once more to his semi-obscurity. However, in the General Election of the following year he was again returned as a Member of Parliament.

A few days later another of the surprising, somersault turns in his fortunes occurred. At a meeting of the Parliamentary Labour Party he was chosen – by a narrow margin over the much respected, pro-war rival contestant, John Clynes – as the party's leader in the House of Commons. This elevation was promptly followed by another. For the first time in history more Labour than Liberal Members had been returned to the House, and the Labour Party therefore became the official Opposition to the new Conservative Government. Thus MacDonald became the Leader of the Opposition.

There were more profound reasons for this success than his attractive personal qualities. One was the fact that the results of the vengeful Versailles Treaty made an increasing number of people begin to wonder whether he had not been right in his war-time advocacy of a negotiated peace. Another was that the re-thinking which the shocks of war had stimulated among large sections of the public caused a swing away by many trades union leaders from their old radicalism towards his socialist ideas. Moreover events in the last few years had enabled him to reinforce another significant contribution to the political thoughts of his fellow-countrymen which was of extreme importance for the Labour Party and for Britain. The Russian Revolution in 1917 had provoked considerable searching of conscience in the Labour movement. The victory gained by violence by the Bolsheviks made many ardent socialist spirits in Britain (as well as in other countries across Europe) revive the notion that the Labour Party was wrong to suppose it could achieve its aims by peaceful constitutional means, and that it should follow the Russian lead. A heated argument between the philosophies of Revolutionary Communism and of Evolutionary Socialism was renewed. Left-wing extremists argued that the notion of gradually attaining a socialist society by Parliamentary processes must be scrapped, and that instead an unremitting class war should be waged by strikes and other industrial action with a view to a sudden, unconstitutional take-over of power. These enthusiasts urged that traditional reformist British socialism should be given a new, more virulent, and if necessary violent Marxist look. Many people in the Labour rank and file were tempted to accept this plausible suggestion.

More than any other individual MacDonald defeated the revolutionary tendency, and persuaded an overwhelming majority of Labour Party and Trades Union supporters throughout the country to maintain their faith in peaceful Parliamentary methods. He did not believe that the waging of a class war was either right or necessary. For him socialism was a faith which could unite people in all classes who performed useful services to the community – professional men and women, farmers, industrial managers, shop-keepers and artists as well as factory hands, coal-miners, agricultural labourers and other manual workers. Society was a brotherhood in which a variety of characters made different constructive contributions. And there need be no forcing of a crisis, no violent overthrow or collapse of the capitalist system; gradually step by step the economic and social structure could be changed into the socialist forms which modern circumstances required. He recognised that other methods might be unavoidable in certain foreign lands ruled by tyrannical regimes; but not in Britain, where democratic institutions would enable a peaceful evolution to occur. Steadily, by reasonable persuasion, the Labour Party, the Trades Unions and the Co-operative Societies – the trinity of allies composing the Labour movement – could increase the multitude of their supporters among the electorate until, by a bloodless revolution, a majority of socialist members sat in Parliament to guide the pace and nature of the transformation.

He preached his doctrine by various means – arguments in conferences, speeches to public audiences, articles in journals and magazines, and every other constitutional method of propaganda. Always a hard worker, he was tireless in his advocacy. Through those years we children saw him each morning at breakfast at eight o'clock, when we exchanged with him our various scraps of news of the last twenty-four hours, and then not again until the next morning except for a moment when we went to say good night to him in his study. His lamp always continued to burn until midnight or beyond as he sat reading and writing. Through the rest of each day he attended committees and other working groups in London, and every week-end he went away to address public meetings elsewhere throughout the land. We had left our cottage in Buckinghamshire after our mother's death, and his only variation in this busy routine was the rare occasion when he took a brief semi-holiday in Lossiemouth. There he would continue to work through every morning and evening, but took us on walks along the sea-shore or across the countryside in the afternoons. Once each year he also led us on a two days mountaineering expedition in the Highlands. During all those outdoor roamings he would chat with us about our schools, recreations, literature, history and other topics, just occasionally touching on his own political preoccupations. In the early evenings before resuming his official toil he would read books aloud, as had been his custom in our childhood, or would play card games with us. He was invariably a most affectionate parent – but his dedication to the Labour movement commanded almost all his time.

Through each week he worked about sixteen hours every day, and he was no less energetic on his week-end speaking tours in different parts of England, Scotland and Wales. Most of his activity in his bookcase-lined study at home was writing. He wrote countless memoranda, pamphlets and newspaper articles, and many books. Altogether he published more than twenty volumes, chiefly on political theory and practice. Those produced during the immediate post-1917 years presented the case against Revolutionary Communism and in favour of Evolutionary Socialism in Britain: and so, through a crucial period of its development, he helped to steady the British Labour movement, preventing it from either compromising with Communism or being seriously split between rival schools of socialist thought. By maintaining its loyalty to traditional democratic British forms of political action he and his principal colleagues enabled it to win ever growing support among the electors. And his intellectual and personal pre-eminence in the team revived his popularity to an extent that enabled him – after eight years in the wilderness – to recover its leadership.

He did not question that other, non-constitutional methods might sometimes be inevitable in the different conditions prevailing in certain other countries; but he argued that in Britain the Parliamentary method was best, and that it would result in due course in the socialists achieving their aims. The Labour Party's dramatic gains in the 1922 Election seemed to foreshadow that he would be proved right.

The memory of his dominant role in those times is still cherished by many. I am touched by the numbers of now elderly people – retired school teachers, members of office staffs, barbers, taxi-drivers, manual labourers, old-age pensioners and others – who, when they somehow discover that I am a son of Ramsay MacDonald, speak of him with nostalgic affection. Some of them are critical of his action in forming the National Government in 1931, but they all recall vividly and gratefully his handsome appearance, richly melodious voice and compelling eloquence at public meetings. Almost all of them say that he converted them to socialism. He was their political teacher, their crusading leader; and to this day he remains for them the outstanding figure among the pioneers of the Labour movement.

*

His power of moulding contemporary thought in that critical period was considerable not only in Britain but also in socialist circles across Europe and beyond. Some of his books were translated into several foreign languages, and were widely read abroad. Indeed, his success in combating Communist doctrines earned him the bitter enmity of Russia's new leaders. In particular their most brilliant propagandist, Leon Trotsky, poured contempt on him in many vitriolic public utterances. I am not sure to what extent he was in communication with representatives of Russian Bolshevism before, during and after the 1917 Revolution. Naturally he knew some of them because he and they had been fellow delegates at international socialist conferences prior to the war. Certainly he kept to some extent in touch with them, for I remember an incident in which I became personally involved. One evening at our house in Hampstead he handed me a few stamped letters to post in a nearby pillar-box, with an additional, unstamped envelope containing a note for me to deliver by hand to Mr Litvinov in person at his home in Highgate. As I approached the pillar-box I met a friend, and we started a pleasant conversation. By the time we parted my mind had drifted far away from my instructions about my parent's correspondence, and thoughtlessly I popped all the letters into the box. Only when I returned to our house did I remember that I was supposed to deliver one of them to Litvinov; and I promptly went to explain my mistake to my father. He expressed concern, gave me the pennies necessary for Litvinov to claim the unstamped envelope when a postman brought it to him in due course, and asked me to hasten to Highgate, tell the Russian emigré what had happened, and ask him to secure the communication without fail, since it must not fall into the hands of the authorities. I performed this duty faultlessly – and incidentally, that was my first meeting with the distinguished Russian. A score of years later I negotiated with him as his country's Foreign Minister at the League of Nations in Geneva. But I still do not know what were the contents of that mysterious letter!

*

After the 1922 Election events moved rapidly. At the end of 1923 another General Election was called; and when the results were announced the Conservative, Labour and Liberal Members in the House of Commons numbered 258, 191 and 151 respectively. Thus the Tories had lost their overall majority; and the Liberals declared their readiness to support a Labour government. Such an Administration would be a minority one dependent on Liberal votes for survival, which would prevent it from having any real security in office, and also from introducing certain socialist items of legislation. It had no mandate from the voters for such law-making. In those circumstances one body of opinion in the Labour Party urged that its leaders should refuse to accept office; but MacDonald and a majority of his colleagues decided that such a course would be shirking their responsibility, and would plunge the country into a political crisis. The other two possibilities of minority Conservative rule or an immediate fresh Election were both undesirable, for in each case the Labour Party would be blamed for refusing office, and would lose the confidence of many supporters who wished it to make an effort at government. It is difficult for people living in Britain in the early 1970s to realise the very strong, frightened prejudice against the Labour Party which was widespread fifty years ago. A favourite popular slogan throughout the constituencies in the 1923 General Election had been 'Labour is Not Fit to Govern', and multitudes of voters believed that if a socialist Prime Minister entered 10 Downing Street the nation would promptly be plunged into incompetent, irresponsible and extremist administration. MacDonald and his colleagues thought it essential that they should prove to the electors that the party was capable of giving the nation orderly and wise progressive rule. They also believed that their foreign policy would help to improve a difficult situation in Europe. They therefore agreed to form a government even though its minority status would seriously cramp its style, and probably shorten its life.

*

An interesting episode occurred at that time which illustrated the extraordinary social as well as political change which had taken place in Britain during the previous three decades. Horrified hostility to the establishment of a Labour Government was so great among sections of the British public that King George V decided to help restore confidence by demonstrating his own trust in the new administration. He took the unprecedented step of giving a State Banquet at Buckingham Palace in honour of the new Prime Minister and the group of ex-coalminers, ex-railwaymen and other, mostly ex-manual, workers who were to be his Cabinet team.

At the vast, glittering dinner table MacDonald sat at the Queen's right hand. As course followed course through the meal his attention kept wandering towards the face of a handsome man wearing on his court dress the medals, ribbon and star of many Honours, who sat some distance away on the opposite side of the table. The countenance seemed familiar – and yet MacDonald could not recall its identity. It haunted him; he tried in vain to remember where he had seen it before; but with a sense of frustration he in the end abandoned the effort.

After dinner the King sat on a sofa at one end of a long reception gallery whilst all the men present gathered in a gossiping throng at its other end. Officers of the court conducted selected individuals one by one to talk with His Majesty; and the Prime Minister was the first among these. When their conversation ended he rose and started to walk back the length of the chamber to rejoin the other guests.

As he approached them a man disengaged himself from the crowd and advanced to meet him – the handsome, much decorated fellow whose face had tantalised him throughout dinner.

The stranger extended a hand in greeting and said, 'I want to express my warm congratulations and delight that you're our Prime Minister. It's a grand day of peaceful Revolution.'

MacDonald felt touched, and thanked him.

'I'm afraid you've forgotten me,' the other remarked.

'No, I've only half forgotten you,' MacDonald replied with a laugh. 'I remember your face, and kept staring at you during dinner, trying to recall where we last met. Where was it?'

The man smiled.

'Do you remember a night about thirty years ago when three poverty-stricken young men who had come to London to seek their fortunes went together to hear a lecture by Huxley at the Royal Institution; and when the lecture was over, and they left the hall and put their hands in their pockets, they found they hadn't enough pennies between them to pay their bus fares home. So they walked miles through the night back to their lodgings.'

'Yes, of course I remember that night,' said MacDonald. 'Smith was one of the trio; but he died some years ago. The others were young Dr Dawson and myself.... Are you Dr Dawson?' he added with dawning recognition.

'Well, not exactly,' the other replied with a chuckle. 'I'm Lord Dawson of Penn.'

In the intervening years, during which they had not met, one of the poverty-stricken youths had become the King's Physician and the other was now his Prime Minister.

*

The Labour Government's minority position naturally created great difficulties for it; and in the end it lasted only nine months. This is not the place to tell its story. In the subsequent Election towards the end of 1924 the Conservative Party recaptured many constituencies, mostly at the expense of the Liberals; and it regained a clear majority in Parliament. However, the government's performance had favourably impressed many previously doubting electors, and although the Labour Party lost about forty seats in the House of Commons, it increased its popular support in the ballot-boxes by more than 1,100,000 votes. As a result the Liberal Party dropped much further into the political background, and the Labour Party was decisively established as the only possible alternative government. Another important milestone in its progress had been passed.

In the short Labour Administration MacDonald had held the post of Foreign Secretary as well as that of Prime Minister. He did not originally intend to assume the two portfolios, but personal and other difficulties arose whilst he was composing his cabinet team which compelled him to do so. The double office was an almost intolerable burden; but his conduct of foreign policy produced results very beneficial to Europe. He played a decisive part in abating the unhappy bickerings and tensions which were an aftermath of the Versailles Treaty, and in starting a rapprochement between the mutually opposed European powers. Even strong critics of him as Prime Minister agreed that he was a fine Secretary of State for Foreign Affairs. Over the years a keen study of international problems had become one of his primary interests, and the promotion of world peace one of his chief concerns. His gifts of diplomacy were such that in my opinion it was in some ways a pity that he had to be Prime Minister in the first two Labour Governments of 1924 and 1929–1931, spending a lot of his energies in trying to settle the small internal party quarrels as well as the major national problems which preoccupy the head of a government. If he had been free to conduct Britain's overseas policy through that critical period, the international situation might have taken a lasting turn for the better.

I must not in this essay trace events between 1924 and 1931, when MacDonald was first Leader of the Opposition for five years, and afterwards Prime Minister of another Labour Government. Although on that second occasion his party for the first time gained more seats in the House of Commons than the Conservatives, it still commanded only a minority of votes against them and the Liberals combined, and so was once more dependent on the latter for support. Moreover, it had the ill fortune to assume office just when the grave economic depression which started in 1929 began to afflict the world. This created very difficult problems for many nations round the globe, and led to an extreme financial crisis in Britain in August, 1931. Then MacDonald took the second violently controversial action of his political career, when he resigned as Prime Minister of the Labour Government and formed a National Government instead.

His motives were so viciously misrepresented at the time by many leaders in the Labour Party – perhaps not unnaturally in the circumstances of party politics – that his attitude has been largely misunderstood ever since. Some of them even declared that he had deliberately premeditated and plotted the overthrow of the Labour Government and the establishment in its place of a government of national unity under his own Premiership. He took little trouble to answer the personal accusations against him, because he wished to concentrate his energies and capacities on helping to overcome the desperately grave danger which threatened the nation. Nor was he inclined to exacerbate unnecessarily the quarrel between himself and the Labour Party. His fundamental political attachment was still to that party with most of its Members of Parliament, and especially to its massive rank and file throughout the country. But he thought that some of its leaders had cravenly shirked their duty, and had misled it on an issue of unavoidable, urgent patriotic importance.

The following facts will help to clarify his motives and actions at the time. I know them to be correct. Although before 1929 my association with him as a member of our family was naturally close, I was not intimately connected with his political activities until I myself became a Member of Parliament in that year. From then onwards I was allied with him in his official life, and can write with first-hand knowledge about his intentions.

Far from plotting to overthrow the Labour Government, during its last days of life he strove hard to prevent its collapse, using every endeavour to persuade the cabinet to stay in office and shoulder responsibility for overcoming the economic crisis. He and Philip Snowden (who was Chancellor of the Exchequer) gained the support of a majority of their Ministerial colleagues for a programme of severe economy measures involving financial sacrifices by every section of the population, including a temporary cut in the benefits paid to the unemployed. However, a considerable minority led by Arthur Henderson opposed this last suggestion. I was told by some high civil servants in the know at the time that MacDonald was so anxious that the Labour Government should perform the honourable, even if in some ways unpopular, task of saving the national situation that he actually kept it in office a day or two longer than the official financial experts advised was prudent, in a final attempt to persuade the minority to agree. They stayed adamant, however, threatening to resign as a group if the cabinet persisted in the proposal touching the unemployed, and to rouse an agitation in the Labour Party which would mobilise the support of the unprecedented multitude of workless and their more emotional sympathisers – and so split the party in two. Against the better judgment of a clear majority in the cabinet that minority thus forced the whole government's resignation.

I should, of course, remark that the minority were sincere – though partly also timid or opportunist – in their conviction that a temporary cut in unemployment benefits would be wrong. Earlier in the discussions Henderson, their leader, had in fact supported such a cut in a different form, but afterwards he changed his mind. Moreover, they did represent a similar view held by large sections of Labour's supporters in the country, including most of the members of the T.U.C. general council, and if the government had proceeded with the proposal, there would have been trouble in the party. But MacDonald, Snowden and other Ministers believed not only that the cabinet should do its duty, but also that if their team was sufficiently united, this trouble could be reduced to manageable proportions.

Other strong reasons made my father anxious for the Labour Government to stay in office. He foresaw that 1932 would be a decisive year for some very important international problems such as disarmament, German reparations, and India's political future; and he greatly wished these to be dealt with in accordance with its enlightened policies. However, the minority stayed obstinate in spite of all his arguments.

When it became clear that the Labour Government must resign, MacDonald's first intention was to leave office with his colleagues. I was a back-bench M.P. at the time. Parliament had started its summer recess, so I was holidaying in Lossiemouth; and during the crisis my father telephoned me once or twice each twenty-four hours to tell me the latest developments. On the morning when the decision to resign appeared inevitable he told me that within a day or two he would join the rest of our family in Scotland. His plan was to surrender not only the Premiership but probably also the leadership of the Labour Party in Parliament, since if the government of Conservatives supported by Liberals, which would presumably assume office, introduced similar economy measures to those prepared by a majority in his Labour cabinet, he would feel in honour bound to support them. Such action by him as Leader of the Opposition might embarrass, and indeed cause strong protests from, many members of the party who were averse to cuts in unemployment benefits; and so he thought he should reduce as far as possible the danger of a serious split in the Labour ranks by himself leaving the front bench, taking a seat 'below the gangway', and from there voting for the new government's measures. On all other questions he would remain a loyal member of the Labour Party.

But that was not to be. In a later telephone conversation he told me that numerous authorities were questioning whether a mere coalition government of Conservatives and Liberals would be strong enough to rally the widespread popular approval through the country necessary for the unpleasant measures required in the emergency, and that he was being pressed to head a National Government which, as a result of his leadership, would command a lot of Labour as well as other support. Indeed the King himself had intervened to urge that this was his duty. He clearly felt reluctant to agree – but a few hours later he telephoned me again to say that he had decided he must accept the plea. The problem must have caused him a heart-rending searching of conscience.

So he became Prime Minister of a National Government. At that time he expected it to remain in office for only five or six weeks, simply to pass and implement the crucial legislation required to resolve the nation's immediate troubles, and then to resign. Normal party warfare between the Conservative, Labour and Liberal forces would be resumed, and a fresh General Election would be called. Having done his duty in the crisis, he expected to retire from public life, where there would be no further place for him.

He found that four of his Labour cabinet colleagues were determined to enter the National Government to help him achieve his purpose – two of the most eminent old Labour leaders, Philip Snowden and J. H. Thomas, and a pair of newer members of the party, Lord Sankey and Lord Amulree. His and their influence in the country would be powerful enough to give the government adequate authority to perform its task. They might well be repudiated by the official Labour Party itself, but their opinions would carry such weight with vast numbers of Labour voters throughout the land that the administration's severe measures would gain wide support.

Beyond achieving that immediate and, he believed, essential purpose he had no wish to make difficulties for the Labour Party. On the contrary, he hoped that – although he himself might be expelled from it – it would maintain its unity, recover its strength, and return to power in either the next election or the following one. So he made no attempt to weaken it further. In particular he refrained from recruiting supporters among back-bench Labour Members of the House of Commons. If he had tried to do so, he undoubtedly could have detached considerable numbers, and caused a serious breach in the party. Immediately after the formation of the National Government a meeting of all Labour M.P.s was called to consider the situation. Henderson and his colleagues who had formed the minority in the recent cabinet would of course be there to expound their point of view. MacDonald could have attended to state his – but he stayed away. This was partly because he was so preoccupied with his immediate official work that it would have been difficult for him to spare time for other tasks, but mostly because he did not wish to split the Labour Party. He knew that if he went to the meeting and presented his case, he could swing a lot of sympathy to himself – and the conflict between the party's principal leaders would shatter its unity and strength. Many of its members were devoted to him, felt sadly perplexed at the situation which had arisen, and would readily have followed his lead had he asked them to do so. He therefore stayed away, and Henderson's statement of the problem went virtually unanswered. Neither Snowden nor Thomas attended the meeting, and only Sankey made a short speech taking a different line. His remarks were few and cautious, however, for he could not reveal secrets about the discussions in the Labour cabinet which would give a more accurate picture of the issue at stake than Henderson's argument presented. Moreover, Sankey was a recent convert to socialism, and did not command the prestige and authority among its adherents which MacDonald, Snowden or Thomas could have asserted. I myself went to the meeting, and from my knowledge of the facts knew how one-sided Henderson's speech was, and how unfairly it dealt with my father's attitude; but I, too, could not reveal confidential information which would have given the audience a fairer picture of the two sides of the question.

Even so, a considerable number of Members came privately to the Prime Minister to express their sorrow at the dilemma in which they found themselves, and to seek his counsel. He advised them to stay with the Labour Party, and to do their utmost to persuade it to pursue a responsible, constructive policy through the current crisis.

I was one of the Members to whom he offered this advice. When I returned from Lossiemouth to London immediately after his new government's formation, and told him that I would support him, he was concerned, although personally pleased. He said that I need not do so, and that in many ways it would be better if I stayed in the Labour Party, to help to sustain its strength beyond the current crisis. He observed that his own political career was almost finished, but that mine was just beginning; and he expressed a hope that I would always remain with the Labour Party, and help it to achieve the socialist society in Britain which its first two short-lived minority governments had scarcely begun to establish.

However, I abided by my decision. I trusted his judgment as to what was necessary in the immediate situation. I also felt that he was the man who mattered most in Britain at the moment, that he was passing through a period of personal and political anguish owing to his breach with his old friends and followers, that he was contemplating a cruel self-sacrifice compelled by his sense of public duty, and that his son should not add to the bitterness of his situation by leaving his side.

About a dozen Labour M.P.s resolved on the same course, and all of us were promptly expelled from the Labour Party. During the next few days quite a number of others, including several ex-Ministers, told me privately that they agreed with MacDonald's personal action, that with his unique responsibilities as Prime Minister he had done the right thing, and that they wished they could express this opinion in public – but that the virulence of certain other ex-Ministers was making this impossible for anyone whose political future lay with the Labour Party. Several of those sympathisers spoke confidentially to him in the same strain; and he repeated to them that he fully understood their position, and that they were acting properly in staying with the Labour Party.

On the morning following the formation of the new government I happened to meet Herbert Morrison, the most important as well as capable of the younger ex-Cabinet Ministers, walking across Westminster Bridge; and we stopped for a talk. He told me that during the last few days of the Labour Government's life my father had been magnificent, again proving himself 'a very great Prime Minister'. His policy through the crisis had been very wise, and his patience and persuasiveness in cabinet had almost succeeded in preventing the minority from deflecting the team from its rightful course. But in the end the timidity of certain Ministers about defending the cuts in unemployment pay had won the day.

I learned later that Morrison had wished to join the National Government, and had offered to do so, but that my father at once urged him not to, saying that whereas Snowden, Thomas and he himself were elders whose time of leadership was nearly over, Morrison was one of the ablest of the younger leaders whose influence through many more years would be invaluable to the Labour Party. So Morrison changed his mind, and joined the Opposition in the House of Commons.

MacDonald and Snowden persuaded their Conservative and Liberal colleagues to adopt precisely the same programme of national economies as had been agreed by a majority of the late Labour Ministers. No doubt they hoped that one result of this would be to enable those ex-Ministers to make the Opposition's hostility to the proposals less uncompromising. But this did not happen. Every one of the ex-Ministers opposed the plan when it was debated in Parliament; and soon afterwards some of those very same men were fiercely denouncing and misrepresenting the Prime Minister in their speeches throughout the country. Such is party politics.

I shall not consider here whether MacDonald was right or wrong in deciding to become Prime Minister in a National Government. It was one of those situations in which there is no absolute right or absolute wrong. We can leave the historians of the future to form impartial judgments. What I am principally concerned with in this essay is the character of the man who took the decision. His action demonstrated once more his courage, sincerity and disregard of self. He knew that it would lead to misunderstanding and perhaps vilification by large sections of the people whose good opinion he most cherished, and he assumed that his decision would bring a quick end to his career. But those considerations did not sway him. As in his opposition to Britain's entry into the war in 1914, so again in the crisis of 1931 he acted in accordance with principles which he believed to be right.

*

The remainder of his story is a mixture of success and failure, of glory and sadness. As I have mentioned, at the time of the formation of the National Government he and his colleagues reckoned that it need continue in office for only about six weeks, to put through Parliament the measures necessary to overcome the economic crisis, and then to resign. I remember this vividly because I was made a junior Minister in the new administration, and expected to hold that post for only those few weeks, and then to leave political life for ever. My expulsion from the Labour Party made my re-admission to it impossible, and I would never join any other party. So I began to consider what new career I should seek in some entirely different field of endeavour.

However, that expectation about the government's brief life-span turned out to be a serious miscalculation. Owing to various circumstances beyond its members' control – including the vehement opposition of the Labour Party to its emergency measures – it could not end its existence abruptly after the few weeks required to enact the crisis legislation. As things turned out it continued in office for several years, and MacDonald remained Prime Minister for almost the first four of these.

His government achieved some fine things which I need not catalogue here. One example was its decisive contribution to India's advance towards Independence within the Commonwealth, a cause which was particularly dear to his heart. Indeed, the powerful part that he had played, from the time of his first visit to India in 1909, in assisting the Indians to achieve their freedom was so conspicuous that some commentators sought to explain his decision to keep the National Government in office as inspired mostly by a desire to maintain the drive towards India's Independence which he initiated as Labour

Prime Minister when he presided over the 1930 Indian Round Table Conference.

Incidentally, when I became Britain's High Commissioner in Delhi a quarter of a century later I was often reminded by his Indian admirers of the consistent help he gave to their achievement of freedom. One such occasion occurred on a day when I got delayed for an hour at Madras airport because an aircraft arrived late. An elderly Tamil approached me in the lounge, remarked that he thought he knew my face, and asked my name.

I replied, 'Malcolm MacDonald.'

'Are you the British High Commissioner?' he enquired.

I said I was.

His eyes opened wide with pleasure as he exclaimed, 'Are you Ramsay MacDonald's son?'

Once more I said that he was correct.

He clasped me with both hands in warm friendship, and expressed delight. Then he explained that in 1911 he had been an undergraduate at Madras University, where he and many other students became enthusiastic supporters of the Congress Party's agitation for Indian home rule. 'We were very impressed,' he continued, 'by a book called "The Awakening of India" published that year, written by someone described on its cover as "Ramsay MacDonald". It was such a good, sympathetic account of our Indian problems and aspirations that we did not believe its author could be an Englishman. He must be an Indian – and we supposed a misprint had been made in his name, and that it should read "Ramaswami MacDonald".'

My father's staunch liberalising activities in various Imperial and international affairs will hold an important place in history's final appreciation of him as a creative statesman. One of his last contributions in that field was his leadership of the British delegation at the useful Lausanne Conference of 1932. Not long afterwards, however, the situation in Europe began to deteriorate, and the prospect for harmony between its principal powers gradually disappeared. I recall a comment he made to me on the day in 1933 when Hitler assumed supreme power in Germany.

'Now I shall never see peace in my lifetime,' he said sadly. 'I hope you'll see it restored in yours.'

Later he favoured the strengthening of Britain's military forces as a deterrent against an outbreak of war; and one of his last acts as Prime Minister was to publish the 1935 White Paper announcing a programme of rearmament – a decision for which he was criticised by politicians in various circles.

*

Well before that a serious ebbing away of his own personal abilities had begun. He was tired, overworked and ageing; and the strain on him was reinforced by a deep sorrow lodged within him. Twice in his career his heart was broken – although his spirit was never broken with it. The first heartbreak came in his private life when his wife died, and the second in his public life twenty years later when he was separated from the Labour Party. He kept that second sorrow largely to himself, expressing it only in confidence to intimate associates. He had not revised his view about the correctness of his action in 1931, but remained extremely unhappy at the irreconcilable breach it caused between him and his old colleagues. He hated speaking in House of Commons debates against his life-long friends ranged on the Opposition benches, and this deep, hidden feeling speeded a decline in the quality of his Parliamentary performances. Although he enjoyed individual friendships with his new Conservative and Liberal associates, I do not think he was ever really happy working in political alliance with them. His affections stayed with the masses of his old comrades in the Socialist movement.

I personally wish he had retired much earlier from the Premiership and government. After his death I once expressed this view to detached, sagacious Maurice Hankey, who as the Cabinet Secretary had been one of his wisest official counsellors from 1924 onwards. 'Yes,' answered Hankey, 'it was a pity from his personal point of view; but from the national point of view he could never be spared. There was never a moment in those critical years from 1931 onwards when his knowledge, wisdom and prestige were not invaluable to the governments not only of Britain, but also of the Commonwealth. He always seemed indispensable.'

I wonder? Indeed, I do not agree. I think this might have been true if he had preserved intact his earlier abilities; but after a while the strain of his life and work took a serious toll. Perhaps partly as a result of his declining capacities he lingered too long as Prime Minister, and afterwards as Lord President of the Council. Had he retired two or three years earlier, reasonably soon after the government completed the emergency task for which it was formed, and whilst his qualities as a statesman remained unimpaired, his reputation would not have suffered the damage which later struck it.

Another thought troubles me. Sometimes when I speculate why he tarried so long in office I wonder whether one reason might have been a paternal wish to sustain my political career. He may have reckoned that his departure from the Cabinet would herald the National Government's end, and that my position in public life could then also collapse, since I would have no association with any major party. Perhaps he recalled my loyalty to him in 1931 and wished to support me in a similar way.

Whatever his reasons, I think that his staying in office after the early 1930s was the greatest mistake of his life. As a result his public image at the time of his death was too much affected by people's recollection of his failings in his last few years. It is fairer to remember him as he was during his long, fruitful strivings throughout the previous half century.

*

Some of his personal assets, which did remain unimpaired until he drew his last breath, were his remarkable grace of body, charm of character and culture of mind. His good looks were famous: he was perhaps the handsomest Prime Minister in the long succession of those great figures in Britain's history. His personality was captivating, combining gentleness with strength, seriousness with gaiety, and simplicity with brilliance. Almost always he showed a generous kindliness which touched people's hearts; and his fine oratory, political skills and wisdom gave all those gifts extra magic. As for his intellectual distinction, it revealed itself in various fields besides politics. Indeed, it was partly by accident that he entered public life at all, for when he was a young man his first love was the natural sciences, and he intended to make a career as a scientist. However, a serious illness at a time when he should have been sitting examinations made him miss the opportunity. Balked in his prime desire, he was forced to turn to other occupations – and in due course developments led him into politics. But he never lost his deep interest in the sciences, and several of the great physicists, chemists and similar personalities of his generation were among his good friends, such as Rutherford and Einstein. Indeed, his deep interest in biology and related subjects laid the foundations of his belief in Evolutionary Socialism, for he felt that in a freely growing society such as existed in Britain economic and other developments would enable socialism to arrive by gradual means if its advocates guided popular opinion peacefully in its direction.

His other intellectual enthusiasms ranged in a more amateur way over the fields of history, literature, philosophy, music and the aesthetic arts. Of course he had his faults, both as a Premier and as a man. For example, national and international economics were not one of his particular interests, and his understanding of them was limited at a time when they were becoming a principal concern of government leaders. This was a serious shortcoming in a Prime Minister, especially as it made him depend too much on the occasionally dubious wisdom of intellectually powerful but out-of-date financial pundits like Snowden.

Again, he was sometimes inclined not to confide his thoughts on important current issues adequately to his colleagues. A certain duality existed in his nature, a trait of the mystic, the dreamer lying alongside the practical realist. These contrary elements perhaps sprang from his mixed Highland and Lowland Scots ancestry on his father's and his mother's side respectively. As a result of the former he was sometimes too reserved at critical periods, withdrawing within himself and failing to share his innermost feelings and reflections with others. His wonderfully friendly, outward-going wife had largely eliminated this strong tendency to reticence, but it reasserted itself during his loneliness after her death. Moreover, the mystical trait sometimes made him express his thoughts in ambiguous, and even apparently confused terms, although usually he expressed himself with clarity. This led some critics to regard him as a deliberately cunning charlatan, and others to judge him a muddle-headed fool.

Another frailty in him was a streak of vanity. Some people who knew him well denied that anything of the sort existed. Certainly it was not offensively obtrusive, and has become greatly exaggerated in the minds of people who did not know him. Yet I think it was there, and it sometimes puzzled me, for it seemed incompatible with other strong elements in his character. Perhaps it was an instinctive self-defence mechanism in the make-up of an individual who was sensitive in spite of the tough fibre that he displayed in public life, and who had suffered a succession of fearful wounds such as the hurt of illegitimate birth, the premature loss of his beloved wife, his political outlawing during the first World War, and later his tragic triumph in 1931.

In essence he was a simple, unpretentious man. He spurned all titles and honours such as the Earldom offered him when he resigned the Premiership. Although his wide circle of friends included many illustrious statesmen, philosophers, men of letters and other celebrities, it also embraced countless humble folk. Some of the middle- and upper-class intellectuals who joined the Labour Party after its pioneering years felt jealous of his capacity to be on intimate terms with working-class people.

He was as able an intellectual as themselves – although, unlike them, he was largely self-taught – and they resented the fact that he aroused much more affectionate, tumultuous responses from massive audiences than they did. Some of them invented a theory that he broke with his socialist colleagues because he had grown disdainful of working folk, and felt happy only in the mansions of rich aristocrats. Certainly he enjoyed parties in those stately homes when the company was interesting and the conversation stimulating; but he was bored by fashionable social functions, and shunned such occasions whenever he could. Although he felt at ease in ducal palaces, he was equally at home in workmen's cottages, where he also shared many thoughts and feelings with his hosts. Wherever he went on his widespread propaganda campaigns he stayed in the dwellings of Labour supporters – coal-miners, railwaymen, factory hands, agricultural labourers and the like. His origins and many of his experiences were similar to theirs; he was one of them; he and they were kin. And he never felt so much at home as when he sat gossiping with his fisher-folk cronies in his native Lossiemouth. Often he would stay for hours with them at their firesides exchanging talk about all sorts of common interests.

Almost always after his wife's death he returned to Lossiemouth for any holidays he could snatch from official labours. Sometimes also he would escape briefly to its peaceful, friendly atmosphere for two or three days of concentrated work at critical moments in his career, such as when he was forming his governments in 1924 and 1929. And he left instructions that when he died his cremated ashes should be borne there for burial in the cemetery at nearby Spynie, where his wife's remains already lay. Always he visited her grave when he went to Lossiemouth, carrying a bunch of heather or other flowers as an expression of his abiding love. When he arrived in his native burgh for the first time after becoming Prime Minister in 1924 a jubilant reception party presented him with a posy of roses, which he later laid on her gravestone.

No arrow was too poisoned for some critics to shoot at him.

One of the most cruelly barbed was the innuendo that his political action in 1931 was influenced by his fondness for a lady of aristocratic Conservative connections, the Marchioness of Londonderry. The suggestion was completely unjust; his friendship with her, as with her husband, was sincere and genial, and he made no attempt to conceal it, for there was nothing to hide. Like some other widowers or similarly solitary men deprived of intimate female companionship, he enjoyed feminine society, and several of his affectionate friendships with other intelligent women, such as the socialist writer Mary Agnes Hamilton, the pianist Harriet Cohen and the authoress Princess Marthe Bibesco, were as cherished by him as the one with Lady Londonderry. Every one of them was entirely Platonic.

Of all the many happinesses in his life the highest was his marriage with his beloved Margaret, and of all its profound tragedies the deepest was her premature death. He and she were two halves of a vivid, brilliant whole. The 'Memoir' of her which he wrote soon after she died became renowned as one of the most moving books of its kind ever written, and it was reprinted in new editions over and over again.

I remember a day in 1936 when a foreign visitor asked him in the course of a cheerful conversation over lunch, 'Why have you never re-married?'

The smile suddenly faded from my father's lips, his face became sad, and he answered, 'My heart has been in the grave for a quarter of a century.'

If she had lived to be at his side through all the subsequent strenuous and difficult years, I believe his great qualities would have had an even more consistently fine flowering than they achieved.

Eamon De Valera

'De Valera came to visit me one Sunday at my country house in Essex.'

WHEN I became Secretary of State for Dominion Affairs near the end of 1935 Eamon De Valera had already been for some time Prime Minister, or Taoiseach, of the Irish Free State. During many earlier years I had read about him as the arch-traitor among Irish rebels against the British Crown – an unscrupulously mischievous enemy of my country, my compatriots (including presumably myself) and everything else British. I therefore felt intrigued at the prospect of not only meeting but also dealing officially with this obstreperous character – if he would consent to deal with me. My predecessor in the Dominions Office, the capable Trades Union leader and 'right-winger' among Labour politicians, J. H. Thomas, had been involved in various dealings with him, and regarded him with considerable disapproval. Recalling the ancestral Spanish blood that flowed through his veins, Thomas sometimes referred to him with a laugh as 'the Spanish onion in the Irish stew'.

I began to study in official documents the latest situation in the notorious, seemingly endless and perhaps insoluble Irish Question – to consider what I might say to De Valera about it if and when we met. Although the earlier hot quarrel between our two countries had been distinctly cooled by the Treaty negotiated in 1921 by which the Irish Free State became a self-governing Dominion within the British Commonwealth, it had warmed up again because of actions taken by De Valera after he assumed office in 1932. Always a bitter opponent of the 1921 agreement, as soon as he became Taoiseach he began to undo some of its provisions. Against strong protests from the other party to the Treaty, the British Government, he abolished the Oath of Allegiance to the King which members of the Free State Parliament had previously taken, reduced the duties of the

Governor General who represented the King in Dublin, withheld payment of Land Annuities due to Britain, and initiated other policies in defiance of Thomas's objections.

These unilateral acts did remove some of the points in dispute between the Irish Free State and Great Britain, but in a way that soured their relations. And several matters of more significant disagreement remained unsettled, threatening to cause continuing friction between the two countries. For example, De Valera and his Ministers were staunch Republicans averse to the King of Britain continuing as King also of Ireland; they felt passionately opposed to the division of their country by which Ulster remained part of the United Kingdom of Great Britain and Northern Ireland separate from the Irish Free State; their nationalist susceptibilities were grossly offended by the British navy's occupation of certain sea-ports along supposedly independent Southern Ireland's coast; and the dispute about land annuities had caused a trade war between the two countries. The Taoiseach and his cabinet were in no mood to allow these matters of discord to be forgotten, or even temporarily pushed under a diplomatic carpet.

My study of the problem made me feel that, although certain of these questions could not be solved quickly or easily, some room for manoeuvre might exist in the case of others. I also knew that De Valera had indicated a desire for friendlier relations with Britain. I therefore sought an opportunity for a wholly private meeting with the Irish leader, first to get to know him, and then to explore informally with him the possibility of some move towards at least partial agreement. Before long a chance for this arose. I learned that he would stay for a night in London on his way from Ireland to Europe for a visit to an oculist in Switzerland. Already in those days he suffered from the eye trouble which has afflicted him ever since, and which gradually made him virtually blind.

I put the idea to Stanley Baldwin, my Prime Minister, and gained his cautious assent. I then told John Dulanty, Dublin's High Commissioner in England, that I would like to make De

Valera's acquaintance, and suggested that if it were agreeable to the Taoiseach he and I might meet whilst he was passing through London. I stressed the need for secrecy because if our meeting became known to the press they would at once speculate about its significance, and a violent public controversy as to its wisdom could arise. I mentioned to Dulanty that some of my Conservative colleagues in the British government were still so vehemently opposed to De Valera and all his works that they might feel deeply critical of my contacts with him – an attitude which would be shared by many Members in both the House of Commons and the House of Lords. Perhaps the Taoiseach would be equally embarrassed by disapproval from some of his extremist political followers in Southern Ireland. I added that I hoped our initial talk would open the way for further exploratory exchanges which could lead towards a settlement of some of the outstanding questions dividing our two countries, but that any chance of such a result would be destroyed if our meetings were exposed to hostile comment by newspaper reporters, Members of Parliament and other critics in Britain, Ulster and the Irish Free State. In that case neither De Valera nor I would be free to consider mutual compromises in the interests of an acceptable 'package' agreement which we might otherwise be disposed to contemplate.

Dulanty was very pleased with my suggestion, and reported it in a private message to De Valera, who replied that he would gladly see me in his room in a hotel where he would stay overnight on his way to Europe.

With great caution Dulanty and I planned the rendezvous; and after dark a few evenings later he and I met outside a basement entrance to the hotel. A guide led us through the kitchen quarters and up back-stairs to the floor where the Prime Minister was lodged. Our knock on his door was promptly answered, and a moment later Dulanty was introducing me to De Valera.

I was familiar from newspaper photographs with the tall, austere figure and seemingly always prim, stern countenance of my host; so I was taken by surprise by the friendly smile which lit his face as he greeted me. He could not have given me a more affable welcome.

We had a pleasant talk, starting with an exchange of rather formal diplomatic courtesies, but then settling into more relaxed conversation. We touched in broad terms on the problems of Anglo-Irish relations, but did not probe deeply into them. I told him that I intended to explore with my cabinet colleagues the possibility of finding mutually satisfactory solutions to at least some of the matters in dispute; and he responded amicably to this. Before parting we agreed to keep in personal touch through Dulanty with a view to perhaps arranging a further meeting when we could start a serious examination of the whole controversy. He said he planned to make periodic visits to Switzerland for treatment by his oculist, and that he would always be glad to talk with me. He accepted that, for the present at least, our meetings should be secret.

I felt slightly encouraged by this first confrontation with the reputedly tough, fanatical Irishman.

*

If our further conversations were to open the way towards official negotiations, his task in seeking the approval of his Ministerial colleagues would naturally be in some ways easier than mine. He was the Prime Minister and unchallenged leader of a government who could almost certainly count on gaining the support of his cabinet for any propositions he wished to make. Indeed – if I may anticipate for a moment – even if his Ministers felt sceptical about a policy which he advocated, he was apt to get his way. In the negotiations between our two governments that opened almost two years later his fellow Irish delegates occasionally appeared to be in partial disagreement with him on some point. After a protracted argument among them at a meeting I asked his colleague Sean Lemass privately, 'What happens when Mr De Valera takes one view on a controversial problem and all the rest of you in his cabinet take a different view?'

He laughed and replied, 'The cabinet then takes its decision by a minority of one.'

I, on the other hand, was not the Prime Minister in Britain – very far from it! In Baldwin's government I belonged to a small minority faction, the National Labour representatives as distinct from the larger and more powerful Conservative and National Liberal groups. Some of the influential Tory Ministers would (I knew) be opposed to the sort of settlement with De Valera which I was considering, and which I intended to recommend to the cabinet if I felt sufficiently confident that De Valera would ultimately consent to it. My first need was of course to gain Baldwin's sympathy.

I reported to him the substance of my talk with De Valera, and expressed the opinion that, in spite of all the difficulties which lay ahead, we should make a sustained attempt to reach agreement with the Irish on as many outstanding issues as possible. I indicated the lines on which I thought this might be practicable. Baldwin was cautious and non-committal in his response, partly because of scepticism about the Irish leader's willingness to make adequate concessions to our points of view, but also because he was more familiar than I with the strong hostility which my suggestions would arouse among some of our Conservative colleagues in the government. Nevertheless, he did not discourage me unduly, and agreed that I should work out my proposals carefully with a view to our considering their presentation to the cabinet.

During the next few weeks I examined every issue involved. On certain matters I consulted other Ministers whose departments were concerned. Gradually I formed my ideas about various alternative solutions which might prove expedient on this and that question, and I wrote a document containing a statement of the whole problem which led to a series of recommendations. Baldwin approved its circulation to our colleagues – but refrained from promising me positive support in the heated arguments which it would provoke among them. With a friendly, enigmatic smile he said he would leave me to make my case.

At the next cabinet meeting Ministers did not discuss the subject, deciding instead to refer my paper to a cabinet committee for thorough examination before the Government should consider any decision either for or against my proposals. Baldwin was chairman of the committee, and its members included all the most important Ministers.

The committee met one afternoon in the Prime Minister's room in the Parliament building, where our presence was required to vote in a series of divisions which would take place on a bill being debated in the House of Commons. Baldwin called upon me to open the discussion. I could see one or two grim faces among my colleagues, who evidently found the occasion displeasing, and were preparing to protest at my policy.

I spoke at moderate length, analysing the difficult Anglo-Irish problem in broad perspective, and presenting the main arguments for my recommendations. I did not go into many details, feeling that I could deal with them when our deliberations turned to particular matters. After I ceased speaking the Prime Minister asked me a few questions, seeking further information, but in a manner unrevealing of his own opinions. Other Ministers made tentative comments on this or that detail of my proposals. Then the Lord Chancellor, Viscount Hailsham, weighed in with a statement of his opinions.

His lordship was as dyed-in-the-wool a Tory as ever sat on the woolsack or anywhere else; and his views on the Irish problem were rabid. He and I happened to be good personal friends, but there were few, if any, political questions on which we saw eye to eye.

After some diplomatically kind words about me, he launched into a strong attack on my entire policy. A very able advocate, he built up a powerful case, indicating among other things his contempt for De Valera, and his doubts about my wisdom in having anything to do with that traitorous rascal. I could see on some other Ministers' faces the partial sympathy which his blistering dismissal of my arguments aroused.

Whilst he spoke I turned over in my mind the replies that I would make, and scribbled an occasional note on a piece of paper to remind me of points with which I should deal. His onslaught was so weighty that the situation was critical, and I must make a good, persuasive case if my policy were to stand a real chance of gaining favour.

As it happened, the division bell rang soon after Hailsham fell silent, summoning us to go and vote. Our meeting adjourned; but I presumed it would be only briefly interrupted, and that we should continue our discussion ten minutes later when we had voted. I also assumed that in its course Baldwin would give me an opportunity to reply to the attack made on my proposals. I therefore felt astonished when he announced that we would not meet again after the division, and that he would consider when we should resume our examination of the matter at some future date. I was very disappointed, wondering whether his inclination was perhaps to postpone it for ever.

As we walked to the division lobby Neville Chamberlain, who was Chancellor of the Exchequer and a member of the committee, asked me to come for a talk with him in his room after the voting. Until then he and I had not often spoken to one another, except for an occasional exchange of brief, formal pleasantries. He was a very reserved man, and I did not know him at all well. I could not think what he wished to discuss with me, and agreed with puzzlement to go to his room.

When I entered it, he motioned me to occupy an armchair beside the desk where he was sitting; and then he said in a cool, objective tone of enquiry, 'Tell me what you would have said in reply to Hailsham's attack on your policy if the P.M. had given you a chance to answer him.'

I was surprised, and glad that the Chancellor should be sufficiently interested to seek my views. My mind was filled with thoughts on the subject, all arranged in the coherent order in which I had hoped to express them at the resumed committee meeting. So I poured them forth without hesitation.

Chamberlain listened carefully to my lengthy statement, neither interrupting me to ask a question, nor betraying any sign of his own opinion on the subject.

When I ceased speaking he smiled in his charmingly restrained manner, and said, 'I entirely agree with you, and you can count on my support throughout future discussions.'

My heart leapt with pleasure. Knowing the considerable influence which Chamberlain exerted among Conservative Ministers, including the Prime Minister, I felt encouraged.

*

He was as good as his word. Throughout the vigorous arguments about our Irish policy which ensued in Ministerial circles over the next many months he gave me firm support. This may well have helped to tip Baldwin's views definitely in the same direction, and the Prime Minister's aid was of course particularly valuable. Yet perhaps Baldwin never really needed much persuasion, and his sometimes apparently undecided attitude was tactical rather than genuine. His role as the head of a coalition government was delicate on such a controversial question, and he had to steer our discussions in ways which would avoid a grave split in the cabinet, and prevent the alienation of a section of Conservative Ministers who could mobilise strong support among Members of their party in Parliament if they decided to withdraw. Baldwin's conduct of our conferences was therefore necessarily cautious. His cutting short of the first exchange of arguments in our committee was probably deliberately designed to prevent an early vehement confrontation which might cause rises of temper, and to allow time for cool, protracted consideration of the problem. In fact he played a difficult political game with characteristic shrewdness and even cunning. During it Chamberlain's more clearly outspoken support for my policy was of great assistance to him.

After our initial discussions in the cabinet committee Baldwin agreed to my having another talk with De Valera, provided the Taoiseach understood that our conversations were exploratory and non-committal as well as secret – conditions which De Valera readily accepted. He and I therefore planned to meet on the night when he next passed through London. Our talk would be a serious start to exchanges of opinions on every aspect of the Anglo-Irish question, which would inevitably continue through many months with a view to finding the maximum amount of agreement – if any! – that appeared practicable.

I thought the best opening move in the talk would be for me to repeat my sincere wish for such an agreement, and then to ask De Valera to make a broad statement of his views on the major issues in dispute between our two countries. I would ask questions and offer comments which might open the way towards the sort of conclusions that I had recommended to my British colleagues.

Before the meeting I told Dulanty of this intention, and his reaction was very sceptical. He thought De Valera's natural guardedness would make him chary of starting with a revelation of his thoughts. The Taoiseach might suspect that I was laying a trap for him. Indeed, Dulanty anticipated that our conversation would probably last for only half-an-hour.

In fact it continued for four hours. During much of the time Dulanty stayed in the room with us, but for longish periods De Valera and I talked alone. He readily accepted my suggestion that our talk could be most fruitful if we both expressed our opinions in an informal, personal, almost unofficial as well as entirely candid way – 'thinking aloud' as the saying goes. And he responded to my invitation to open it by a comprehensive statement of his views. Whenever I threw in a question he answered it promptly, and afterwards he listened interestedly to my comments. Mutual understanding and friendliness – though by no means accord on several matters – grew between us. At the conversation's end we decided that our officials should meet to examine in greater detail certain questions we had considered, and that later a further discussion between us would be useful.

Several times in the next eighteen months we held our secret rendezvous in London, and we also conferred when we were fellow delegates at a session of the League of Nations Assembly in Geneva. During those discussions we considered every important question in dispute between our two governments, shirking nothing, expressing our views with complete candour, arguing on certain topics with mutual firmness, but on others discovering possible means of perhaps reaching a measure of agreement. De Valera repeatedly and fervently urged that the vital need was to end partition and create a United Ireland. With equal conviction I expressed my opinion that – although several British Ministers including myself would like to see this achieved in due course – there was no possibility of attaining it in the immediate future. The British government could not force that solution on an unwilling Ulster, which would moreover be supported in its resistance by a majority in our present cabinet and Parliament. De Valera kept reiterating that all other questions were of lesser importance; to which I replied that the only way to move towards union was by settling those other matters first, in the hope that greater friendliness would then grow steadily between the Irish Free State on one side and Northern Ireland as well as Great Britain on the other, and perhaps gradually make a United Ireland practical politics. To this De Valera answered that it would be extremely difficult, if not impossible, for his government to make any concessions to us on other questions – whether concerning finance, trade, defence or anything else – so long as partition continued. Partition had been one of the British rulers' most hostile acts against the Irish people in a long succession of such unfriendly deeds, and whilst it lasted really good neighbourly relations between our two nations could not exist. He emphasised his strong, sincere desire for such relations.

With good sense and tolerance he was nevertheless ready to consider with me in an exploratory way possible solutions to the other outstanding problems. However, he retained a tough attitude on them all. I made various proposals for compromises on them which I need not describe here, for this essay is not an account of British policies regarding them, but a sketch of De Valera's personality.

During our talks I gradually got to understand it more fully. He was a transparently honest and sincere man who never concealed, or even half-hid, his beliefs and aims. Most of his opinions were rigidly as well as ardently held, springing from the deep-rooted convictions of a passionate Irish nationalist. When he presented his arguments for them his face appeared unchangeably solemn, and although his voice was never raised in anger, usually staying quietly reasonable, it was sometimes vibrant with intense emotion. On those occasions he was apt to treat me to long monologues, and his attitude remained completely uncompromising. On other aspects of our problem he was more disposed to admit the possibility of a divergent view from his own, and was prepared, perhaps rather reluctantly, to consider suggestions for a modification in his original outlook. At all times he was ready to be as patient a listener as he could be an exhaustive talker, letting me state my opinions and arguments at any length I liked. Occasionally he revealed a pleasant sense of humour which was inconsistent with the grim image of him portrayed in the British press. Then his sombre face suddenly became lit by a smile, and he might break into restrained laughter. Invariably he was courteous, and considerate. He never stood on ceremony, being always at ease, initially no doubt because of his absolute confidence in himself and the rightness of his cause, and later perhaps also because of the trust he grew to feel in my sincerity.

I learned to have a high respect and indeed affection for this austere, impassioned old Sinn Feiner who was at the same time a quietly charming man.

*

A few months after my first personal contacts with him a delicate problem suddenly arose which could have increased the difficulties between our governments. This was the constitutional crisis that led to King Edward VIII's abdication.

His Majesty was of course King not only of Great Britain and Northern Ireland, but also of all his Dominions: Canada, Australia, New Zealand, South Africa – and the Irish Free State. The situation was therefore one of deep concern to the governments and peoples of each of those lands. Moreover, as their constitutional monarch the King could take no decision one way or another in such an important state affair except on the advice of all his proper councillors, who included the Prime Ministers of the other independent Commonwealth nations as well as of Great Britain.

As Secretary of State for Dominion Affairs in London I therefore had the fascinating, if rather sad, task during the next fortnight of maintaining contacts through each day and half of every night between all those scattered statesmen, acting with the King's consent on his behalf as well as that of the British cabinet. In cables couched in the form of messages from Baldwin to them (which needed extremely careful drafting, a work in which Neville Chamberlain and John Simon – who was Home Secretary – gave me constant help) I informed them in confidence of every development, and sought their latest private thoughts or official advice for consideration by King Edward as well as by British Ministers at each stage of the crisis. Incidentally this duty was made all the more interesting because not only the personal characters but also the political beliefs and religious sects of the half-dozen Premiers were very different from one another. Some were Conservatives, others Liberals and one a Socialist, and they belonged to a variety of Christian churches ranging from the Roman Catholic through the Anglican, Wee Free Presbyterian and Methodist to the Dutch Reformed. Moreover, two of them – Hertzog in South Africa and De Valera in Ireland – were Republican in sentiment, opposed to monarchy in any shape or form. At the beginning of the crisis I wondered whether the King's dilemma would become chaotically confused by conflicting advice from this heterogeneous team. However, with the exception of one difference of opinion by one or two Premiers on one important matter in the first twenty-four hours – which was quickly resolved by agreement – our communications produced spontaneously and consistently unanimous counsel to the King at every stage of the difficult and in some ways dangerous affair.

Here I am concerned only with my contacts with De Valera. The issue at stake naturally caused him acute embarrassment. He, his government and his supporters in the Irish Parliament were Republicans to a man, disliking the institution of monarchy in general and the British monarchy in particular. Only with extreme reluctance had they ever consented to acknowledge the King of Britain as their own ruler, partly because he was the King of the much wider Commonwealth to which they wished their country to belong. In 1936 even fully independent membership of the Commonwealth still involved allegiance to the crown, for the era of republics co-existing side by side with monarchies in that remarkable international partnership had not yet arrived.

The Dublin government had been careful to perform the minimum of actions implying allegiance to the King; and in normal circumstances extremely few occasions arose when any public demonstration of it was required. Now, suddenly, the abdication crisis threatened to change all that. As I have already mentioned, King Edward could reach no final decision in the matter except with a knowledge of the advice tendered by all his Prime Ministers – including De Valera. Yet that staunch Republican wished to avoid any act which would commit him to positive approval of the monarchy. Quite apart from his own conscientious objection, such a deed on his part could arouse awkward criticism from important sections of opinion among his fellow-countrymen.

He and I therefore agreed on a procedure which would give him the maximum information on what was happening, whilst causing him the minimum of involvement. Partly by word of mouth through a private emissary I – acting in Baldwin's name –

kept him acquainted with every significant development, including the King's and all the other Prime Ministers' views, on the understanding that we in London would not seek any formal expression of opinion from him unless a situation arose in which it seemed constitutionally absolutely necessary that His Majesty should receive official counsel from him as well as the rest of the group. Short of this we had an unwritten understanding that – unless he sent a message of disagreement – he would acquiesce in whatever decisions were evolving.

The arrangement worked satisfactorily until the moment when the King resolved to abdicate. This conclusion required formal and public action by each Commonwealth government – action which would be extremely embarrassing to the Taoiseach of Southern Ireland. To make the abdication legally effective the Parliament at Westminster must pass an Act declaring that on a certain date King Edward the Eighth stepped down from the throne and his successor, King George the Sixth, ascended it. But whilst this statute would achieve its purpose so far as the United Kingdom was concerned, it could not do so for the other kingdoms in the Commonwealth. Since they were all independent sovereign states, the Parliament in London could not make laws for them except where they asked it to do so. Otherwise each Legislature must pass a similar Act confirming the abdication for its own nation.

In preparation for this I had already sent the Dominion Prime Ministers the text of a Bill which we in London would introduce into our House of Commons if such a situation arose; and I suggested that on the same day as the action was taken in the Palace of Westminster our partner governments (except those in Australia and New Zealand, who asked that our law should cover them) should present identical items of legislation to their respective Parliaments, so that the abdication of one King and the succession of another would take place simultaneously throughout the Commonwealth. I had of course despatched this information and proposal to De Valera as well as to the other Premiers.

As soon as King Edward took his decision I informed each of them of the date and hour when we in London proposed to secure the passage of our Bill, and asked them whether that moment would be convenient for them to do likewise.

In the meantime Baldwin had received a private message from De Valera saying that he and his government could not at any time in any circumstances take the action proposed. It was unthinkable that they should make themselves responsible for putting one British King off a throne in the Irish Free State only to elevate another. De Valera added that whatever the British Government proposed to do, he and his colleagues would therefore do nothing.

This could have created a very difficult situation. However, I sent a secret comment to my Irish friend stating the prospect in simple terms. I said that if his government refrained from action, this was entirely their own concern, and I pointed out the consequences. If the Parliament in Dublin passed no legislation, at a given moment King Edward the Eighth would cease to reign and King George the Sixth would succeed him in every part of the Commonwealth – except the Irish Free State. In that land Edwardus Rex would continue to be King. Moreover, presumably as soon as he married Mrs Simpson she would become Queen of Southern Ireland.

This must have shaken De Valera. Soon afterwards I learned that he proposed to speed-up the introduction into the Irish Parliament of constitutional legislation which he had contemplated for some time, but which would not otherwise have been produced until several months later. By it, all the King's functions in the internal affairs of the Irish Free State would be abolished and only those concerning external relations maintained. This raised a delicate question as to whether Southern Ireland remained a monarchy or became a republic, and therefore whether its partnership with Britain and the other Dominions in the Commonwealth could continue, since the Imperial Conference of 1926 had declared that all the Commonwealth members were 'united by a common allegiance to the

Crown'. With a courtesy which he invariably showed, De Valera had informed King Edward and Ministers in London earlier in the year of his intention. I put to him then the British Cabinet's critical views of the proposal, with friendly warnings of the possible unhappy consequences if it should result in the Irish Free State ceasing to be a member of the Commonwealth.

As Dominions Secretary and a loyal subject of the King, I was honour bound to do everything I could to preserve his position as the sovereign who linked half-a-dozen different independent peoples in a unique community of nations. However, no argument that anyone could produce would deflect De Valera from his purpose; and he and his colleagues were clever to use the abdication crisis to achieve it, since other governments concerned were so preoccupied with various urgent problems created by the emergency that this Irish action provoked less public controversy than it would otherwise have done. In the circumstances the matter got settled quietly on the understanding that the Irish Free State remained sufficient of a monarchy to continue in the Commonwealth. The Royal Title which described our ruler as King of Great Britain, Ireland and the British Dominions beyond the Seas stayed unchanged, and the functions regarding external affairs which he performed for the Free State were important. The abolition of his functions in its internal affairs did raise an interesting question about the exact constitutional position of the Crown in independent Dominions which stimulated fresh thinking on the subject. But I need not enlarge on that issue here.

De Valera's policy involved a voluntary concession on his part. No doubt he and his colleagues would have preferred to introduce a new constitution which established their country as an unqualified, unquestioned Republic. However, their primary desire was to attain a United Ireland, and presumably they felt that a complete elimination of the Crown would be so offensive to a majority of Ulster's population that this prospect might disappear for ever. They hoped that an arrangement which preserved a special association in external affairs with Great

Britain through the King would prove to be a conciliatory gesture which made a Union possible.

So far as King Edward's abdication was concerned, the form of the constitutional amending legislation in Dublin made unnecessary any law replacing one King by another on a throne there. A slight difficulty did arise. Even the hasty acceleration of the new law failed to achieve the change on the same day as the abdication occurred in Britain, for it did not get finally passed until about twenty-four hours later.

We Ministers in London shrugged our shoulders at this slight difference of time-table; it did not greatly matter. George the Sixth would become King for certain purposes in the Irish Free State a day after ascending the throne in other kingdoms of the Commonwealth – so what? It would be odd, but not disastrous. Indeed, by this ingenious, rather typically Irish solution, the Commonwealth passed unscathed through an extremely critical episode which could have broken that valuable brotherhood of nations. And those other doughty Republicans, the Afrikaaner Ministers in South Africa, thought up a similar device about timing. Baldwin received a message from General Hertzog saying that they agreed to introduce into their Parliament an Abdication Bill similar in substance to ours, and that it would come into effect a day before the British statute. No doubt this was to establish beyond any shadow of doubt South Africa's absolute sovereign independence. The sum total of these exchanges was therefore that the transfer of the crown took place on one day in South Africa, the next day in Britain and three Dominions, and the following day in the Irish Free State. Everyone's honour was satisfied.

The small differences in the time-tables did, however, have a significant constitutional consequence. Previously many lawyers had argued that in spite of the fact that each member of the Commonwealth was an independent nation, the group were collectively one united monarchy whose peoples owed allegiance to the same Crown. Those legal luminaries asserted that the crown was as indivisible as the head of the individual who wore it. But whatever might have been said earlier for their theory, the actions of the Parliaments in Dublin and Cape Town knocked it into a cocked hat – or rather, into six crowns.

I personally was not worried by this development. On the contrary, I welcomed it, for I felt that the prospective evolution of the Commonwealth made such a definition desirable. I looked forward to a time when the independent members of that partnership would cease to be limited to a few nations of white peoples, and would include several nations with populations of many different coloured skins. It seemed to me that such a multi-racial Commonwealth could perform immense services to the human race. I hoped that before many years had passed India would become a fully sovereign member of it, and that afterwards various other dependent peoples in the British Empire would likewise graduate to independent status in the Commonwealth. But I reckoned that if this were to become possible we should have to concede that some of them could be Republics, for I did not think that certain of them in Asia and Africa, for example, would acknowledge an alien monarch of a totally different race as the ruler to whom their fellow-countrymen must owe allegiance.

After the abdication I therefore began to advocate in private conversations with some of my influential cabinet colleagues that if – as seemed likely – the Dublin government decided in due course that it must 'throw off the yoke' of the British monarchy and establish a Republic, this should not mean the Irish Free State's automatic departure from the Commonwealth. I urged that if the Irish would like then to continue as loyal members of the association, we should agree to them doing so. In fact the test for membership should not be allegiance to a crown, but allegiance to certain principles in which the British and their Commonwealth partners all believed, and for the upholding of which they would co-operate. I argued that if we refused to allow an Irish Republic to stay in the partnership, that could be an unfortunate precedent which would make it difficult for us to agree to a Republic of India or a Republic of

Nigeria remaining in the Commonwealth if and when those states emerged.

However, when I ventured to suggest this rather radical notion in the mid-1930s, it was frowned upon by some of my Tory colleagues. I remember their abrupt, contemptuous rejection of it when I mentioned it to them in informal talks. Other Ministers were more non-committal. They felt sceptical about the idea, but were ready to keep open minds, and to consider the problem in the light of the current circumstances if it should ever arise.

As things turned out it never did arise whilst I remained Secretary of State for the Dominions. De Valera's government enacted their promised legislation, and for many years afterwards continued an unobtrusive but courteous recognition of the Crown for certain purposes. Only much later did Southern Ireland become a Republic.

*

The Irish government's action concerning the King's functions disposed – however unsatisfactorily in some British authorities' eyes – of one controversial issue which might have prejudiced the chances of De Valera's and my discussions on other matters producing constructive results. When the abdication crisis ended I resumed my efforts towards securing cabinet approval of negotiations on lines which his and my exchanges, supplemented by talks between our officials, were gradually revealing as practicable.

During the crisis I had learned more about the Taoiseach's unyielding nature. I now realised that I had made mistakes in some of my earlier judgments about the extent of the concessions he would be prepared to make on this or that question, and had been too optimistic in my advice to the cabinet. I had hoped the Irish Premier would prove to be a normal political leader ready to give and take in negotiations, with a view to the two sides eventually reaching an accord in which they met each other more or less half way. But I discovered that he was so utterly convinced of the rightness of his opinions, and so dedicated – some people would say fanatically dedicated – to them as matters of principle that he would make very few substantial concessions. He expected us British to do almost all the giving, and to hope for only the gift of Irish goodwill – of course, a very valuable gift after generations of ill-will – in return.

He did keep telling me that his government could move much further towards meeting us on certain other matters if a United Ireland were established forthwith. They would be ready, for example, to conclude something like the co-operative naval and military defence agreement which we desired, since this would then become in Ireland's as well as Britain's interests. However, there was nothing that we in the British government could do to modify partition in the existing circumstances; if we had thought the slightest chance of our doing so existed, we would have sounded the Ulster Prime Minister on the subject. So De Valera and I had no choice but to agree to disagree on that very obstinate problem. He reluctantly accepted that progress on it must be indefinitely postponed. This prevented him from making the considerable concessions on some other questions which he would otherwise have favoured. The fact is that partition stood in the way of the comprehensive, wise accord on all the outstanding matters, including defence co-operation, which our two governments could probably otherwise have reached.

Slowly our exchanges produced a tentative understanding on the broad substance of possible pacts on other matters. These were much less satisfactory than I had hoped for; but still, on balance, they seemed to me worthwhile if the British people did receive in return distinctly more friendliness from their Southern Irish neighbours. Nevertheless I had to be careful not to appear to give way to De Valera's stubbornness too easily, or I would have lost the trust of my colleagues who were supporting me in the cabinet committee. I therefore continued to press him, and left his persistent refusal to alter his attitude to persuade them to face the facts of Anglo-Irish life as he had created them.

Eventually, towards the end of 1937, our two governments agreed to start formal negotiations. Some months earlier Baldwin had ceased to be Prime Minister in Britain, and Chamberlain occupied 10 Downing Street in his place. So when a team of Irish representatives under De Valera's leadership came to London in January, 1938 for the conference, Chamberlain led our British delegation.

A light-hearted incident occurred at its first meeting which illustrated a little known trait in the Irish chief's character. He was reputed to be an uncompromisingly solemn man who could make only long-winded, turgid statements of his opinions on any political subject, without any glimmer of a sense of humour. It was also popularly supposed that whenever he spoke on the Anglo-Irish Question he began by reciting the whole list of his countrymen's complaints against us British, commencing with almost prehistoric events, dwelling at length on Oliver Cromwell's alleged oppression of Ireland, and proceeding tediously through every unhappy incident of each subsequent century.

Our two delegations held their first session one afternoon in Downing Street, and after we had discussed various procedural matters De Valera began to state his government's views on the half-dozen issues which we had met to consider. He made no reference to past history, concentrating in a businesslike way on the practical aspects of each problem. He had not quite completed this comprehensive opening statement when we adjourned.

The two teams had asked me to write before the end of each meeting a brief draft communiqué which they could consider issuing to a crowd of journalists who were eager to learn at every stage how our discussions were proceeding. Shortly before that first adjournment Chamberlain therefore read out a text which I had scribbled. It merely announced that the conference had started, listed the Ministers who attended on each side, reported that the British Prime Minister had spoken words of welcome to the Irish members, and then recorded that Mr De Valera opened the discussion with an introductory statement of the Irish delegation's views which was not completed before the meeting ended, and which would be continued when it resumed.

As Chamberlain finished reading De Valera beamed a smile and said, 'The newspapers will comment that by the end of a long harangue I was still describing the wrongs done to Ireland by Oliver Cromwell.' He suggested adding a few words to avoid this accusation. All those present burst into laughter, and accepted his amendment. The negotiations had got off to a good start.

They continued at meetings held through the next three months, with periodic recesses whilst the Irish delegates returned to Dublin for consultations with their colleagues. In the London discussions De Valera urged again the supreme desirability of establishing a United Ireland, and Chamberlain (though he personally agreed with the proposal in principle) had to explain the impracticability of attaining this in the foreseeable future. The issue almost caused our negotiations to collapse; but eventually an Agreement was concluded which settled virtually every other outstanding question. Indeed, it all but ended the bitter Anglo-Irish quarrel which had plagued the two peoples for centuries. Their unhappy feud would have gone on simmering, and could have flared up seriously and perhaps disastrously during the Second World War if our 1938 Agreement had not resolved the Treaty Ports question in particular. I shall write more about that later.

The main credit for the settlement belonged to Chamberlain and De Valera, both of whom showed sensible, practical statesmanship through the negotiations. As regards De Valera, without abandoning any of his principles about Irish freedom and unity, he revealed a mellow streak of pragmatism alongside his rigidity in handling a supremely difficult problem.

*

One incident that occurred during the negotiations might have prejudiced their successful outcome. Two or three troublesome points of dispute were eased towards agreement by a long talk which De Valera and I held when he came to visit me one Sunday at my country house in Essex. Our earnest discussion continued through much of the morning and afternoon, but was interrupted for a while by the arrival of friends for lunch. Among the drinks which I proposed to offer my guests was whisky; and – suppressing my Scottish prejudice and bearing important diplomatic considerations in mind – I told my butler that only Irish whiskey should be served. This display of ignorance on my part about the geographical origin of the Irish concoction was by good chance prevented from upsetting progress in De Valera's and my later talk, because I went into the dining-room before the meal to make sure that the table arrangements were all that they should be – and to my horror noticed that the whiskey bottles had 'Belfast' printed in large letters on them! At once I ordered their banishment, and the substitution of politically harmless Scots whisky in their place.

After the negotiations ended, I told De Valera that I would like to present him with a handsome gift as a memento of our work together, and I asked him whether there was anything he especially wanted. He demurred, saying that the Agreement was the most perfect souvenir of our efforts, which he would always remember with pleasure. I refused to accept his self-denial, and enquired again whether there was any particular article that he would like as a present.

After a jocular expression of surprise that a Scotsman should think of giving a free gift to anyone, he told me that he was in fact greatly tempted by a treasure which he had seen for sale in a second-hand bookshop along Charing Cross Road. It was a copy of the first edition of an important early work on the elements of quaternions. Reminding me that he had only entered politics because of his outraged Irish nationalist feelings at the time of the Carson-led rebellion in Ulster which threatened a schism of Ireland, and that his other supreme interest in life was mathematics – of which he would have liked to be a professor – he said that the volume was rare and valuable, and that he would prize it more than anything else I could give him.

Delighted at the proposal, I went to the dealer in ancient books armed with the several pounds in cash which I presumed would be necessary for the purchase. On enquiry I found that the volume was indeed an extremely precious one for those interested in mathematics, but that the public demand for such items was so small that the gem would cost me only five shillings.

The incident was a charming example of the grand Irishman's consideration for a Scottish friend. Incidentally, it could also help to explain the somewhat rigid, logical, uncompromising mind which he was inclined to display in all matters, including political problems. If I understand mathematics correctly, it is a science which calculates with exact, irrefutable precision the right answer to be drawn from any and every combination of circumstances. Two and two make four, and nothing anyone can say or do will alter that inexorable fact. It does not admit of any compromise.

*

Chamberlain had overcome successfully all the objections of our right-wing Conservative colleagues to negotiations with the Irish. Afterwards some strong criticisms of the Agreement were voiced in the House of Commons, its most vehement opponent being – as I shall have reason to recall later – Winston Churchill. In Ulster, too, the accord was denounced; but the government leaders there were not unduly concerned, since they appreciated the firmness with which we had resisted De Valera's attempts to modify the partition between Northern and Southern Ireland.

Before the formal negotiations with De Valera started I had told the Prime Minister of Northern Ireland in strict confidence about the cabinet's plans and purposes, in the hope of gaining his understanding, if not his tacit consent. He was that rather tough, die-in-the-last-ditch-if-necessary Ulsterman, Lord Craigavon – a grim-faced, burly man whose most memorable physical feature was a broken nose. Rumour whispered that the nose had been fractured by a kick from a horse, and that this contact with his lordship's stony countenance broke the horse's leg.

He and I met privately in London, and I explained to him in detail our proposals for a settlement with the Southern Irish government, of course assuring him that it would leave the division of Ireland unchanged. He listened courteously and attentively. At the end of my exposition he nodded silently, and offered no other comment.

I remarked, 'I suppose you think I'm a crazy fool to believe an agreement worth making with the government of the Irish Free State.'

He smiled with surprising warmth and answered, 'No, not quite so bad as that; I just think you're another Lossiemouth sentimentalist.'

Lossiemouth was the small fishing town in the north of Scotland where my father was born.

*

De Valera returned to Dublin with the Irish Agreement and the mathematics book in his pocket.

Not long afterwards an official statement published in the English press announced that Sir Samuel Hoare, the Secretary of State for Home Affairs, would soon introduce into Parliament a Bill containing proposals for reforms in the administration and conditions of prisons throughout Great Britain. A few days later I received a message from De Valera saying that he was extremely interested to read this news, that as an old inmate of our gaols he had many ideas about desirable changes in their management, and that if I thought my colleague would be interested in studying his notions, he would send me a memorandum expounding them. I asked Hoare whether he would like to consider our pristine foe's suggestions, and he at once answered that he would welcome them.

I let De Valera know this, and not long afterwards received a document composed by that celebrated old gaol-bird containing numerous authoritative proposals for changes in the running of our prisons. I passed it to Hoare, who studied it carefully with his officials. He told me that he found it an invaluable treatise on the subject, and that he would embody many of its suggestions in his draft legislation. For various reasons the bill's introduction into the House of Commons got delayed, but in due course it became an Act of Parliament. So no doubt all the subsequent inhabitants of our prisons have benefited from the experience of their distinguished predecessor.

*

After the Agreement negotiated between Chamberlain and De Valera relations between Britain and the Irish Free State distinctly improved. The Southern Irish never changed their view that the partition of Ireland was improper, but they ceased to treat it as an issue which should provoke constant political bitterness, no doubt hoping that better neighbourly co-operation would in due time help to solve the problem along the lines they desired. With this in mind De Valera sensibly took the heat out of the controversy, not abandoning his unalterable opinion on the rights and wrongs of the matter, but trusting that more cordial relations between Dublin and London would also mean friendlier relations between Dublin and Belfast, and lead eventually to a United Ireland.

The next critical problem which could have brought confrontation between the British and Irish governments arose in 1938 during the historic talks between Chamberlain and Hitler at Munich. The issue was crucial: would peace prevail or war break out in Europe? And this aroused another important issue: if Britain became involved in war, would its Commonwealth partners join it as allies or stay neutral?

I must not write at length here about the discussions within the Commonwealth which took place, and shall only remark that at every stage of the growing European crisis, and especially through its climax during the Chamberlain-Hitler exchanges, I kept the Dominion governments fully informed of every development, sending them an almost non-stop succession of telegrams and receiving from them in return statements of their views. I also maintained close personal contacts with all their High Commissioners in London, including Dulanty, meeting them as a group every day – and sometimes two or three times a day – to exchange official information and opinions. The Irish Government was not the only one which urged us British to avoid war. All the other Dominions took the same line very emphatically. Indeed, if Chamberlain's policy had resulted in war on the Sudetenland issue, all the other Commonwealth governments would have been placed in a dilemma. My estimate was that, should Britain go to war, only New Zealand would readily join us as an ally; for although its government was strongly averse to war, its leaders and people were so sentimentally attached to their old Mother-Country that they would have supported us in any and every circumstance. The position in the other Dominions was different. I reckoned that the Australians would on balance fight, rather reluctantly, at our side, whilst the Canadians would possibly feel unable to do so. In South Africa and the Irish Free State the prospect was clearer: both those countries would stay neutral. Great Britain would therefore have received the active support of perhaps only two Dominions, and if the Canadian government had in fact decided to become a belligerent, its Parliamentary and public support would have been so dubious that Canada's military effort would be gravely prejudiced. All this could well have been fatal for the Commonwealth, and perhaps also for Britain. The widespread Commonwealth would scarcely survive in such circumstances, and Britain's power to win the war might have been crippled beyond repair.

That was a principal reason why I for one supported Chamberlain in his Munich policy. To misquote Winston Churchill, I had no intention of presiding over the disintegration of the British Commonwealth. Whatever else can be said for and against the Munich Agreement, it saved that important partnership.

The outcome of course further strengthened De Valera's

respect for Chamberlain, and reinforced good relations between their two governments and peoples.

*

A year later the situation had changed. Britain declared war against Germany on a less controversial European issue which persuaded all the Dominions save one to become her allies. Only the Irish Free State stayed neutral.

I held office as Secretary of State for the Colonies for several months after the outbreak of hostilities. Then, when Chamberlain ceased to be Premier and Churchill took his place in May 1940, I became Minister of Health instead.

Not long afterwards the new Prime Minister asked me to come for a talk with him. When I entered his room in 10 Downing Street I found that Chamberlain was the only other person present. Churchill put to me the proposition that I should fly to Dublin for a secret talk with De Valera, to try to persuade him to join us in the war.

As I have already mentioned, Churchill strongly opposed the Agreement with the Irish Free State for which I had laid the foundations in my talks with De Valera a few years earlier. His chief reason was the British government's relinquishment of our navy's occupation of certain sea-ports along Southern Ireland's coast. He felt that if we became involved in war our use of those ports would be invaluable – indeed, perhaps vital – in action against enemy submarines and other ships seeking to blockade our island. This was certainly an extremely important consideration. However, in my and most of Chamberlain's cabinet's judgment – supported by the unanimous opinion of the Chiefs of Staff – the very importance of those ports in the event of war threw the balance of argument, paradoxically, on the side of our voluntarily resigning our Treaty right to occupy them.

Of course, if De Valera had been ready in our negotiations to confirm that right, the situation would have been different, and we would have welcomed its renewal by him. But, not unnaturally, the provision gave great offence to the Southern Irish.

They were supposed to be a fully independent nation, yet their sovereignty was limited by the freedom of a neighbouring power to use several of their harbours for military purposes in both peace and war. I felt that this could gravely prejudice our island's security in time of war. If the Irish Free State were an ally of Britain, no difficulty would arise; but supposing it were neutral? The hostility which the Treaty right aroused among the Irish would then make them vehemently oppose its exercise, and any assertion of it by our navy could provoke an antagonism throughout Southern Ireland which might even force them into the arms of our enemies. This would enable the Germans to use not only their country's ports but also other military establishments such as airfields – with extremely dangerous consequences for Great Britain. I therefore judged it more prudent to resign the Treaty right voluntarily, and to seek to win the Dublin government's friendship in the hope that in case of war we could enjoy the use of the ports with their goodwill.

Indeed, I hoped that in the event of war De Valera and his Ministers would feel that their own national interests required them to be an ally on Britain's side. This turned out to be wishful thinking – a tendency which was occasionally one of my failings in the conduct of affairs. It was not always a mistake, for sometimes that very indulgence in wishful thinking made me continue hopefully trying to persuade my adversaries to accept a certain solution to a problem — which they suddenly, almost unexpectedly did! – when a more rational approach might have led me to abandon the effort long before. At other times my optimism turned out to be misplaced. However, in 1937 I judged that even if the Irish Free State remained out of a war in which we British were involved, a benevolently neutral neighbour would be preferable to a hostile one. If it did mean that our fleet could not use Southern Irish ports, they would also be denied to our enemies, whilst our ships could deploy from the Northern Irish coast. Indeed, when we agreed to leave the ports De Valera gave us an assurance that his government would not allow any enemy to use them for an attack against Britain.

However, in the supreme crisis of 1940, when Britain was fighting for its life and Nazi naval activity in the Atlantic Ocean was a grave threat to our survival, Churchill deplored our inability to take counter-action from Southern Irish sea-ports, and resented the Free State's neutrality. He therefore proposed that I should pay a visit to Dublin to try to bring about a change of heart in De Valera.

I felt sceptical about the chances, but of course agreed to go and do my best. During the next two days I held interesting discussions with De Valera, sometimes accompanied by one or two of his cabinet colleagues. He expressed readiness to consider the proposal that the Irish Free State should become our ally – but on one condition. This was that Ulster should immediately join it in a United Ireland. Probably he realised that the idea was impracticable; but his prime, almost all-engrossing aim in public affairs was still the union of the whole of Ireland. In the course of our talks he suggested the following series of developments: first, that Ulster should be constitutionally separated from Britain and become at least momentarily neutral; second, that it should then at once join the Irish Free State in a Union; and third, that the parliament of this newly enlarged nation would promptly – within twenty-four hours – meet to consider the question of declaring war on Germany. He did not rule out the possibility of such a declaration, although he thought the odds were probably on Ireland remaining neutral.

I told him that so extreme a proposition was unrealistic, since the population of Northern Ireland would vehemently and uncompromisingly oppose it. We could not provoke their wrath in the crisis of war. De Valera did not demur, but he refused to accept certain less extreme proposals for much closer co-operation between Ulster and the Irish Free State with a view to their union at some later date, which Churchill had authorised me to put to him. He said firmly that his government and people could not contemplate abandoning their neutrality at once in return for a vague promise of future Union which might never get implemented. They could only do so if Ireland were definitely united forthwith.

He then argued in serious, friendly vein that in any case a neutral Irish Free State would serve Britain's interests better than an allied one, since in the difficult and indeed desperate circumstances of the time a non-belligerent neighbour could give Britain greater security than a belligerent. He declared emphatically that he and his fellow countrymen were just as eager as any Ulsterman for us British to win the war, since a Nazi victory would be disastrous for all the small free nations. But (he urged) if his government were to declare war on Germany, Hitler would quickly send an army to invade their militarily weak island as a stepping stone to an invasion of Britain itself across the narrow Irish Sea. On the other hand if Southern Ireland remained neutral, the Germans would not dare to attack it. His country therefore provided an area of protection on Britain's flank. He added that his government would give us British every help that a neutral nation could discreetly provide. For example, it would allow its citizens without restriction to join the British army, navy and air force as volunteers; it would permit British soldiers, sailors and airmen to take leave in the Irish Free State provided they wore civilian clothes; and it would convey to the authorities in London any intelligence it could about German naval activities off Southern Ireland's coast. He could scarcely have promised more benevolent co-operation short of declaring war against the enemy.

I personally felt that there was quite a lot of sense in what he said; but when I returned to London and reported the result of my talks to Churchill, he was deeply disappointed, and bitterly critical of De Valera.

*

Owing to my almost continuous absence from Britain in a succession of posts in Canada, Asia, Europe and Africa throughout the last thirty years, I have never seen De Valera since. But from a distance I have watched his activities with keen sympathy. No doubt his personality remains unchanged, for no character whom I have met was cast in a stiffer mould. He maintained certain ideas and beliefs firmly, and unalterably. Some critics might say he was too rigid, too obstinate, too inflexible in his attitudes. However that may be, my comment is that he was the most consistent and honest statesman in his adherence to policies and principles whom I have known in any part of the world.

His greatness as a leader is confined within certain limits. At times he played a distinct part in Commonwealth and wider affairs, but he is not an international giant, only a national one – a great Irishman who has made a unique contribution to the liberty of his fellow-countrymen. So far he has been thwarted in his desire for a United Ireland, but the work which he has done for the people of the Irish Free State has been remarkable not only in its quality but also in its astonishing duration. Today, more than fifty years after he became a rebel Irish leader, and forty years since he was first chosen as Taoiseach of the independent Free State, he is still its popularly elected President. Scarcely any other leader in the past or present has been so long and so consistently acknowledged as the living Father of his People.

Winston Churchill

'He was in his element — a born warrior whose chief interest from childhood had been fighting battles.'

THERE is less need than usual for anyone else to write about Winston Churchill because he himself penned so much on that subject which is authoritative, revealing and fascinating. Indeed, he acted as his own Boswell to his own Dr Johnston – and no more zealous Boswell ever scribbled about a grander Johnston. His series of vivid books, from the single volume *My Early Life* to the six-tomed account of *The Second World War*, describe not only many of the principal events during the dramatic near-century through which he lived, but also his own roles in them. He was a gifted writer of history as well as a notable maker of it; and he felt enthusiastically conscious of his former as well as his latter calling. I remember an afternoon in the House of Commons when he was strongly attacking Stanley Baldwin, then our Prime Minister, on a question of government policy. 'History will say,' he declared, 'that the Right Honourable Gentleman was wrong in this matter.' Then, with a broad grin he added, 'I know it will, because I shall write that history.'

This naturally does not mean that he was an accurate historian with a well-balanced or objective judgment on the affairs he describes. On the contrary, most of his narratives are subjective, and when he recounts significant events in which he was himself involved they tend to be prejudiced and even sometimes misleading. They will need careful study by professional historians with access to many other contemporary sources. Nevertheless, his numerous literary works are a powerful contribution to history, and especially to our and posterity's understanding of that supreme leader of the free world in a moment of fateful peril, Winston Spencer Churchill.

I shall do little more than add a few personal anecdotes to the vast library of Churchilliana being contributed by various authors. My contacts with him were sometimes close, but rarely intimate; and until the outbreak of war in 1939 they were characterised by opposition rather than co-operation. In my essay on Eamon De Valera I have already mentioned the difference of opinion which arose between us regarding the Irish Agreement of 1938. Equally contrary were our views on the Palestine problem in the late 1930s. I was then Secretary of State for the Colonies, and so responsible for British policy on that difficult question, since the Holy Land was a mandated territory under Britain's rule. Churchill was an uncompromising Zionist who believed that the decisive direction concerning Palestine's destiny lay in the Balfour Declaration of 1917, and that the Arab case must be virtually ignored and the Jewish case accepted without qualification. I felt great sympathy with the Jewish cause – especially in view of the Nazi persecution of them which had recently started – and accepted the powerful legal and moral force of the Balfour Declaration. But I also had to recognise assurances given to the Arabs. My deep compassion and liking for the Jews should not make me break Britain's promises to those other people. One trouble was that some of these were in conflict with the Zionist interpretation of the Balfour Declaration, which should not be implemented without proper regard for our wider responsibilities. Indeed, it seemed to me difficult to reconcile completely the two sets of undertakings; and in this situation I realised that the conflict between the Jewish and the Arab points of view was not one between Right and Wrong, but one between Right and Right. In my opinion, therefore, negotiation was necessary to seek a mutually agreed compromise settlement which would be fair to both parties.

Early in 1939 I chaired a Conference for that purpose, composed of representatives of the Jewish Agency on one side and the Arab states and Palestinian Arabs on the other, with the British Government as a conciliator between the two. We conferred in St James's Palace in London, and our discussions continued for about a fortnight. Yet the Jewish and Arab delegates hardly ever met! So bitterly antipathetic were they to one another that they rarely consented to appear in the same room together. As a consequence I and my British colleagues – Lord Halifax, the Foreign Secretary, and R. A. Butler, his Parliamentary Under-Secretary of State – used to meet one group by itself every morning and the other every afternoon, exploring the outlook of each, reasoning with them, reporting the arguments of one side to the other, and endeavouring to find some patch of common ground between them on which to lay the foundations of an accord. From the start our efforts seemed to be almost hopeless; but twice we did manage to reach a point of possible agreement sufficiently promising to persuade leaders of the two teams to sit at the same table under my chairmanship, and to exchange views. On both those occasions – after some initial cold diplomatic courtesies and cautious political probings – our slender hopes were dashed. The meetings adjourned with no result except an obstinate agreement to disagree. Thus the chance of discovering an amicable solution of one of the world's most delicate international problems was lost, perhaps for ever. It was one of my great failures in statecraft.

A later attempt that I made to achieve a compromise solution by virtual arbitration was an equal flop. My most potent critic in Parliament, Winston Churchill, was neither surprised nor disappointed. As I have written, he was wholly committed to the Zionist side; and in more than one House of Commons debate he and I clashed as the chief protagonists of two points of view. He felt passionately on the subject, and viewed me with distinct disapproval.

After one of those debates he and I continued our contentions in the division lobby. He was in ill temper, and his eloquence took a gruff turn. After making some extremely contemptuous remarks about the Arabs, he charged me with breaking the British nation's word to the Jewish people. I answered with what I thought were quietly reasoned arguments, but he was in no mood to consider these, and replied in words of unqualified condemnation. Among other vicious statements he declared that the Arabs were barbaric hordes who ate little but camels' dung. Our exchanges became ever more animated, but consistently fruitless, and I felt they would lead us nowhere. So, after one particularly vehement pronouncement by him, I changed the subject.

'Winston,' I remarked, 'I wish I had a son.'

He glowered at me uncomprehendingly and asked, 'What do you want a son for?'

'Because I'm reading at the moment,' I answered, 'a book called "My Early Life" by a certain writer named Winston Churchill. It's superb, and I'd like to give it to my son and say to him, "Go thou and do likewise".'

Churchill beamed a broad smile, tears moistened his eye-lids, and he gripped my arms in both his fists. In cordial phrases he expressed his gratitude.

On the following day I received a copy of his latest book, 'The Life and Times of John Churchill, Duke of Marlborough', autographed in generous terms by its distinguished author.

*

This friendly incident made no difference, of course, to his views on the Palestine problem – or on me! One of his compelling qualities was his capacity to champion every cause he espoused with unquenchable fervour and dedication.

I have mentioned the speeches which he and I used to make against each other on that Palestine issue. During one of my earlier statements in a House of Commons debate he interrupted my peroration with a mischievous interjection which convulsed our fellow Members with laughter – and ruined the peroration.

The date was November, 1938. A few weeks earlier the famous meeting between Neville Chamberlain and Adolph Hitler at Munich had taken place. On his return to London the Prime Minister made his imprudent remark prophesying that the agreement he had reached with the Führer could mean 'Peace in our time', and a false glow of optimism about the possibility of curbing Nazi Germany's European ambitions without resort to war inspired many Members on both the

Government and the Opposition sides. Churchill was not one of their number.

I had become Secretary of State for the Colonies a few days earlier. My speech was largely analytical of the grim, confused Palestinian problem. In it I sketched first the Jewish and then the Arab case, described the great difficulty of reconciling the two, and declared that nevertheless the Government would devote all its resources and energy towards this reconciliation. Then, as a peroration, I indulged in a flight of somewhat religious appeal. Reminding my fellow Members that Palestine was a Holy Land, I urged that our responsibility for its fate had an especially sacred quality. Working up towards a climax of reverent reflection, I said to a hushed House, 'I cannot remember a time when I was not told stories about Nazareth and Galilee, about Jerusalem and Bethlehem, where the Prince of Peace was born.'

I hesitated a moment for effect before pronouncing a final eloquent sentence of Christian pleading. But the silence was promptly punctuated by Churchill's voice muttering in a stage whisper which all could hear, 'Good Heavens! I never knew Neville was born in Bethlehem.'

The crowded House roared with laughter, and my closing sentence was an anti-climax. Unfortunately the official Hansard report of the debate primly ignored that classic interjection.

*

There were many other reasons why Churchill despised my politics. He and my father had always been good friends, but they usually represented opposite schools of thought in public affairs – and I was a faithful disciple of my parent. So on socialism, India and various other national and international problems he and I disagreed.

Nevertheless, when he became Prime Minister in the war-time crisis of 1940 he invited me to join his government. In the previous cabinet he had been First Lord of the Admiralty; and on the day of his elevation he formed his new Administration in his Admiralty office before moving into 10 Downing Street. One after another he summoned all his Ministerial partners-to-be, to tell them which posts he wished them to fill. I arrived a minute before my appointed hour, and was ushered into his assistants' ante-room. A private secretary told me that Mr Leo Amery was with the Prime Minister at the moment, but that he would emerge very soon.

Not long afterwards the door into Churchill's room opened, and through it came a smiling Amery, seeming rather pleased with himself.

I entered the presence. The great man was striding up and down the chamber with his head thrust forward in deep thought on his massive shoulders and his hands gripping the lapels of his jacket, as if he were making a speech in the House of Commons.

He looked round, caught sight of me, and said rather oratorically without halting his pacings, 'My dear Malcolm, I'm glad to see you. I've nothing to offer you except . . .' For a moment he hesitated deliberately in his utterance.

I felt disappointed, thinking he could have no more senior office to give me than that of Postmaster General or some similar minor job.

Then he continued, '. . . blood and toil, tears and sweat.'

I was taken aback, wondering whether he had created a new war-time Ministry, and was asking me to become Secretary of State for Blood, Toil, Tears and Sweat.

He glanced at me to observe my reaction, stood still, and then in a voice suddenly changed to friendly informality remarked, 'I want you to be Minister of Health in my government.' He added that this would be an important task because Hitler might soon be in a position to start an all-out onslaught on Britain, and the Ministry of Health would be responsible for many services protecting and sustaining our population through the crisis.

I of course accepted the proposal. Afterwards the Prime Minister and I exchanged a few pleasantries, and then I left the room whilst he recommenced his pacings to and fro, again with his hands gripping the lapels of his coat.

Amery awaited me in the private secretary's office. He looked at me enquiringly, and I told him that I was to be Minister of Health.

He expressed satisfaction, and then asked, 'Did he also offer you blood and sweat and toil and tears?'

I answered 'Yes'; and Amery remarked that he had received the same proposition. 'He must be rehearsing his speech for Parliament this afternoon,' he commented.

Miss Ellen Wilkinson arrived in the room, and was shown into the Premier's study whilst Amery and I hastened away to start our new jobs without delay.

A few hours later we all sat in a crowded House of Commons listening to Churchill making his first speech as Prime Minister. In the middle of it we suddenly heard him utter the well-rehearsed and now immortal phrase, 'I would say to the House, as I said to those who have joined this Government, I have nothing to offer but blood, toil, tears and sweat.'

*

I was not a member of his War Cabinet. That small, select group of Ministers was confined to his most important colleagues like Max Beaverbrook, Anthony Eden, John Anderson and a few others. I therefore did not often have the privilege of joining in their discussions about the strategy and tactics of first defending Britain and afterwards assaulting Nazi-held Europe which took place in the cabinet room, and during which the Prime Minister talked sometimes at great length, and always with formidable eloquence about the military and diplomatic conduct of hostilities. Only now and then, when the affairs of my Department were closely involved, was I summoned to take part.

The most memorable occasion when I listened to one of Churchill's confidential discourses to a group of Ministers was on the historic day in 1940 when the Allies' resistance to Hitler's armies on the Continent had finally collapsed, and the British expeditionary force was being evacuated from Dunkirk. He invited all his senior colleagues who were not members of the

War Cabinet to meet him in his room in the House of Commons. About a score of us attended, and we sat round a table at which he presided. The mood of the company was tensely anxious because of the very bad news from Europe, which caused a combination of apprehension at the appalling defeat that the Allies had suffered, and of pride at the heroic if humiliating episode in which our troops were now engaged. I remember vividly that the sky out of doors was a mixture of blue heaven and grey clouds which caused sunbeams to keep alternately slanting brightly and dissolving gloomily through tall windows into the room – a display of Nature's indecisive mood of mixed optimism and pessimism which seemed appropriate to the occasion.

Churchill addressed us. He started by giving the latest information from Dunkirk and expressing a cautiously confident hope that all our surviving soldiers would be safely embarked for Britain before the enemy caught up with them. Then he declared his own decision – despite the current tragedy – to continue the war against Germany without any thought of seeking a negotiated peace. He observed that Hitler would probably be ready to make such a peace, since he was now about to gain all that he wanted in Europe, for the time being at least, and had no particular ambition to conquer Britain. But the Prime Minister added that in his judgment the prospect of Nazi rule throughout the Continent was intolerable, and that its protracted existence would become a steadily increasing threat to Britain itself and to British Imperial rule overseas. Therefore he thought we should not contemplate any negotiation, even though we could probably secure a quite honourable settlement from our short-term point of view. In his opinion we must continue to fight in spite of the fact that we should be struggling physically alone against a powerful and so far victorious foe. We would of course receive moral and some material support from fellow members in the Commonwealth like Canada and Australia, and from certain benevolently neutral powers such as the United States; but apart from that we would be battling entirely on our own. At this point he remarked that if any of his Ministerial colleagues thought his decision wrong, and favoured an effort to make peace, he would understand and respect their point of view, even though he disagreed with it. They were free to resign from his Government with every mark of friendship from him.

He did not attempt to deny that his determination to continue fighting, with virtually the whole of Europe now under enemy control, would face the people of our little island with appalling dangers. And he proceeded to describe those dangers. The first was the possibility of an early military invasion from across the English Channel. This could not be ruled out, for Hitler commanded forces which would make his chance of success quite formidable. On the other hand our navy was in good shape, and should inflict considerable losses on the Germans whilst they crossed the sea, even if they did succeed in landing some troops in Kent or Sussex, and in reinforcing them afterwards. Moreover (Churchill observed) one should not be too much guided by precise calculations based on irrefutable facts about comparative military strengths: in war incalculable elements sometimes intruded to exert unforeseeable influences. Thus the frequently changing moods of the English weather could play a decisive part in any attempt to invade Britain from the opposite French coast. A few days of stormy seas might coincide with the dates that the Nazis chose for their operation, and throw it completely out of gear.

The Prime Minister then reviewed other possibilities of an attack on England. He said we must be ready to face massive bombing assaults from the German air force. We should be prepared to live and work for days on end in air-raid shelters underground, at the same time remaining actively alert to counter all the destruction which would be wrought above ground. He felt sure that our own Air Force would give a good account of itself. Perhaps, if we were to contemplate a long-drawn siege, we should plan the evacuation of vast sections of our population across the Atlantic Ocean.

Afterwards his speculations roamed over the outlook in greater detail. Assuming that the enemy could land armed forces on our shores, he spoke of the resistance we must organise. He talked of us fighting on the beaches, and in the fields, and along the streets in towns and cities – in much the same dramatic language as he employed in a famous speech shortly afterwards in Parliament. His imagery was based on the possibility that for a while at least the invaders would meet with success, and that we must obstinately oppose every step of their advance. In his next few sentences this notion was carried to a further, graver conclusion when he declared that perhaps the foe would eventually smash all opposition within our homeland and become complete masters of the British Isles. Concerning this prospect he commented that we should never surrender, and that we would therefore withdraw our remaining forces to Canada and other friendly countries in order to continue the war relentlessly from overseas, with confident certainty of ultimate victory even if we had to wait for several years. He felt sure that the customarily free peoples of Europe would not tolerate indefinitely slavery under a dictatorship by Huns. Underground movements, secret subversion, open rebellions would occur, growing steadily in power until the tyranny was overthrown.

With a gleam in his eyes during his passages about fighting on the beaches and in the streets, he spoke of himself carrying a gun and shooting at the enemy – almost as if this would be the most enjoyable moment in his whole life.

For a long time he talked with passionate, pugnacious eloquence, never seeking to minimise the troubles which we should face if we refused to make peace with Hitler on the morrow of Dunkirk. He foreshadowed a long and gruelling struggle, declaring that this was essential to defend the British way of life and the British Empire against extinction, and expressing unquenchable optimism that in the end we should gain victory.

I think this was the most unforgettable hour I have ever spent in a career generously sprinkled with memorable experiences. Needless to say, when Churchill finished speaking, none of his Ministers offered his resignation.

*

Not long afterwards the Prime Minister asked me to come for the talk with him and Neville Chamberlain about the secret visit by me to Dublin which I have already described in the previous chapter. Tirelessly, ceaselessly he was probing every possibility of increasing our strength against the enemy.

He had now reached the climax of his amazing career. After a long life's journey which carried him through a lot of uphill and downhill political country he had at last – at the advanced age of sixty-six – arrived in the foothills of the supreme mountain range for which he had always been hopefully searching; and he started to scale heights which during the next year would carry him to a summit of historic glory. He revelled in the adventure, for which all his previous strivings had been an instinctive preparation.

The nation's situation was desperate, and the way ahead appeared extremely difficult and dark. But Churchill had the sort of vision which could penetrate the darkness, perceiving narrow paths through and beyond it; and his eloquence enabled his fellow-countrymen to catch glimpses of the same prospect. He was in his element – a born warrior whose chief interest from childhood (when he loved playing with tin soldiers) had been fighting battles – and military battles in preference to mere political ones. Though he deplored the turn of events in Europe, he nevertheless delighted in its consequence for himself. At last his genius as a war leader could receive uninhibited expression.

When he became Prime Minister it was by no means certain that Britain could survive the trials which loomed ahead, and which became ever more evident during the next several weeks with the conquest of France and the subjugation of virtually all Europe to Nazi Germany. Nor was the organisation of our nation's war effort such that the qualities of the British people as fighters could be adequately asserted. The administration in Whitehall was still working in too low a key; the parties in Parliament were divided in their loyalties, and the population as a whole felt uncertain about what to do and how to do it. Latent in them were their native virtues of courage and tenacity, but these were not fully mobilised, nor roused to an unconquerable pitch. They needed awakening and leading. Within a few days Churchill had begun to achieve this. He galvanised the machine of government into top gear; he created a united government, Parliament and nation; and he infected the masses of the people with his own optimism about ultimate triumph. Nor did he do this by misleading them with false hopes of easy or early success. On the contrary, he was completely candid about the difficulties, dangers and even defeats which lay ahead, and about the obstinate refusal to surrender which would be necessary to snatch victory from many grim setbacks. He himself felt confident about ultimate success, and he inspired his fellow-countrymen with the same confidence. In the early months he did this chiefly by the spoken word. His gift of oratory was like a magic wand which he waved miraculously. Those dramatically eloquent, grim and gay, defiant and exhorting speeches through the crisis of 1940 turned the tide of war, and transformed the British nation's moment of greatest peril into its 'Finest hour'.

*

The emergency through the crucial summer of 1940 required continuous hard work by every member of the Ministerial team. We all toiled mornings, noons and half the nights. The Prime Minister was a tough task-master, often sending us enquiries throughout the days, far into the evenings and during the small hours of a morning about details of our policies. The heaviest strain fell upon him; so much depended on the powerful impetus of his leadership. He never flagged in any of his waking moments. In spite of his advanced years he possessed Titanic energy, and was the guiding head and heart of the nation's resistance. At that fateful crisis in modern history he was the one indispensable man who could save Britain from destruction.

It was therefore of paramount importance that he should stay fit and strong. After the first three hectic months of preparation for the expected Battle of Britain – which in one form or another was bound to erupt before long – Parliament was about to adjourn at the end of July for its recess. A day before the adjournment the War Cabinet met in 10 Downing Street with a small group of other Ministers to review the current situation and take some urgent decisions. I was one of those present. At the close of our discussion the Prime Minister addressed us. He said we had all worked admirably through a most difficult period, but that our greatest trials and tribulations still lay ahead. He expected they would begin in the early autumn, when the enemy would almost certainly attack our island. We must be ready for that supreme test, which would be prolonged; and so we must keep in the best of health to respond to the challenge whenever it came. He therefore hoped we would all take advantage of the Parliamentary recess to enjoy a bit of a holiday. 'Don't all go away at the same time,' he said with a grin. 'Arrange to disappear in turns, each of you asking a colleague to act for you during your absence.'

When he finished speaking Lord Halifax, the Foreign Secretary, replied that we would all obey his instruction, provided that he himself did likewise. Halifax said that Churchill's robust health was what mattered most to the nation and all free mankind, that he had carried the greatest burden throughout the last several months, and that it was of paramount importance that he should seize the opportunity for a brief, refreshing respite. 'We're ready to follow your good example in all things,' he ended. 'So if you'll take a holiday, we'll all take holidays as well in turn.'

Churchill listened courteously to this appeal, and then gave a broad smile as he remarked, 'My dear Edward, my life is a perpetual holiday.'

*

He proved right in his forecast that the Germans would strike at Britain in the autumn. On the afternoon of September the 7th groups of Junker bomber aircraft launched the first serious air raid on London; and from that date onwards almost daily assaults occurred there and elsewhere in the island.

Two Ministers in particular were responsible for the protection of our civilian population against the effects of enemy attacks: Sir John Anderson as Minister of Home Security and myself as Minister of Health. Anderson and his officials were in charge of all the Civil Defence arrangements, whilst I and my officers administered the emergency medical and hospital services, the public air-raid shelters system, the food-and-rest centres for people bombed out of their homes, the scheme for evacuating children, old folks and other non-essential urban residents into the safer countryside – or across the Atlantic Ocean – and various similar projects. Anderson and I worked in the closest co-operation, meeting with our principal advisers at the start of every morning to consider the current situation and settle quickly any problems which had arisen during the last twenty-four hours. Late in 1940 he was moved to another important post in the cabinet, and Herbert Morrison succeeded him as Minister of Home Security. Morrison and I continued the same fruitful collaboration.

They were times of dedication to the task of saving the nation. Not just a few leaders at the top, but millions of people at every level of society were involved in this vital purpose. Air-raid wardens, first-aid teams, stretcher parties, fire fighters, doctors, nurses, hospital staffs and other types of civil defence workers, as well as gunners in anti-aircraft batteries and air- and ground-crews of the Air Force were engaged through much of the night following their normal daytime toil on the battlefields of the exposed towns and cities.

For myself, my duties took me night after night on tours of inspection in London boroughs expecting or actually suffering assaults, and sometimes into damaged industrial centres elsewhere in the country. These visits gave me an insight into the workings of our Civil Defence plans during the height of each battle which few others possessed; and periodically Churchill summoned me to tell him my views on this or that aspect of England's protection. One evening, for instance, he invited Morrison and me to dine with him in the well protected quarters which he and his wife occupied near their official residence at 10 Downing Street. He wished to hold with us a thorough discussion about our future London defence policy.

His portly figure greeted us dressed in the zip-fastened siren suit which he usually wore for convenience at home in those hectic times. Throughout an excellent dinner his conversation was genial, for he was in cheerful mood. The day happened to be a significant one in the history of the war, since news of the capture of Tobruk by our forces had just arrived in London. The Prime Minister discoursed at length on the strategy and tactics of our campaign in North Africa, spreading a map of the Libyan desert on the table among the knives, forks and dishes, and describing the vicissitudes of the Tobruk affair. For the first two hours he dismissed from his mind our problems on the home front.

Then he swept the map aside and said, 'Now tell me what's happening in the East End of London. The battle of Stepney is just as important as the battle of Tobruk.'

And for the next few hours we discussed exhaustively the civil defence of Britain, examining all sorts of problems which would arise as new German offensive devices developed and our counter measures needed continuous adaptation to match them. Churchill cross-examined me about my most recent visits to various parts of the island. At one point in the talk the admirable part which the King and Queen were playing in sustaining the morale of our population was mentioned. The Premier expressed deep appreciation of King George VI's and Queen Elizabeth's tireless devotion to duty. He remarked that during the Abdication crisis in 1936 he had strongly supported King Edward VIII, urging that he should be allowed to stay on the throne; but he now commented that he had been mistaken, since that monarch and his wife would not have been such a popular rallying pair as the present King and Queen.

Churchill himself had considerable experience of what was happening in bombed areas of the island, for although he was primarily concerned with the prosecution of the war overseas he made frequent journeys to important centres in the country, including visits to London boroughs which had been recently bombed. Those personal appearances by him did a tremendous amount to raise even higher the defiant spirit of the population. One story that I was told at the time illustrated his unconventional touch with the masses of ordinary men and women. He went to a district which had been badly damaged in an air-raid during the previous night. The local cockneys – many of whose homes had been destroyed – crowded round him, thrilled by his presence. At the end of his tour of battered streets he stood with his back to a large heap of rubble where twenty-four hours earlier a public building had stood, and signalled to the crowd for silence. He made a short speech to them. In characteristically robust phrases he expressed his admiration for their steadfastness, uttered defiance of 'Lance-corporal Hitler', and commented that the ruined edifice behind him was of no account – its destruction could be treated with contempt, for it made no difference to the British nation's resolve to continue fighting until they gained victory. He then raised one hand aloft with two fingers stuck up in his famous 'V' sign of Victory, turned his back on the audience, and with his other hand undid the front buttons of his trousers and relieved himself on the rubble. The multitude of people were convulsed with laughter and cheers.

*

Churchill was tireless in his travels through various parts of Britain, inspecting army units, naval establishments, air force stations, munitions factories and other manifestations of the national effort. Wherever he went crowds of people gathered to see and applaud him.

One day he visited Scotland with General Sikorski, the leader of the Polish government in exile, to review Polish troops in training there. On their return to London the General told me about the occasion, which had been a distinct success. Churchill was obviously impressed by what he saw of the allied soldiers, and Sikorski felt very pleased. Indeed, he thought the Prime Minister was in such affable mood that this would be a good moment to seek his aid on a difficult problem which had arisen for the Polish authorities.

The matter concerned finance. Sikorski's government naturally needed a lot of money to perform its administrative tasks, maintain its military forces, and support all the other war activities in which it was engaged. Its financial resources were limited, however, for away from its homeland it had no population to tax, and few other sources of income. It therefore depended on help from friends. At the time of Churchill's Scottish visit Sikorski was trying to raise a loan in the City of London; but difficulties had arisen. The bankers were proving reluctant to lend cash on terms agreeable to the General and his colleagues.

He therefore broached the question with Churchill, explaining the situation to him, and asking him whether he would use his unique influence with the powers-that-be in the City to grant the Poles' request. Sikorski could speak no English, and talked with the Prime Minister in French.

In reply Churchill shook his head sorrowfully, and remarked in his slightly halting, schoolboy-accented French, 'Non, mon General; quand je suis avec les Vieux Dames de Threadneedle Street je suis impotent.'

*

After a while he began to send some of his Ministers of Cabinet rank overseas to represent the British government in the capitals of important allied or friendly powers. Thus Lord Halifax became our Ambassador in Washington, Duff Cooper went to Singapore, and later such men as Philip Cunliffe-Lister, Oliver

Lyttleton and Harold Macmillan were posted to various parts of Africa. In March, 1941 he asked me whether I would go to Ottawa as High Commissioner, explaining that our relations with Canada were becoming more and more important in certain fields of the allies' war effort, and that when he had suggested to MacKenzie King, the Canadian Premier, that I might come to Ottawa as a liaison between them, MacKenzie King had expressed pleasure.

At first I resisted the proposal, for I felt extremely reluctant to leave besieged Britain unless I did so as a soldier proceeding overseas to fight the enemy. At the beginning of the war I had begged the then Prime Minister, Chamberlain, to let me resign my cabinet office and join the army; but he refused to let me go, asserting that my experience as a Minister would make me more valuable to the nation as an administrator in Whitehall than as a Tommy in a training camp. Now again I urged Churchill to grant me freedom to join the armed forces rather than retreat to North America, however important the job to be done there might be. I said I would feel miserable if I left the black-out of London for the lights of Ottawa.

Churchill expressed sympathy with this sentiment, but urged that I should nevertheless go to Canada. He commented that MacKenzie King would feel very upset if I refused his plea, and asked me to think the matter over for twenty-four hours if I was not ready to give an immediate positive reply. I agreed to do this, and after a day's agonised reflection decided that every one of us must be ready to work in whatever capacity Churchill judged would be most useful to Britain's cause. So I reluctantly accepted his suggestion, and prepared to sail across the Atlantic Ocean.

On the day before my departure I lunched with him in Downing Street. The only other guest was Lord Beaverbrook, who was of course proud of his Canadian ancestry and his birth in Nova Scotia. The three of us discussed certain questions touching Anglo-Canadian co-operation in the manufacture of essential war supplies, and in the expansion of the vitally important Commonwealth scheme for training Air Force pilots and crews which was being developed across vast, safe Canada.

At the end of the meal, when I was taking leave of Churchill, he said with mock seriousness as he glanced at Beaverbrook, 'The first duty you must perform when you get to Canada, dear Malcolm, is to visit Nova Scotia and lay a bunch of flowers on the doorstep of the house where Max was born.'

I must confess that I never carried out this instruction. I always felt that one symptom of the less attractive side of the Prime Minister's character was his long-standing, close friendship with Beaverbrook. Nonetheless, I was told by some of his intimates that the notorious press lord performed a unique service for the nation through the darkest days of the war. Churchill was temperamental, like many other prima-donnas, and every now and then he sank into profound despondence about the progress of the war. In these moods he was apt to lose confidence in himself, to think he was perhaps making grave mistakes in the conduct of affairs, and even to be morosely pessimistic about the chances of victory. And at those times Beaverbrook would have long sessions *à deux* with him over drinks of brandy, and would tactfully humour him, telling him that he was the greatest Englishman who ever lived, and prophesying that his place in history would be peerless. After a while those sentiments reassured the leader, pulled him out of his depression, and restored his customary buoyant spirits.

*

I sailed across the Atlantic in a battleship. Soon after settling down in my new post in Ottawa I went to visit Lord Halifax in Washington so that we could discuss with the American authorities certain problems of Canadian-American co-operation in support of Britain's war effort. The United States were still neutral, and this occasionally caused delicate situations to arise.

President Roosevelt invited Halifax and me to lunch with him at the White House. The meal was served in his private study, where the three of us could hold our confidential conversation without interruption. For me the occasion was a fascinating first glimpse of the remarkable American leader. He was in light-hearted mood whilst waiters handed round our food and drinks; but as soon as they left the room he switched his talk from some amusing personal reminiscences to the current state of the war. He remained cheerful, for in spite of all the formidable difficulties around and ahead of us he evidently felt no shadow of doubt about our ultimate triumph. Though his country was carefully avoiding any involvement in hostilities, he, its President, spoke throughout as if his government and people were fully committed allies of Britain. He explained to me that one of his embarrassing problems was American public opinion, majority sections of which were strongly averse to entry into the war; and he observed that he must therefore be careful not to offend this sentiment, although he was determined so to guide the thoughts of his countrymen that at some appropriate future moment he could declare war against the Nazis.

He did not in fact achieve this until several months later, when the Japanese bombing at Pearl Harbour gave him the opportunity he patiently waited for. Yet one would hardly have guessed this from the way he talked that afternoon. For example, whilst we were discussing the ways and means by which an allied army could eventually mount an invasion of Europe, he expressed the view that at the right time large landings of additional fighting men should be made in North Africa, to drive the enemy completely from the southern shores of the Mediterranean and so free that sea for action by our naval and military forces against the continent to its north. He wheeled himself in his cripple's chair to a map of Northern Africa hanging on a wall, pointed to the Tunisian coast, and said emphatically, 'I think that's where we should land' – using the word 'we' to include American as well as British troops.

If some of his Senators and Congressmen had heard their President speaking with us on that mid-summer's day in 1941, they would have been profoundly shocked!

*

Churchill's popularity as our war leader was not always unchallenged. Every now and then a situation arose which caused him to be criticised. He was aware of the ups and downs that occurred from time to time in the confidence he commanded among his fellow countrymen. In one of our talks he said to me, 'I'm like a bomber pilot. I go out night after night, and I know that one night I'll not return.'

Such a slump in his popularity had occurred when I flew to London for consultations about a year after I first went to Canada. The important fortress of Tobruk in Africa had been re-taken by the enemy. This was a grave, unexpected blow; and a sense of unease affected public opinion throughout Britain. Many people felt that serious mistakes were being made in the conduct of hostilities; and the Prime Minister himself became a target for attack. Certain Members of Parliament were inclined to think that his influence in guiding military strategy might be too strong, too amateur and too dictatorial, that he was in danger of being a liability instead of an asset as Prime Minister, and that someone else should replace him. Not many important persons thought this, but the notion began to circulate in a few high places.

On my return from Canada I was surprised to learn that one of his close partners in the War Cabinet held this view. I was even more surprised by the source from which I heard the news – the Minister concerned himself, Sir Stafford Cripps. Soon after my arrival in London he asked me to come for a talk with him in his Whitehall office, and in the private of his room he confided his opinion to me as a strict secret. What astonished me most of all was the name of the man whom he thought should succeed Churchill – none other than Cripps himself.

He asked me whether any of his colleagues were expressing the same thought to me. I answered that I had arrived in London only on the previous morning, that I had therefore talked with no more than two or three Ministers so far, and that none of these had mentioned any such notion.

Cripps commented that he believed several members of the

cabinet might seriously consider the proposal; and he suggested that it would be useful if I – as a friend of many influential men both inside and outside the government, and as an experienced and now detached High Commissioner in Canada with no personal axe of my own to grind – felt able to float the idea with some of those concerned. I was amazed by this proposition, and answered that I thought it would be wrong for me to get involved in such a delicate political matter.

I had a high regard for Cripps, who was a man of outstanding ability, integrity and courage. Perhaps at that moment he allowed the personal ambition which is inevitably an element in the make-up of most successful politicians to influence his thoughts unduly; but no doubt he also felt genuinely worried by Churchill's tendency to thrust his military ideas on the Chiefs of Staff and the cabinet, and was anxious lest this should prejudice the safety of the nation.

However, I did not agree with his suggestion for a change in the Premiership, and I refrained from pursuing the matter. Several days later I returned to Canada, and on none of my subsequent visits to England did I hear so much as a whisper either from Cripps or anyone else to the effect that Churchill should be replaced by another Prime Minister.

I sometimes wondered whether Churchill became aware of Cripps' private plan, and whether this knowledge prompted a mischievous remark which he muttered to a friend during a later debate in Parliament. A difficult situation for the Government had arisen in the House of Commons, and as Leader of the House Cripps took charge of the altercation which developed. He was somewhat arrogant in his handling of the incident, and as a result it continued longer than it need have done. Arguments and counter-arguments flew between him and several Members; but in the end he got his way, and the House accepted the government's policy. Cripps strode haughtily out of the chamber.

Churchill was sitting with other Ministers on the front bench. As Cripps walked past them he nudged Ernest Bevin reclining bulkily at his side, jerked a thumb towards their withdrawing colleague and asked, 'Do you see who that is going out, Ernie?'

Bevin looked up, glanced at Cripps, and said, 'Do you mean Stafford?'

'No,' answered the P.M. with a solemn shake of his head. 'There, but for the grace of God, goes God.'

*

Often whilst I lived in Canada I flew across the Atlantic for consultations in London. It was essential for those of us who held responsibilities in North America to keep in close contact with our colleagues in Whitehall. On every visit I had a good talk with Churchill about current events, and similar discussions with other Ministers.

On one such occasion I had an interesting chat with an old friend, General 'Pug' Ismay, who throughout Churchill's wartime Premiership was a vitally important member of his staff in Downing Street. A soldierly official with no particular genius, but with considerable experience, shrewdness and common sense, Ismay also understood how to deal tactfully but firmly with people, including his masterful boss. His particular duty was to act as a liaison between the temperamental Prime Minister – who always had strong views of his own on military matters – and the Chiefs of Staff, the very eminent soldier, sailor and airman who were his top professional advisers on the waging of the war. Many arguments between the Prime Minister and this trio occurred at their meetings, and the great man used sometimes to disagree quite sharply with the advice they offered him. Ismay's supreme service to the nation was the maintenance of harmony among them all.

'How sound is Winston's wisdom in great military affairs?' I asked him. 'How often is his judgment right, and how often wrong?'

The General replied, 'I'll give you the answer in a horse-racing analogy. When Winston is betting on a classic race he nearly always spots the winner, and is proved right. But often when he's betting on an unimportant race he allows his imagination to play tricks with his cooler judgment – and he backs a loser!'

*

Periodically I flew from Ottawa to Washington for consultations. My stays there were always intensely interesting, and none more so than an occasion in 1942 when Churchill went for a few days as Roosevelt's guest at the White House. The two leaders, their joint Chiefs of Staff and other of their principal advisers held a summit conference to consider the current war situation and determine its future conduct. The United States had by then been Britain's active ally for a considerable time, and their partnership was becoming ever more formidable.

MacKenzie King joined the party, and I also was asked to come from Ottawa for talks about the increasingly helpful part which Canada was playing in contemporary developments. Now and then during those days I chatted with Churchill, but usually our conversation was brief because his American hosts filled his time with not only a succession of long official discussions, but also interviews with influential Congressmen and Senators. However, he was anxious for a fuller exchange of views with me, and he invited me to come and see him early one morning before his other engagements were due to commence.

I arrived at the White House, was met in its hall by a member of his personal staff, and guided upstairs to his private suite on the first floor. The aide opened a door, motioned me to enter, and closed it behind me, himself staying outside. I presumed that I should find Churchill within; but the room was empty. I had also assumed that the chamber would be his study or sitting-room; but I found that it was his bedroom. Pillows, sheets and blankets lay in disarray on a broad four-poster bed, and among them nestled two large red boxes which I recognised as repositories for secret official documents. Otherwise the couch was unoccupied, having evidently been vacated by its sleeper shortly before. On a nearby chair lay some discarded evening clothes, along a sofa a clean shirt, undergarments and socks were neatly arranged, and on a dressing-table were scattered Churchill's gold watch, cigar case and other similar properties.

I became aware of the sound of splashing issuing through a door slightly ajar in one wall, which evidently led into a bathroom. Sure enough, a few moments later the door opened, and through it stepped an immaculately dressed man-servant whom I recognised as the Prime Minister's valet. He said that his master would not keep me waiting more than a minute, since he was just getting out of his bath. Soon afterwards Churchill appeared wearing nothing but a towel wrapped round his middle. His naked skin was dripping wet, and he started to dry himself as he greeted me. Unfurling the towel from his body, he vigorously rubbed his ample torso and limbs, and began to ask me questions about the current situation in Canada.

The valet was meanwhile brushing a suit which Churchill would wear, and arranging it for putting on. He then unfolded a pair of underpants lying on the sofa and held them up for Churchill to get into as soon as he was ready. When that moment arrived the Prime Minister turned his back on me, threw his towel aside, and stepped into the drawers. Twisting round again, he held out his two arms to let the valet fit first a vest and then a shirt upon him. Throughout these processes I sat on a stool beside the dressing-table whilst he and I maintained a running conversation about the latest developments in Canada's war activities. Churchill fired pertinent questions at me without cease as his servant fitted on his socks, helped him into his trousers, handed him a tie for his own knotting, buttoned a waistcoat on him, placed his shoes on his feet and tied them up, and finally handed him his jacket – which the great man condescended to put on himself. His comments on my answers were vigorous, apt and sometimes humorous. Our conversation continued whilst he collected some money, a handkerchief, his case of cigars and a few other requirements, and put them in his pockets. Then he sat relaxed on a chair for another twenty minutes telling me of the main questions being settled in his discussions with Roosevelt.

It was a pleasant mixture of private domesticity and official confabulation. Eventually a knock sounded on the door, a private secretary poked his face into the room to announce that the President was ready downstairs for the resumption of their talks – and Churchill bade me goodbye. He asked the secretary to rescue the official red-boxes lying among the blankets on his bed, and started to light a cigar as he strode from the room.

*

The recollection of that scene reminds me of a story I was told some time later about how the name of the United Nations Organisation came to be invented. The incident occurred during one of Churchill's stays in the White House. According to my informant, one evening after dinner the President and Prime Minister sat discussing how the world should be reshaped after Hitler had been overthrown and peace restored. Among other topics they exchanged views about the international body which should take the place of the old League of Nations to organise peaceful co-existence among all the peoples round the Earth. After reaching agreement on various proposals regarding its constitution, they turned to the question of the most appropriate title for it. The body could not be re-christened the League of Nations, since that description was now rather discredited. Both Roosevelt and Churchill offered various suggestions, but none of them seemed quite right. The hour became late, and they decided to adjourn their discussion, sleep on the problem, and resume consideration of it the next day.

Churchill slumbered as soundly and unconcernedly as usual; but the President lay awake pondering on the question of a suitable name. Sometime in the small hours of the morning he hit upon a bright idea, and decided to put it to his guest as early as possible. He then fell asleep; but as soon as he woke he slipped out of bed into his wheel-chair, trundled himself along a corridor to Churchill's bedroom, and knocked on the door. Not waiting for an invitation to enter, he opened it and manoeuvred himself inside. The place was empty. However, he saw that the bathroom door stood ajar, and he shouted through it, 'Winston, are you there?'

'Yes, Franklin,' called a voice. 'Come in.'

Roosevelt wheeled himself into the inner chamber, but at first could see no sign of its occupant. Guiding his vehicle alongside the bath and glancing over the tub's edge, he caught sight of the Prime Minister lying full length like a lazy hippopotamus in the water.

'Good morning!' said the President. 'I came to tell you I think I've got the right name for that international institution we discussed last night.'

'What is it?' asked the other without stirring from his recumbent position.

'The United Nations,' announced Roosevelt, eagerly watching his colleague's face for his reaction.

He saw Churchill's head sink completely beneath the water, with its eyes staring and its mouth pouting at him through the liquid. Then the face rose again with slow deliberation to the surface, like some submarine animal emerging for a breath of air. Protruding his lips, the Prime Minister shot a high fountain of splashing water into the atmosphere and exclaimed approvingly, 'It'll do, Franklin; it'll do.'

Thus the hope of humanity has been known as the United Nations Organisation ever since.

*

On one of his visits to North America Churchill came to Ottawa in mid-winter for consultations with the Canadian Government. The temperature out-of-doors was far below freezing point, and snow lay thick everywhere. The eminent visitor arrived at Rideau Hall, the Governor-General's residence, where he was to stay as a guest of its occupants, the Earl of Athlone and Princess Alice. They greeted him in its imposing entrance hall with its portraits of past and present British monarchs, pieces of courtly furniture, and rich carpets. Those rugs could be somewhat treacherous in icy-cold weather, for when new arrivals from outside walked across them, the friction of their shoes on the carpet somehow engendered electricity in them, with the result that when one person held out his hand to another for a welcoming shake an electric spark flew between their fingers just before they touched. We who lived in Ottawa were accustomed to this phenomenon; but to strangers it was surprising, and often caused them momentary fright.

When Lord Athlone and Churchill extended their hands in mutual greeting, sure enough a spark flashed between them.

Churchill betrayed surprise, but no shock. He merely raised his eyebrows in astonishment, grinned broadly and remarked, 'This wouldn't be a good house for a courting couple.'

*

The war moved steadily towards a favourable outcome, and in September, 1944 Churchill and Roosevelt came to Canada as MacKenzie King's guests to hold a conference in the historic Citadel at Quebec. On the first evening Lord Athlone and Princess Alice gave a dinner party for the three statesmen in the fortress's banqueting hall. The invitation list was select, being confined to the President and Mrs Roosevelt, the two Prime Ministers with Mrs Churchill, and the most important of the American and British chiefs' counsellors. To meet the convenience of such busy men engaged in crucial war-time discussions, dress was informal. The season happened to be the height of summer, the temperature hovered in the nineties, and Churchill wore a thin white tropical suit. He looked a bit exotic – but of course never minded cutting an unusual sartorial figure.

I recall that in the middle of the meal he looked across the table at me, and asked my age. When I answered that I was forty-three his eyes gleamed, and he expressed his envy. Remarking that I would surely lead a very interesting life in the peaceful world which he proposed to establish after we won the war, he deplored the fact that he himself had already overshot man's allotted span of three-score years and ten.

Immediately after dinner the Governor-General, Princess Alice and the ladies withdrew, leaving the statesmen to start their deliberations. Over glasses of port and liqueurs they began to consider the agenda for the meetings which would commence on the morrow. Afterwards the supreme military, naval and air force chiefs of America and Britain went into the conference room for a preliminary exchange of views, and the rest of us adjourned for conversation in a small lounge. Only eight of us were present, including Roosevelt, Churchill and MacKenzie King. Another member of the party was the President's close confidant Harry Hopkins.

For several minutes two or three groups engaged in separate social chatter, but then Churchill took command of the occasion. Rising from his armchair, he started to strut slowly to and fro along the length of the room, forcing the rest of us to become a silent audience. The theme of his remarks was the military development of the war throughout the previous few years up to the present moment, with an analysis of the current state of play on the various battlefields. It was, of course, a masterly performance uttered with all his powerful eloquence. For a considerable time his companions sat motionless, listening fascinated to his exposition; but later they began to show signs of weariness. He continued his oration rather too long. Roosevelt – who betrayed symptoms of frailty, a portent of his later fatal illness – shifted uneasily as he sat upright in his cripple's chair, MacKenzie King looked slightly though politely tired, and Harry Hopkins produced more candid evidence of growing boredom. Whereas hitherto he had sat relaxed in a corner of a sofa, he now stretched himself full length on the couch and closed his eyes as if in slumber.

I have already mentioned that the evening was hot. The torrid atmosphere made some members of the party loosen their neck-ties and open their shirt collars. Churchill, however, continued to pace unconcernedly up and down the room, pouring forth his torrent of words. His portly figure appeared distinctly ungainly in its light tropical attire. Patches of perspiration formed beneath his armpits, his unbuttoned jacket was rather too small for him, and the trousers were stretched very tight across his bulging stomach. Evidently the suit was an old one tailored many years earlier when his figure was less corpulent. Now it made a very unsatisfactory fit, and in particular the buttons down the front of his trousers were stretched in their button-holes almost to bursting point.

Suddenly he ended his long soliloquy on the current state of the war, halted his striding, turned towards the rest of us and exclaimed dramatically, 'And now, what's going to happen next?'

Clearly he intended to answer this rhetorical question himself, expounding in a further lecture his ideas about the proper tactics and strategy for the impending, probably final phase of hostilities. But Harry Hopkins stirred on his sofa, opened his eyes, scrutinised Churchill from head to foot, and remarked in an emphatic tone, 'I'll tell you what's going to happen next.'

Churchill looked at him with a hint of annoyance at this interruption, and asked, 'What?'

'Your flies are going to burst and your pants will tumble down,' replied Hopkins.

There was a shout of laughter in which Churchill joined. Before he could resume his oratory general conversation started again.

*

When that Quebec Conference ended Roosevelt returned to Washington and MacKenzie King to Ottawa, whilst Churchill with his team of British advisers caught a train for a sea-port in Nova Scotia where a battleship waited to take them back to London. The Prime Minister asked me to travel with them to the coast, since he wished to speak confidentially with me.

The two of us had a long conversation in his private railway carriage. He opened it by saying that he proposed to make changes in his government in the near future, and that he wished me to return to England then to become again a Minister. He added that the reinvigorated Administration would first finish the war victoriously, and afterwards engage in the two crucially important tasks of negotiating a wise peace in Europe and reconstructing British life following the tribulations of the last few years. He said that he could offer me only the comparatively minor post of Minister of Civil Aviation in the immediate future, but that later, in a major re-forming of his cabinet at the commencement of peace, he would promote me to a very important office.

I did not feel sure that I wished to return to politics after the war, and in any case felt dubious about the wisdom of Churchill remaining head of a government then. I thought his views on many national and some international problems would be unpalatable to me; and so, with warmly sincere expressions of thanks, I refused his offer. He was greatly surprised, and argued strongly in its favour. But when he realised that I was not to be persuaded, he abandoned the attempt.

Our conversation then became a more objective discussion about the future political prospect in Britain. I ventured to express my opinion that he should not long remain Prime Minister after the end of the war. For one thing it seemed to me that it would be difficult, and perhaps wrong, to maintain a coalition government in peace time. Owing to major disagreements between the Conservatives and the Socialists on some vital questions of post-war rehabilitation, there would almost certainly be a return to party politics; and I thought it would be a personal tragedy if he declined from being the heroic leader of a united nation and became instead a partisan chief of one quarrelsome party, either in or out of office. He should withdraw gracefully from factional disputings, retaining his unique prestige and playing a part in public life as a universally respected Elder Statesman.

He demurred, declaring that it would be his duty to remain Prime Minister. He agreed that the Labour Party might break away from the government after the war, but said that he would nevertheless form a broad-based coalition which would win the next general election. His position as the leader of a virtually united nation would therefore be preserved.

I repeated my view that there would be a quick return to unrestrained party politics when the war ended, and that it would be a thousand pities if he then descended from the summit of the Mount Olympus on which he now presided rather like a god, to become an ordinary mortal involved in the 'mud-slinging' of party bickerings.

With a chuckle he commented that he very much enjoyed the mud-slinging of such political battles; and I saw a gleam of reminiscent pleasure light his eyes. But again he denied that this would be the prospect, reiterating that a powerful coalition government would survive the war and continue ruling Britain far into the years of peace.

In the course of our talk I remarked that I had hoped he would give himself leisure after the end of hostilities to write his History of the Second World War, which would be a work of classic importance. Then I added, 'I suppose you're already busily writing it in spite of all your heavy preoccupations.'

'Yes,' he replied, 'I write about 4,000 words of it every day.'

I felt astonished at the magnitude of these literary labours – and then remembered an occasion in 1940 when I had attended a meeting of a group of Ministers under his chairmanship. In the middle of our discussions he scribbled a note on a sheet of paper and pushed it across the table to me. I read it, saw that it asked a question about a topical problem, wrote my answer, and passed it back to him. He scanned my scrawl, nodded in assent, folded the bit of paper, and put it in his pocket.

A moment later Lord Halifax, who sat a few places away from me, passed me a note. It read, 'Be careful what you write to Winston. He'll publish it in his volumes about the war when it's over!'

The fact was that every instruction, telegram, minute or other document which he composed was drafted with two purposes in mind: first the achievement of his immediate aim in prosecuting the war, and second the piece's suitability for publication in the pages of his later memoirs.

*

Churchill – the passionate student of war – had probably lived much of his life with the hope that one day he would lead mankind through a historic military conflict. When at last the opportunity for this arrived he no doubt felt that he was indeed a Man of Destiny whose existence hitherto had been designed by Providence as a preparation for this grand climax to his career. In spite of all the anxieties, difficulties and even disasters which the situation kept hurling at him, he revelled in the experience – and hardly ever doubted its happy ultimate outcome. He relied for this not so much on the benevolence of Providence as on the genius of Winston Spencer Churchill.

Nevertheless, I feel sure that a certain tale which circulated about him at the time was apocryphal. This story declared that before he fell asleep each night he knelt beside his bed and uttered up the fervent prayer: 'Oh God, thank you for giving me life during the greatest war that has ever been fought. Thank you, too, for making me Prime Minister during that war. And please God, may the war go on for ever and ever, Amen!'

In any case the conflict did not continue for ever and ever. In due course the Nazis were overthrown, Europe was released from their yoke, and the victorious British people resumed all their cherished freedoms. One of the most extraordinary exercises of their liberty that has ever occurred took place shortly afterwards, when the voters in a General Election rejected their deliverer Churchill, and put his peace-time political rivals into office in his place.

I was told that when King George VI then proposed to bestow on him the noblest distinction which lay in the monarch's prerogative, offering him a Knighthood of the Garter, Churchill replied with sombre jocularity, 'No, Your Majesty, how can I accept the Garter from you when your people have just given me the boot?'

*

Perhaps I might mention in passing that towards the end of the European war I received a personal message from him saying that he would like to give my services a fitting reward, and that he therefore wished to recommend me for instalment as a Knight Grand Cross of the Most Distinguished Order of St Michael and St George. As I have always been averse to acquiring a title, I sent him an appreciative but negative answer. Next time that I saw him he looked at me with a gleam of humour in his eyes, and remarked, 'I hear you've refused the pearl I offered you.'

I laughed, wondering whether his earlier disapproval of me had revived at my rejection of his various friendly offers, and whether he meant to hint politely that I was the sort of lowly four-footed creature which refuses pearls that are cast before them.

*

After Attlee succeeded Churchill as Prime Minister, and when the Japanese as well as the German war ended some months later, I was transferred from my post as High Commissioner in Canada to that of Governor General in Malaya, Singapore and British Borneo. For the next ten years I lived and worked in South East Asia, although I continued to fly periodically to England for official consultations in Whitehall.

I hardly ever saw Churchill during those years, but did keep in touch with various other political personalities. On one occasion when I came to London in the late 1940s or early 1950s Halifax invited me to lunch with him and his wife Dorothy. The three of us sat together and exchanged our latest news. In the course of the talk Halifax narrated the following incident.

He said that Winston Churchill was not doing well as Leader of the Opposition in Parliament. Indeed, he had become 'rather a bore' in the job. With advancing years his powers were failing and his faults growing ever more apparent. As a consequence most of his front bench colleagues and many back-bench Conservative Members in the House of Commons were increasingly critical of his leadership, and wished him to retire. Yet he showed no inclination to do so. On the contrary, he appeared determined to remain the party's chief throughout the present Parliament and into the next General Election, in the expectation of then becoming Prime Minister once more. None of his partners in the shadow cabinet dared suggest to him that it was time for his withdrawal, for they were too afraid of a vicious reaction. At the request of several members of that team Halifax therefore agreed to talk privately with the great man, and to put the proposition to him. He was one of the few Tory politicians who was always ready to stand up to Churchill, and to tell him exactly what he thought on any subject.

A few days before our luncheon he had taken an opportunity to speak with Churchill alone, and he did so with the completely candid sincerity of their long-standing friendship. Emphasising that he was talking on behalf of many of their partners in both Houses of Parliament, he suggested that Churchill should now resign from the Leadership of the Opposition. He mentioned frankly some of Churchill's growing faults as a chief, and commented with charming candour, 'Winston, you're not doing yourself any good, you're not doing the party any good, and you're not doing the nation any good.' He explained that Churchill's followers were so fond of him, and so respectful of his grand qualities that none of the others could summon up sufficient impertinence to tell him what they thought, but that he himself always felt able to talk to him with the licence of an intimate colleague.

Then he indulged in a little flattery, although speaking also in all sincerity. He said that no one disputed Churchill's pre-eminent greatness, for everyone agreed that in the war he had been the nation's saviour to whom the British people owed the preservation of their lives and liberties. His fellow countrymen admired him tremendously, and this was one reason why they deplored his descent from the unique height of his position as leader of the entire Free World to become a mere cantankerous headman of a minority party in Britain. Halifax was careful to add that although their associates wished Churchill to resign from the Opposition Leadership, no one wanted him to abandon his membership of the House of Commons. On the contrary, they were eager for him to remain in Parliament, and to raise his stature once more to that of the world's finest Elder Statesman, transcending party and indeed national differences. He need not then join in the petty squabbles on comparatively unimportant subjects which lowly politicians fought; instead he would make speeches on only the greatest problems facing Humanity; and those eloquent pronouncements based on his unrivalled experience and authority would ring round the world.

Churchill listened with kindly patience throughout his discourse. When he finished speaking the old man picked a cigar from his mouth, blew a quivering ring of smoke into the air, and observed with a grin, 'My dear Edward, you can tell our colleagues that one of the unalterable rules of my life is never to leave the pub until closing time.'

He said no more . . . and for the next few years continued to command the Conservative Party in Parliament, first as Leader of the Opposition and afterwards again as Prime Minister.

*

I left South East Asia towards the end of 1955, and went to India as High Commissioner. Several months earlier Churchill had ceased to be Prime Minister. One day a while later I received in Delhi a telegram from London asking me to discuss with Mr Nehru the arrangements for Churchill's funeral. The message explained that the ex-Premier was still remarkably hale and hearty, and that his burial would probably not take place for some years, but that whenever the event did occur it should be a State Occasion, for which elaborate detailed preparations were already being made. The cable requested me to convey the plans to India's Prime Minister, and to invite him on behalf of the British Government to attend the funeral in due course, since the authorities hoped to make it not only a great national but also a great Commonwealth and International event.

When I put the proposition to Nehru he readily accepted, agreeing to fly to London as soon as the illustrious old Briton breathed his last. The fact that Churchill had been a consistently bitter foe of Gandhi, Nehru himself and their followers throughout the struggle for Indian Independence made no difference to his decision. Although he strongly disapproved of Churchill's pre-war policies regarding not only India but many other issues, he recognised that our war leader had played a decisive part in the defeat of Hitler's Germany and therefore in the liberation of all mankind, including the Indian people, from the threat of Nazi tyranny. For that reason he was ready to pay homage on behalf of all his fellow-countrymen to their great deliverer.

I felt a suspicion that the arrangements for his State Funeral were being stimulated partly by Churchill himself; and it therefore gave me great pleasure to send a message back to London announcing the Indian Prime Minister's willingness to make a special journey across half the world when the time came to pay him those final honours. . . . However, when Churchill did eventually give up the ghost, Nehru – like many other distinguished world figures who had presumably accepted similar invitations to the funeral – was already in his own grave!

By then I no longer lived in India, and was working in Africa. I had recently ceased to be Governor-General of Kenya, and was assuming office as British High Commissioner there. In accordance with the carefully laid plans, the Churchillian obsequies were made a solemn State Occasion to which many distinguished overseas statesmen were invited. The government in Nairobi decided that their Vice-President, the well-known Mr Oginga Odinga, should represent the Kenyan nation. I conveyed the invitation to him in person, and he accepted with enthusiasm.

'When Churchill was your Prime Minister,' he said to me, 'I was pro-British. It's only since he ceased to lead your country that I've become critical of Britain.'

This remark of course oversimplified the facts, for Odinga's hostility towards British policies sprang largely from his hatred of the Imperialism which Churchill championed. That made all the more impressive the admiration which Odinga, like Nehru, felt for the one time principal enemy of the freedom of African, Asian and other Colonial peoples who later became a saviour of all humanity from a much more vicious tyranny.

*

As I mentioned at its beginning, this essay makes no attempt at a considered appraisal of Winston Churchill. It is a lightly drawn sketch of him as I saw him from time to time over many years, which perhaps adds a few items of information to the vast accumulation of facts about his character and attainments. At the time of his death, and for quite a while afterwards, his reputation was naturally exaggerated, almost as if he were a paragon of all the virtues in both peace and war. In my chapter about my father I have commented how a few years of comparative failure towards the end of his career made people forget or ignore his earlier lifetime of constructive successes. In Churchill's case the opposite is true; a few years of triumphant success in the latter part of his career made people overlook his earlier decades of comparative failure. Gradually, as the emotions aroused by the Second World War subside, and his life can be viewed objectively in its proper perspective, this too flattering estimate of him is being revised. He is becoming recognised as a brilliantly capable yet in some ways foolishly narrow-minded and out-of-date politician in peace time, but a superlative leader in war – one of the greatest of such heroic figures in the story of mankind. Perhaps he had certain vicious characteristics – occasional arrogance, a bullying streak, and other faults. Yet he could also be gentle, kind and sometimes humble. In any case his weaknesses were partly the defects of his qualities – his self-confidence, his unflinching courage, his masterful power.

I shall not start here an examination of his peace-time failures and war-time achievements, for that will be done in many carefully considered commentaries and biographies by more scholarly authorities. I need only say that his indomitable fighting spirit and inspiring eloquence made him for the British people during 'their finest hour' what Pericles was to the Athenians at the apex of their Golden Age.

Achmad Sukarno

'His sparkling eyes, honey-coloured skin and sensuous lips were only the most striking features in an arrestingly good-looking face.'

IN 1946 I went to the Far East as Governor-General of the British dependencies in Malaya, Singapore, Sarawak, Brunei and North Borneo, with certain responsibilities also concerning Hong Kong. Two years later I became Commissioner General in South East Asia, retaining my political duties in those six colonial territories and adding to them diplomatic duties covering half-a-dozen foreign lands in the region.

A historic period in Asia had recently opened. When the World War ended Nationalist movements in various countries that were still subject to rule by one or another of the Western colonial powers vigorously stepped-up their agitation for liberation from alien overlordship. In India in particular the Congress Party led by Mahatma Gandhi was by 1946 nearing the complete achievement of this aim. The government in London agreed with it, and negotiations between the British authorities and the Indian leaders were under way for its early attainment.

In sharp contrast, in the Netherlands East Indies the Nationalist movement was being opposed with fierce obstinacy by the government in Holland. During the war the Dutch rulers had been driven from that wide archipelago of islands, and the Japanese assumed power there. Immediately after Japan's surrender in August 1945, and before the return of Dutch colonial officials and armed forces, the local Nationalist leaders proclaimed their country an independent Republic with Achmad Sukarno as its President. He and his government commanded widespread popular support; but when the Dutch re-established their imperial administration a few months afterwards they at first refused to have any dealings with him, and through the next few years continued by one means or another – often military – to resist his and his colleagues' rebellious struggle to achieve complete sovereignty.

*

One evening in Singapore towards the end of 1946 I broadcast to the Malayan people. My speech contained certain statements which would have been regarded as clichés in many other British colonial territories – where a steady advance to Independence was accepted policy – but which had something of a new ring in the context of the difficult situation caused by the complex multi-racial composition of the population living in Malaya. Less than 50% of those people were Malays, nearly 40% were Chinese, approximately 10% were Indians, and smaller but significant communities of Ceylonese, Eurasians, Europeans and others also resided there. The characters, abilities and aspirations of these ethnic groups were rather different from one another, and their diverse temperaments made certain of them mutually antipathetic and even occasionally antagonistic. Under Britain's rule a more or less fair balance was maintained between their respective interests which enabled them to live and work peacefully together in their common homeland, although now and then unpleasant, vicious incidents had occurred. All this made many knowledgeable authorities believe that the mixture of Malayans could never be moulded into a united, harmonious, self-governing nation. I must not expand here on the considerations which prompted this opinion, and will only say that those who held it therefore assumed it would be imprudent for us British to aim at a steady transition from Colonialism to Independence in Malaya. For various reasons I took a different view, thinking the aim not only right in principle but also – if all of us concerned strove constructively – attainable in practice.

Many Asian nationalists both inside and outside Malaya suspected Britain's intentions there. Aware of the sceptical views held by numerous British authorities, they believed us to be pursuing a policy of 'divide and rule', exaggerating and indeed deliberately exacerbating the differences between Malays, Chinese, Indians and others in order to create an excuse for maintaining British rule indefinitely. They felt that one reason for this attitude was the importance of Singapore as a naval base in our Far Eastern strategic plans.

In the broadcast speech which I have mentioned I sought to refute this charge, and to state clearly the British government's contrary purpose. Among other comments I therefore declared that Britain's aim was steady progress to 'government of the Malayan people for the Malayan people by the Malayan people'. And I stated that our policy was 'not to divide and rule, but to unite and hand over rule'.

When I returned to my house from the studio where I made the broadcast a servant told me that someone wished to speak to me on the telephone. The caller had rung during my absence, and left his phone number. My servant could not tell me who he was.

I dialled the number, and was surprised when a voice at the other end of the line said, 'I'm Dr Sharjir from Indonesia.'

I had never met Sharjir, but of course knew that he was the Prime Minister in Sukarno's government struggling to free their people in the Netherlands East Indies from foreign rule just across the narrow sea from Malaya.

He told me that he was staying briefly in Singapore on his way back from travels elsewhere in Asia, and that he would stop overnight in the city before flying back to Java on the following day. He said he had listened to my radio speech, and wished to congratulate me very warmly on it. When I invited him to come to breakfast with me the next morning, he promptly accepted.

Early the next day we sat eating scrambled eggs and chatting about South East Asian affairs on a verandah overlooking my sunny tropical garden. Sharjir was a small man, almost pigmy in size, but with a big mind, spirit and personality. His intelligence, lucidity and gay wit made his conversation charming and stimulating. He started it by expressing again his admiration for my broadcast on the previous evening.

I replied that the speech was an undistinguished effort filled with a lot of platitudes which added little or nothing to people's knowledge of British policy in colonial affairs.

He commented that, nevertheless, my statements were emphatic and obviously sincere; and he added, 'If any leading Dutch spokesman would talk in the same language to us Indonesians, our quarrel with them would end. We'd cease our hostility, and co-operate with them in the government of our country.'

He explained that all that his fellow Nationalists required was a clear declaration like mine that the Dutch authorities' ultimate aim in the Netherlands East Indies – which the rebels called by the native name Indonesia – was Independence for its people. This assurance would induce them to call off their rebellion and collaborate with the colonial administrators in ruling their widespread archipelago. They were prepared to agree to quite a long transition period before the attainment of full freedom, during which they would gradually assume increasing responsibilities in government until they were sufficiently trained to exercise unrestricted sovereignty. At breakfast that morning Sharjir suggested that this interval could continue for about ten years. Repeating that he and most, though not all, of his nationalist colleagues were in no great hurry for complete Independence, he said they needed to gain considerably more experience in administration before they would become properly qualified to rule by themselves their vast, scattered domain.

'We like the Dutch; they've been friends to us in many ways,' he observed. 'We want the whole process of constitutional evolution to Independence to be gradual and peaceful.'

But he commented sadly that the Dutch were stubborn; they refused to concede that the long-term aim should be freedom for the Indonesians. 'So we're having to fight for our Independence. And we'll win it much sooner than we really need it. They'll be thrown out of Indonesia quicker than need be the case if they would co-operate.'

In reply to many questions by me he discussed contemporary

problems in an enlightening way. It was a good education for me in the attitudes of our Dutch and Indonesian neighbours on the opposite shores of the Straits of Malacca.

As he was leaving to catch his aeroplane he said he looked forward to welcoming me to Indonesia after his countrymen gained their liberty. He added that he would tell President Sukarno about my speech, and that the rebel leader would be happy to meet me. He commented with a smile that I would still then be the Imperialist Governor-General of the British colonial territories in South East Asia because Britain's wise policy meant that the transition to Independence could be much more gradual and friendly.

*

About three years later – near the end of 1949 – I attended the Indonesian Independence celebrations in Djakarta as Britain's representative. Everything had turned out as Sharjir foreshadowed in our talk. The Dutch opposition to Independence was for a while obstinately maintained; the Indonesian rebellion against them was vehemently fought; in due course the colonialists' position became untenable, but by then their hostility had forced the Nationalists to demand absolute freedom much sooner than would otherwise have been the case; and so the Dutch were compelled to agree to a swift grant of complete Independence.

I first set eyes on Achmad Sukarno when I went to present to him as President of the new Republic my credentials as Ambassador Extraordinary representing Great Britain at the historic event. I was struck at once by his distinguished good looks. Then his charming personality captivated me. Several other foreign envoys were present performing a similar duty to mine, and the occasion could have been formal and even pompous. But the President made it relaxed and gay.

He chatted vivaciously with us all. When I was introduced to him he gripped me cordially in both his hands, beamed a broad smile, and said that he highly approved of my policies in South

East Asia 'even though you're a British Imperialist!' I realised then that if he felt inclined to act the diplomat he could be as accomplished a performer of that part as of many other characters which he played from time to time.

Naturally he was in jubilant mood throughout the next few days. At an almost non-stop succession of ceremonial events such as a State Banquet, a Palace Ball and a Military Pageant he revealed his exuberant, dynamic personality. An unaffected self-confidence always radiated from him, and his geniality was infectious. He could charm a bird off a tree, talk the hind leg off a donkey, and make you laugh until tears poured down your cheeks. Those gifts were all aided by his very handsome appearance. His sparkling eyes, honey-coloured skin and sensuous lips were only the most striking features in an arrestingly good-looking face. One element which could have been a defect – his bald head – was discreetly concealed beneath the velvet Muslim *songkok* that he always wore indoors as well as out. His figure was trim and athletic in an immaculate official uniform, a slightly too protuberant paunch being disciplined (rumour whispered) by a tight corset style undergarment. All his movements were natural, lively and full of animal grace. No wonder he was – among other attainments – the greatest lady killer holding a supreme public office anywhere round the world!

During those busy days he made time for a long private conversation with me, as he did with representatives of some other important nations attending the celebrations. Our talk was partly serious about current political affairs in Asia, and partly less so on various other topics. We found that we shared certain keen interests, such as a fondness for paintings and other works of art, a delight in traditional Oriental music and dancing, and a concern for the welfare of the primitive tribal peoples living in the jungly interior of nearby Borneo. Combined with our general accord on international Far Eastern problems, these joint tastes laid the foundations of a friendship which from that moment became very warm.

The climax of the Independence celebrations was a mass rally attended by about 150,000 people in the grounds of the imposing palace in Djakarta which the Dutch Governor-General had just quitted and Sukarno now proudly occupied. There were no formal seating arrangements on the platform – indeed no seats at all – and the President invited me to stand beside him whilst he made a speech to the multitude. At that tumultuous gathering I witnessed for the first time the decisive gift which, on top of his other qualities, made him the unchallenged leader of the 80,000,000 various peoples inhabiting the scores of different islands included in Indonesia. His power of demagogic oratory was terrific. His tones of voice, his grimaces, his gestures, his vivid (though to me incomprehensible) vocabulary, and his every other resource as he spoke to the vast audience that afternoon were unforgettably magnetic. He shouted, he whispered, he conversed, he frowned, he smiled, he laughed, he shook his fists, he clapped his hands, he rose on tip-toe, he danced a little jig . . . and he adopted an assortment of other devices to convey his thoughts and feelings to the crowd, and to arouse certain mass emotions in return. He toyed with them like a producer of a Javanese shadow-play manipulating his puppets. And their response was tremendous. At first he was rather quiet in manner, introducing his theme with sweet, restrained reasonableness. The audience gazed appreciatively at him, nodding their heads at some of his phrases, and occasionally expressing their agreement by applause. Gradually he worked himself and them up into a mood of greater excitement; his voice rose in pitch, whilst their shouted retorts became louder. Ultimately he was yelling passionate sentences at them with contortions of his face and gesticulations of his limbs as if he were an inspired visionary and a raving lunatic combined in one person. At moments he reminded me of Charlie Chaplin playing the part of the orating Hitler in his film 'The Great Dictator'. And the throng greeted his almost every word with storms of cheers.

I felt dubious about some of his tricks. For instance, I remember an episode when he fell silent for many seconds. The crowd waited breathless to hear what he would say next. Then in a gentle, almost casual tone he muttered the word 'Merdeka!' – which being interpreted means 'Freedom!' – and resumed silence. The multitude, somehow knowing instinctively what their leader wished them to do, responded by murmuring 'Merdeka!' in the same almost indifferent tone, but in scores of thousands of voices in unison. He promptly repeated 'Merdeka!' on a slightly louder, less lackadaisical note. After he relapsed into silence they mimicked his expression exactly. He opened his mouth and uttered 'Merdeka!' again, this time more vigorously and forcefully; and they followed suit like a massive class of school children reciting a word they were being taught by their teacher. When the echo died down he reiterated the same slogan once more, shouting it louder and quicker, like a peremptory command. They responded with a precise but thunderous imitation. During the next few minutes he and they repeated the performance over and over again, his ejaculation of the clarion-call becoming sharper with its every repetition, assuming now not a casual but an elated, triumphant tone; and their retorts reflected the same change. Eventually he and they were all yelling 'Merdeka! Merdeka! Merdeka!' incessantly at the tops of their voices, like crashes of cannon-fire in a raging battle. It had been an almost incredible long-drawn, gradually rising crescendo of sound.

I personally thought the President overdid the act. It seemed to me that the monotonous repetitions continued too long, and became a trifle artificial. But the crowd did not agree; and it was their reaction, not that of a foreign spectator like myself, which mattered. They entered into the spirit of his game with mounting enthusiasm, and in the end went wild with frenzy. I realised then how amazingly he could mesmerise vast multitudes of people.

*

Another feature of the celebrations which struck me forcibly was the somewhat glum attitude of many – though not all – of the high Dutch officials attending them. They did not share the Indonesians' happiness at the historic event of government being transferred from their grasp into the hands of the native people. On the contrary, they obviously deplored it. Parading in handsome ex-Colonial officers' uniforms adorned with colourful sashes and glittering medals, they watched the proceedings with solemn, unsmiling faces. Extremely efficient administrators who had done a great deal for the country's economic development and for the local population's well-being in various other ways, they were at the same time honest, rather unimaginative men, incapable of sympathy with anyone else's feelings. Some of them made no pretence of regarding the occasion as anything but regrettable.

Their conduct was in vivid contrast to that of many British officials whom I have watched in similar circumstances at Independence celebrations of their ex-dependencies. Whatever might be the private thoughts of some of those men, they joined fully in the rejoicings of the local populations, clapping, cheering and laughing with the crowds, and in every other way showing appreciation that the occasion was a hopeful as well as historic one for their recent subjects. They were able to put themselves in the shoes of those other men and women, for whom many of them felt deep affection as a result of long years of enjoyable life and work among them.

*

The next glimpse that I caught of Sukarno was through the eyes of Pandit Jawaharlal Nehru, the Prime Minister of India. A few months after the Independence celebrations in Djakarta Nehru came to stay with me in Malaya on his way back to India from Indonesia, where he had been for about a week as the President's guest. He spoke interestingly about his experiences there. He liked the tropical landscapes of Java and neighbouring islands, and admired the attractive, shyly smiling people who lived in them. Their ancient culture, still vividly maintained in traditional music, dancing, painting and other arts, also impressed him, partly because of its bygone Indian associations.

But he made no attempt to conceal his contempt for Sukarno. Before the visit he had respected Indonesia's leader as an Asian Nationalist of considerable political repute, and he still felt regard for some of his qualities. Others, however, he despised. One criticism broke from his lips within a few minutes of his arrival in Singapore. As he and I drove away from the airport where he landed he heaved a glad sigh, and said it was a great relief to sit in a car with a fresh breeze blowing through its open windows – and he added that this had been impossible whilst he travelled day after day through the tropically hot Javanese countryside in Sukarno's company. He told me that whenever he tried to open a window by even an inch to let some air into the Presidential car, Sukarno at once shut it, insisting that they would otherwise risk catching chills, sore throats or some other ailment. All Nehru's protests that the alternative could be death by suffocation were unavailing; his host merely offered him pills – which he himself chewed regularly – to avert that calamity. Nehru regarded Sukarno as a timid hypochondriac.

His criticisms extended to other aspects of the President's character. He expressed disapproval of his smug self-satisfaction, his bombastic, tub-thumping oratory, and his superficial knowledge of various important contemporary international problems. I guessed that these feelings were partly provoked by distaste for the eminent statesman's well-known misconduct in certain private affairs, although Nehru never mentioned that trait in his otherwise candid comments. It was interesting to receive this view of one Asian giant from another during the crucial period of the Asian nations' political emancipation from white rule.

*

I returned to Indonesia quite often during the next few years. Always Sukarno invited me for long talks with him on current Asian affairs, and afterwards we gossiped about our other mutual interests. Often he conducted me through the rooms of his palace to show me the latest additions to his large, ever-growing collection of contemporary paintings, sculptures and *objets d'art* by local artists. Many talented painters and carvers – both Indonesian and Dutch – dwelt in Java, Sumatra, Bali and other islands; and he was an avidly acquisitive connoisseur of their works. His palatial residences in Djakarta and Bogor became attractive art galleries.

Several times he invited me also to gay Presidential parties. Knowing my liking for traditional Javanese, Balinese and other ballets stepped to the accompaniment of *gamelin* orchestras, he arranged superb displays of them for me. The performers were dressed in beautiful costumes; their dramatic acts were as fabulously graceful as could be; and the tunes wailed, beaten and tinkled on flutes, gongs, xylophones and other ancient instruments were enchantingly melodious. No dances anywhere on Earth are lovelier than those of the natives in the Indonesian archipelago.

Sometimes the performances were held out-of-doors in the wide garden surrounding the palace in Djakarta, at other times they took place indoors on the stage of its ample concert hall. I particularly remember one of the latter occasions. I sat with my host in the front row of the auditorium, and the programme of ballets was long and brilliant. Half-way through it an interval occurred during which the artistes could rest their feet and the audience stretch their legs. But Sukarno and I stayed in our seats, engaged in lively conversation. He asked the theatre manager to draw aside the curtains hiding the stage, so that he could tell me about a new mural decoration which – on his instructions – adorned the wall at the back of the platform. Its design was a large map of South East Asia on which the numerous Indonesian islands were painted in gold whilst the other lands were portrayed in black.

Sukarno pointed to it and asked, 'Do you see anything remarkable about that map?'

I tumbled at once to the thought in his head. Those were the days when an increasingly violent diplomatic controversy was raging between the Dutch and Indonesians about the proper ownership of a part of New Guinea which had previously belonged to the Netherlands East Indies, and over which the authorities in Holland still exercised colonial sovereignty. The Indonesian government declared that it should have been transferred to them when the Dutch yielded Independence to all their other possessions in the region, and that it should now be a province of Indonesia called 'West Irian'. The Dutch were doggedly resisting the claim. Incidentally, more than one leading Minister in the cabinet in Djakarta had told me in personal confidence that they felt no particular desire to acquire the place, because its population belonged to a different race from the Malays, and so was not of truly Indonesian stock. They added that the great majority of their fellow countrymen used to share their lack of interest, but that the President had raised the matter without consulting them, and had made such a popular patriotic issue of it in passionate speeches that none of his Ministers could now prudently dissociate themselves from his agitation.

Noticing that on the map behind the stage Dutch New Guinea, alias West Irian, was emblazoned in gold, I asked Sukarno whether his allusion to something 'remarkable' on the mural concerned this fact.

With a gleeful, self-satisfied smile he answered, 'Yes.'

Then he entered upon a discourse on the subject, telling me that those splashes of gilding were correct, that West Irian was a rightful part of Indonesia, and that he, his government and people would never surrender their claim to it. Their demand for its transfer would become irresistible, and the Dutch would have to surrender the place. 'Before many years are passed,' he concluded, 'the territory will be painted the right colour on every map published round the world.'

He then asked me to look at the island of Borneo on the mural, and to note a significant, contrasting feature in it. Borneo was a place for which I felt deep affection because of my friendship with the peoples of Sarawak, North Borneo and Brunei situated along its northern coast. The first two of these territories were British colonies whilst the third was a British protected state, and I often visited them in the course of my official work. So I turned my eyes with interest to their image on the map, and observed that, whilst most of the vast island was coloured gold as part of Indonesia, this trio of small countries were painted black. I nodded approval to Sukarno.

He grinned and said, 'You see, we make no claim to your colonies even though all the rest of Borneo is Indonesian and they still remain under foreign Imperialist rule.'

He then expressed admiration for Great Britain's policy of granting freedom progressively to all its dependencies, one after another everywhere round the world; and he remarked that he especially liked the way in which I guided that policy in Malaya, Singapore and our three Borneo territories. He went so far as to comment that the populations in Sarawak, North Borneo and Brunei felt deep affection for me; and he added that he shared their sentiment. Although I felt touched by this flattering tribute from so formidable an anti-colonialist, I was not unduly impressed by it. Quite apart from his ability to play the part of a genial diplomat when he thought such an act expedient, I suspected that his motive for approving my conduct was partially influenced by another consideration. A short while earlier a photograph of me had appeared in an English newspaper which caused not only a sensation, but even a public scandal. It showed me arriving at a Dayak long-house in the jungly interior of Sarawak holding the hands of two beautiful, almost naked native girls as they guided me over a stony patch of beach from my boat to their home. I realised that the susceptible Sukarno would heartily admire my apparent success in winning the favour of such pretty, exquisitely figured members of the fair sex. Perhaps I should mention in passing that all my friendships with charming, characterful and for that matter strictly moral Dayak young women were entirely Platonic; but I did not suppose that Asia's premier Don Juan could imagine such a relationship possible. Probably he assumed from the photograph that I was a kindred spirit.

Dismissing this flippant thought from my mind, and pursuing the subject which he had opened by drawing my attention to the representation of Borneo on his mural, I asked him, 'Will you never lay claim to Sarawak, Brunei or North Borneo, either before or after they gain their Independence?'

He nodded his head emphatically and replied, 'No, never!'

I recalled that assurance several years later, when he launched his 'Confrontation' campaign against Malaya after the peoples of Sarawak and North Borneo (renamed Sabah) chose to join it in the Federation of Malaysia. That action was not necessarily wholly inconsistent with his earlier undertaking to me – yet it somehow did not seem entirely consistent either!

Soon afterwards the curtain descended once more on the stage whilst preparations were made for the resumption of the dancing. When it rose we witnessed another gorgeous ballet. At its close Sukarno stood up, climbed on the platform, and made a short speech. His oratory was as theatrical as any other item in the evening's entertainment. His gestures were as vivid as those of the steppings of the dancers, and his voice had a lilt as agreeable as that of the orchestra's music. The audience went wild with enthusiasm. As for myself, not being able to speak more than a few phrases in Malay I did not understand any sentence of what he said; yet in spite of this I felt thrilled and uplifted by the sparkle in his eyes, the lively expressions on his face, and the passionate flow of his words.

*

Whenever Sukarno was going to pass through Singapore during his numerous journeys to other lands he sent me a message so that he and I could meet for a talk whilst his aircraft was being refuelled. We usually discussed the current international situation; but I also remember a rather different occasion. He was returning from a pilgrimage to Mecca. As a devout Muslim he went on that important *Haj*, and immediately afterwards flew back to Java. He was due to stop in Singapore for an hour at breakfast time on the morning after he left Jedda.

I went to the airport to greet him. All the members of the staff of the Indonesian Consulate General were also in attendance, with their wives. Sukarno was of course tremendously admired by his fellow countrymen, a feeling which their womenfolk more than shared.

I welcomed him as he descended from his aircraft, and afterwards he exchanged salutations with the considerable group of Indonesian officials. His words and smiles of greeting were particularly affable towards the ladies, all beautifully dressed for the occasion in their loveliest Malay Kabagas and sarongs.

Taking me by an arm, he said, 'Let's go and have breakfast in the airport dining-room. You and I will sit at the same table, but no other men will be allowed to join us. All their wives and daughters will sit with us. I've been in Mecca for the last few days, and haven't been allowed to look at a woman. I'm longing for beautiful feminine company.'

We went into the dining-room and joined sufficient tables together for about a dozen ladies to accompany him and me at the meal. As he feasted his mouth on poached eggs he feasted his eyes on those decorative females. Our conversation was lively and gay. Sukarno was in excellent form, paying compliments right and left, exchanging jests with this young beauty and that, and talking as eloquently with his glad eyes as with his glib tongue.

In the meantime the male Indonesian officials sat at other tables, excluded from their President's company. He did not bother to exchange a word with any of them until we trooped back to the tarmac, where his aircraft had been refuelled and was now ready to depart. Then he stood with them for a few moments making some formally courteous remarks before ascending the gangway into the plane. At the top of its steps he turned round, beamed a ravishing smile, and waved goodbye with both hands to all of us.

I was standing alongside the runway with some of the wives

of the Indonesian officers when the aeroplane rose into the sky. As it disappeared I remarked that I was happy to be able to return them safe and sound to their husbands, for they were so delicious looking that they might have been kidnapped on to the President's craft. They did not dispute my contention, and burst into peals of laughter.

*

Sukarno's popularity with almost all women was phenomenal. Occasionally I discussed the amorous side of his nature with married Indonesian ladies of impeccable respectability, and they readily closed their eyes to the weakness in him. Even if they privately regretted his unabashed promiscuity – and of course would never themselves have joined his long succession of mistresses – they were willing to grant him a licence in sexual affairs which they would not have conceded to any other man. Perhaps this was partly because they realised that his excesses sprang from a quirk in his physical make-up for which his Creator rather than he was responsible; but it was chiefly because they felt their tolerance was a small price to pay for the unique services which the President performed for the Indonesian people, first in gaining their freedom and afterwards in maintaining the unity of their young nation. This was impressive evidence of the peerless position which he held in the admiration and affection of his compatriots.

He himself was completely unashamed of his almost incredible amorous excesses. Indeed, he sometimes boasted publicly of his prowess in that field. More than once he declared openly that among his other high attainments he was 'a great lover'. He simply could not resist the physical attraction of any and every young female beauty who caught his eye, and frequently sought unabashedly to woo them – with only one purpose in mind. Nor did this usually seem to disturb his affectionate relations with his own current wives. He was indeed the greatest, most uninhibited Don Juan of modern times.

*

Sometimes on my visits to Indonesia I escaped for a few days from official duties to enjoy a stay in the delectable isle of Bali lying a short way across narrow straits from Java. In those times that little Paradise on Earth was still unspoilt by excessive hordes of tourists. One of the many remarkable features of the place was the fact that every man, woman and child in its population seemed to be a born artist of some sort. They were painters, sculptors, wood-carvers, dancers, musicians, architects or other such types. Many a village, or *kampong*, was renowned for the distinction of its inhabitants as exponents of one or another of those creative arts, which they usually performed in their spare time after the day's work in padi-fields and households was done. Everything, however simple, that any peasant made with his or her hands was a work of beauty. For instance, the bouquets of flowers and bunches of fruits which they carried each day to the local Hindu temple as offerings for the gods and goddesses were invariably arranged in a gorgeous way which would have roused the envy of the most skilful floral decorators in any sophisticated city of the Western world. They made similar gifts of flowers and fruit to the spirits lodged in shrines in a room or courtyard of every home, however humble or exalted.

One reason why the quality of their arts and crafts was so fine was that most such creative work was more or less an act of worship. Its inspiration was a wish to serve and please the local Hindu deities, and so to gain their goodwill. Naturally any offering which did not attain a high aesthetic standard would earn their displeasure, for those sacred beings were discriminating connoisseurs of things artistic. Unhappily since those times this motive has ceased to stimulate most of the paintings, sculptures and carvings made on the island. A constant intrusion of swarms of tourists has changed the situation. Nowadays the villagers' *objets d'art* are mostly produced not for the worship of the Holy Ones, but for the seduction of those somewhat less holy human beings. So the stimulus is no longer spiritual service, but material profit. And often the result is sad. The taste of trippers is inferior to that of the gods; they are ready to pay inordinately high prices for third-rate souvenirs, which have therefore become the chief output of Bali's once brilliantly gifted but now ordinarily competent artists. The quantity of their productions has enormously increased whilst its quality has grievously declined.

This change had not occurred when I used to pay visits to Bali in the early 1950s; so whenever I went there I not only spent the evenings watching dances performed in the temple precincts of this or that *kampong*, but also devoted mornings and afternoons to making calls on the best painters, carvers and other artists in their homes. I always stayed for several days in the palace of Tjokorda Agung at Ubud. A prince of royal blood, the Tjokorda was a friendly, laughing personality with a scholarly knowledge of local culture; and Ubud lay at the heart of a countryside filled with villages of artistic repute. Each day he and I would meander through the surrounding padi-fields and cocoanut groves beneath a blazing tropical sun, calling in one *kampong* after another for miles around on the principal artists in their cottages. We drank and chatted with them, and inspected their latest works. Always I returned from those expeditions with a small selection of their paintings and carvings, which cost only modest sums of money.

Most of the artists and craftsmen were native Balinese endowed with the creative genius of their race. But a few were Dutchmen or other foreigners who once upon a time had visited Bali for a holiday, promptly fallen in love with the place, and decided to stay in it for the rest of their lives. Among these wise individuals was the talented painter Roger Bonnet, who lived in Ubud. Tjokorda Agung and I always visited him in his studio. One of his characteristics was his encouraging patronage of his native neighbours' works. Indeed, he possessed the finest, most comprehensive collection of paintings by old and contemporary Balinese masters in the world. Talking with him on the subject as we examined one after another of his two or three hundred classic pictures was an instructive, fascinating experience.

Always we would also view his own latest creations. No mean artist in his own right, he displayed a gift for portraying the characterful charm of Balinese villagers who came to sit for him as models.

One afternoon he showed me a particularly lovely sketch which he had drawn of two teenage Balinese girls dressed in the gorgeously beautiful costumes of performers in the famous Butterfly Dance. I should comment that religious custom decreed that only young maidens who had not yet reached the age of puberty should be temple dancers. I could not resist the picture of that enchanting pair, and bought it at a considerable price, cash down. Since I was to continue on long travels elsewhere before returning to my home in Malaya, I did not take it away with me, but arranged for Bonnet to have it packed and sent to my address in Johore.

By chance two days later Sukarno visited Ubud, and dropped without warning into Bonnet's studio. He, too, looked at a show of the artist's recent works – and he likewise admired the portrait of a pair of decorative small girls. It had not yet been removed from the wall for despatch to me.

'I'll buy that picture,' the President said.

Bonnet told him that it was already sold.

Sukarno feigned deafness, and repeated that he would buy the sketch.

Bonnet reiterated that unfortunately this particular picture belonged to someone else.

But Sukarno was not to be deterred. Stating that it made no difference if any other person had acquired the drawing, he declared that he himself was now its owner.

Embarrassed, Bonnet tried another line of persuasion. 'A great friend of yours has already paid me the money for it,' he remarked.

'Who's that?' asked his eminent visitor.

'Malcolm MacDonald,' Bonnet answered.

'You can tell Malcolm,' observed the President, 'that as usual I admire his taste, but that he can't export a treasure like this from Indonesia. It must stay in these islands, and will go into my collection in Djakarta. He's very welcome to come and enjoy it there whenever he likes.'

So that was that. Bonnet could do no more. The dancing maidens never landed in Singapore, but posed instead on a wall in the Presidential Palace in Djakarta. Bonnet wrote me an apologetic letter, and sent me another of his fine drawings in their place; but it never really compensated me for their loss.

Incidentally, I was told later that Sukarno did not pay for his purchase. Sometimes he exercised a Presidential prerogative to take free possession of any property he chose – much as certain Imperialist Royalties used to do!

*

Sukarno's popularity with his fellow countrymen in those years was tremendous, and it extended more or less uniformly among all the ethnically varied peoples who composed the Indonesian nation. Some prominent personages were critical of him, partly for reasons of clannish rivalry because he was of Javanese-Balinese extraction whilst they belonged to a different stock. But the President almost wholly overcame such tribal prejudices among the masses of natives scattered across the archipelago. This made him virtually unique among Indonesia's leaders, since popular support for other politicians was always much more territorially limited. Those men could each claim significant followings in one island or another, but not further afield. By contrast, Sukarno's sway was universal. One of his fine qualities was his capacity to knit together within a common national loyalty many racially diverse, traditionally separate, and even to some extent mutually incompatible peoples. Indeed, in a way he was the only Indonesian national leader, uniting under his personal authority nearly a hundred million Javanese, Sumatrans, Balinese, Kalimantans, Celebeans, Moluccans and other types who had earlier been forcefully but not necessarily willingly combined under foreign colonial rule. Were it not for him, those various elements might have split apart after they gained Independence, so dissolving their union. Occasionally serious threats of this arose. It was his influence as much as any other factor which kept them all together during the initial formative years of the new nation.

He did this partly by his energetic stimulation of the spread of a national language to supersede many local dialects. But his chief weapons were certain of his own characteristics. First, his prestige as the leader of the struggle to throw off the shackles of Dutch colonialism was paramount. Second, his personality was magnetic: if ever a man had irresistible charisma, it was he. And third, his oratory was captivating. By the sheer magic of his words he retained unchallenged popularity long after the inadequacy of his deeds became apparent.

This unassailable political supremacy made unfortunate one of his weaknesses of character. He was vain, and felt jealous of any possible rival. Frightened lest some other leader should arise who would displace him as the national hero, he was inclined to suspect this or that prominent Minister in his cabinet of conspiring to oust him. Several of those men were in fact intellectually or administratively abler than he; and he was conscious of this. A few of them were outstandingly capable, such as Hatta, Sharjir, the Sultan of Jokjakarta and one or two others. In reality I do not believe any of them regarded himself as a candidate for Sukarno's supreme position. From talks with them at the time I felt convinced that they stayed loyal to him because, although aware of his weaknesses in some fields of government, they recognised his unique capacity to maintain national unity through that crucial period of Indonesia's political growth. So they were content to continue serving their country under his Presidency. If he had kept them together as an executive team, the story of Indonesia through the first two decades of Independence could have been much happier and more prosperous than it was. Nature had endowed the country with great economic riches, and if this wealth had been steadily developed by able and honest Ministers and civil servants, the material strength of the nation could have grown immensely.

As a result the Indonesians – who formed the largest nation in Asia after China and India – could have exerted great influence throughout South East Asia and beyond.

But that was not to be. Sukarno felt uneasy at the recognised ability and growing influence of some of his Ministers; and as their personal fame increased he resented it. One after another he contrived or allowed their ejection from power. Lesser, more subservient and sometimes more corrupt men replaced them in his councils – with sorry results for the Indonesian people. By himself Sukarno was no adequate substitute for those earlier colleagues; he lacked wisdom as a policy maker in certain important fields, and his administrative capacity was almost non-existent. In particular he had only a superficial understanding of financial and economic problems, and in any case displayed no serious interest in them. As a consequence mismanagement caused the country's economy to wilt, whilst in other ways too the well-being of the nation gradually declined. Indonesia's potential influence in international affairs never blossomed.

Yet the force of Sukarno's personality continued to prevail. For a long time all sorts of other individuals or groups, both inside and outside the country, got blamed by the populace for Indonesia's growing ills; but the man most responsible – Sukarno himself – eluded their displeasure. A few courageous voices were raised in criticism of him, but they went unheeded. Only much later did public criticism begin to crack his prestige. Until then his magic continued to work.

I think one explanation of all this was a significant element in his make-up as a politician. He was a truly great, fiery leader of a Revolution – but when the Revolution had been won, and other, cooler gifts of leadership were required, he lacked those gifts. Several other renowned nationalist chiefs in Asia, Africa and elsewhere who have gained Independence for their peoples in recent years combined in their personalities the qualities of fine Revolutionary and wise post-Revolutionary leaders, displaying a genius first for agitation against an alien government and afterwards for rule in a native government. Nehru of India and Kenyatta of Kenya are outstanding examples of this. Sukarno of Indonesia was not in the same class as a statesman.

Possibly Mao Tse-tung of China is also a greater Revolutionary than post-Revolutionary leader. As an example of the former type he is of course infinitely superior to Sukarno, having largely devised the intellectual Chinese interpretation of Marxist philosophy which inspired the Communist movement in China, and also invented the political and military strategy by which it achieved power. But when it came to post-Revolutionary rule his zeal for maintaining an effervescent mood of agitation almost regardless of consequences – as during the Cultural Revolution – perhaps made him sometimes a less sagacious leader at that stage of affairs. This thought raises complex considerations which need much more analysis than is appropriate here; but if it is partially correct, Mao compensated for his own defect by his readiness to allow Chou En-lai's administrative ability to play a decisive role in guiding their government's policies through the last quarter century. It is to a considerable extent the partnership between the Revolutionary genius Mao and the post-Revolutionary genius Chou which has carried the Chinese people through this turbulent period of their history.

A similar partnership in Indonesia could have done similar good. But Sukarno's character was such that he would not contemplate any partnership of that kind. He would not tolerate the presence in his cabinet of an outstanding political colleague who might conceivably become a rival to himself. Wishing to monopolise power, not to share it, he so arranged things that he became a virtual dictator.

The fact is that he had little capacity, or even inclination, for practical policy-making, or for conducting the implementation of plans. He was bored by the dull routine of day to day administration. By nature he was an agitator, a fervent agitator, a perpetual agitator. He was conscious of the enthusiasm he could always – or nearly always – arouse by his struttings and shoutings on a stage. And although he could play various parts for brief moments, he kept reverting to the only part he could perform permanently – that of a passionate Revolutionary. So when he had gained victory in one revolution he looked for another revolutionary cause to espouse. Soon after he won his fight for Indonesian Independence he therefore started his agitation for acquiring Dutch New Guinea. And after he secured West Irian he peered around for fresh fields to conquer, and worked up his anger about the prospective incorporation of Sarawak and Sabah into Malaysia. He hoped that his 'confrontation' with Malaysia would lead to those little countries passing under Indonesia's – and his – influence. When he failed in this purpose, he frustratedly contemplated the rest of Asia, which a few years earlier had been seething with revolutionary movements, and observed that almost everywhere the achievement of Independence had caused its governments to subside into the quiet tasks of nation building. He searched for a continuing Revolution somewhere – and saw China. So he allied himself with the Chinese revolutionaries, seeking to associate them and his fellow countrymen as brothers struggling against Imperialism, Capitalism, Revisionism and everything else that seemed averse to a continuation of Revolution.

In the meantime incompetence and corruption in his government led to a steady decline in Indonesia's well-being. More and more people in the know felt that the President was primarily responsible for this. He had outlived his usefulness, and was now not an asset but a liability. Unless and until he could be replaced, there would be no recovery. However, his popularity with the masses remained so high, his political skill so shrewd, and his dictatorial power so strong that for long his removal proved impossible. In the end the army had to act decisively, over-throwing his government by a *coup d'état.* Even then his hold on vast sections of popular opinion continued so firm that General Suharto and his colleagues in the new regime dared not take punitive action against him in person. Many of his aides were tried in court, found guilty, and imprisoned. Others were condemned to death and executed. But he, the principal author of their failures, though not of all their misdeeds, remained free. This was partly because the new government's leaders themselves felt such respect and gratitude for some of his past achievements that they did not wish to hurt him more than appeared necessary. For a while he even continued as nominal, though ineffective President; and afterwards he was left to live in peace in his private home. So he remained until, several years later, he died.

Achmad Sukarno was a giant, but a giant with feet of clay.

Prince Sihanouk

' . . . his black curly hair, chubby face and juvenile figure were pleasant. Charming friendliness glistened in his dark eyes . . . '

As ruler of Cambodia King Sihanouk was heir to one of the greatest dynasties of Oriental potentates in history, the Emperors of the Khmers. His most famous ancestors occupied their throne from the ninth to the fourteenth century A.D. in the majestic capital at Angkor. Afterwards their power declined, and in 1432 aggressive warrior neighbours, the Thais, captured Angkor, forcing the Emperor of the day to flee with his court and government. Khmer monarchs never returned to rule in the ancient city; nor did the Thais stay there. After sacking it they retreated to their own homeland, leaving the place deserted. Its splendid palaces, temples and streets did not long remain empty, for soon an army of jungle vegetation invaded them, and throughout the next four hundred years they were lost in deep forest. Only in 1860 were they rediscovered by a French naturalist seeking rare tropical plants in the woodland, who suddenly sighted the richly ornate towers of Angkor Vat through a screen of trees. Now the mass of semi-ruins standing in their wild setting is one of the noblest groups of historical monuments anywhere round the world.

After the Emperor of 1432 fled from Angkor he founded a new capital 150 miles away on the site of present-day Phnom Penh. Although the great era of the Khmer Empire – which had covered most of South East Asia – was over, he and his descendants continued to rule the people of the smaller land of Kambuja, or Cambodia, until two years ago. The wearer of its crown was not regarded by his subjects as an ordinary mortal. To those simple peasants he remained what his ancestors had been to their forefathers – a King-God representing on this Earth the Holy One who presides in Heaven over mankind's destinies. That attitude suffered little change when a foreign people again conquered them. When the Western Powers were dividing up much of the world among themselves in the nineteenth century, the French took possession of Indo-China, including Cambodia. The ancient kingdom became a Protected State of Imperial France, still retaining its native sovereign, but under the suzerainty of the government in Paris.

*

Soon after I became Britain's Commissioner General in South East Asia in 1948 I went to Phnom Penh to pay my respects to His Majesty King Sihanouk, discuss current problems with the French High Commissioner, and begin to gain a first-hand acquaintance with Cambodian affairs. On the morning of my arrival I paid a call on the king in his palace. As my car drove through the gateway in a high wall surrounding the royal precincts I caught my first glimpse of the charming group of regal buildings scattered among wide lawns and flower-beds. To me they were an exotic sight with their decorated tapering walls crowned by tiers of fabulously carved roofs ascending to gilded spires. Their names were as attractive as their appearances: the Silver Pagoda, the Pavilion of Dancers, the Chamber of Musicians, the Stable of the White Elephants, the Throne Hall, the Royal Treasury, the Private Palace, and other romantic descriptions of their various functions in traditional court life.

I alighted at the foot of a flight of steps climbing to the entrance to the Throne Hall. At its top I was greeted by a young man dressed in Cambodian costume who seemed little more than a school-boy. His black curly hair, chubby face and juvenile figure were pleasant. Charming friendliness glistened in his dark eyes as I bowed respectfully over the hand he extended to me – for I realised that this was none other than the King himself. It was typical of the informal courtesy which he always combined with regal dignity that he sent no court flunkey to meet me outside the door and conduct me to the royal audience, but came in person to perform that service.

He was in fact a few years older than his boyish appearance

might suggest. Aged twenty-five, he had already occupied the throne for seven years. He led me into a spacious chamber with a painted ceiling and frescoed walls, where we strolled along a rich carpet between rows of low-bowing courtiers to gilded chairs standing by themselves at its far end. The King motioned me into one of these as he sat on the other.

Whilst he and I chatted for the next half hour, the array of Officers of State all dressed in Khmer court uniforms sat in prim, pompous silence listening without moving a muscle to our conversation. The scene was reminiscent of an eighteenth century engraving illustrating some Oriental potentate receiving a foreign envoy. Around us in the vast room were arranged majestic items of furniture for use on special occasions during the lives and at the deaths of successive monarchs: the golden throne on which they sat at their coronations, a silken couch where they reclined at particular palace ceremonies, a decorative palanquin on which they were borne in processions through the streets, a nine-tiered umbrella-of-state held over their heads during outdoor festivities, a gorgeous vase in which their corpses were embalmed before being cremated, and the catafalque on which those dead bodies were borne to their funeral pyres. Beams of tropical sunshine slanting through tall windows lit the theatrical scene.

The King's talk was a lively mixture of serious and light-hearted chatter. He asked me various questions about the current situation in South East Asia in general, and offered his own comments on Cambodia's problems in particular. Every now and then he switched the conversation to one or another of his favourite hobbies, such as horse-riding or composing jazz music; but always after these diversions he returned to more solemn topics. At one point he expressed his eager desire that Cambodia should be freed from colonial rule.

At the close of our conversation he rose and led me past the once more bowing courtiers to the top of the steps descending to my car, and bade me 'au revoir'. Afterwards I strolled through the palace grounds, visiting several pavilions. In particular I went to see the inmates of the Stable of the White Elephants, two of those rare living giants being among the king's most prized and indeed semi-sacred possessions.

That evening I dined with him in the Private Palace, a small elegant residence with something of the air of a *Petit Trianon.* Our royal host greeted two dozen guests with genial smiles. He remained relaxed despite the fact that all his fellow countrymen bowed extremely low as they entered the room and virtually crawled in homage towards him until he touched them on a shoulder with a friendly gesture which uplifted them once more.

At a banquet table richly laden with crystal, silver and flowers the company was as decorative as the many lovely works of art which stood around the palace rooms in the forms of ancient Khmer sculptures, Vietnamese lacquers, Thai porcelains, Japanese paintings and Chinese carpets. The diners were a select group of princes, princesses and other courtiers, men of aristocratic distinction and women of delicious beauty. The king was about the youngest person present, many of the others being old enough to be his parents or even his grandparents. Nevertheless he outshone the rest, maintaining a flow of animated, often merry and always interesting talk. Sometimes he monopolised the conversation, everyone else listening to an opinion which he propounded or a tale which he told. He spoke of the contemporary situation in their country, throwing out ideas about its problems and prospects. At one point he referred laughingly to the trials and tribulations of Kingship, remarking that his rustic subjects expected him to perform impossible miracles. He quoted an incident during a recent tour that he made in a remote district where the weather was foul, bandits were on the rampage, and wild beasts gorged the crops. When he appeared among the poor peasants they asked him to put a stop to all these disasters.

'I can't control those things,' he told them.

'But you're the King,' they commented simply.

'Yes, but I've no control over stormy weather, savage beasts and wild men,' he asserted.

They gazed at him dumbfounded.

'I'm the King; but I'm also a mere human being,' he added.

They could scarcely believe this. They assumed he was something more than an ordinary mortal, being a demi-god.

I listened to him, prompted him with questions, and observed his reactions with fascination. I gained an impression of a young man in whom deep seriousness lay beneath an exuberant light-heartedness, inexperience was tempered by innate sagacity, and natural modesty was matched with inherited authority. He presented an enthralling study of a youth prematurely burdened with responsibilities far beyond his years who was deliberately learning the wise exercise of his supreme duties, lacking expert knowledge and yet fortified by instinctive self-confidence. That last quality sprang from his magic attribute of Khmer majesty. Nevertheless, those weighty official traits in his character could not quench the irrepressible boyishness in him, his gift of sparkling youth as well as gradually maturing intelligence.

There was an undeniable touch of Frenchness in the whole proceedings, with no hint of distaste for its alien presence. The dining-room furniture was French in the regal style of Louis XVI; our meal consisted of half-a-dozen French dishes concocted by a chef from Paris washed down with vintage Provençal wines; and throughout it a French military band on a lawn beyond the windows played a succession of gay European tunes. An honoured guest at the table was the French High Commissioner, and all the Cambodians conducted their conversations in impeccable French. If one closed one's eyes one might imagine oneself banqueting in the Elysée Palace.

After dinner we reverted to pure unsullied Cambodia. We went to watch a theatrical performance by the Royal Corps-de-Ballet in the Pavilion of Dancers. Beneath a velvety black sky illuminated by myriads of stars the King led us across lawns to that imposing building. As we strolled he told me interesting things about the plays we should witness, preparing me for episodes which would otherwise be incomprehensible to an Occidental stranger like myself. He was an authority on ancient Kambujan drama, and his explanations were vividly enlightening.

The Pavilion's interior was a mixture of spaciousness and intimacy. It had no outer walls, an ornate ceiling being supported only by tall pillars which exposed the vast chamber to the cool tropical evening air outside. A stage filled the theatre's centre, sunk slightly below the level of the auditorium like the arena in a circus. The place was lit by many hundreds of candles set in glittering chandeliers. As we entered, some two hundred people rose from their seats and bowed to the King; and when we sat in throne-like chairs a hush of expectancy filled the playhouse whilst servants crawled obsequiously to offer His Majesty dance programmes for our instruction.

At one end of the wide stage a native orchestra crouched on the floor, its members quietly fingering their flutes and oboes, gongs and drums, conches and other traditional instruments in readiness for action; whilst at the other end squatted a choir who would sing occasional passages of narrative as the dancers performed their classical masques. Between those two groups stretched an empty space of platform.

Suddenly the hush ended. The orchestra broke the silence with a flourish of music. Flutes and other wind instruments blew gently, ripples of melody rose from bamboo xylophones, and gongs and drums added some well-timed thuds to the noise. It was an exciting overture, filled with a medley of tones and phrases which were novel to my unaccustomed ears. At the same instant as the first note sounded, a group of female dancers appeared at a far end of the stage. Clothed in fabulous velvet, silk and bejewelled costumes, with golden head-dresses gleaming with precious stones, they hastened in two rows like successive waves advancing along a beach, half running and half shuffling across the floor until they came to a halt before the King. Facing him like a platoon of gorgeous Amazons, they fell on their knees, joined upraised hands reverently before their eyes, and made obeisance to him so low that their heads almost hit the ground. Then they resumed a kneeling posture, unclasped their hands, rose to their feet again, turned and departed as swiftly as they had come. As soon as the stage was empty the music ceased.

This introductory homage paid, the performance of ballets could begin. For the next two hours we watched a series of graceful, often slow moving but at other times swiftly capering steppings by the troupe of ballerinas. The only male actors were players of clownish parts; otherwise all the characters of heroes and heroines, princes and princesses, villains, monkeys and other creatures were represented by those pretty girls, sometimes wearing appropriately ugly masks on their faces. They expressed themselves in eloquent movements not only of their bodies and limbs, but also of their fingers and toes, each tiny, fleeting gesture conveying its own distinct significance. The themes of their acts were romantic episodes in ancient Kambujan mythology or history; and these were performed to the constant cooing and wailing, tinkling and rumbling, whistling and sometimes even shrieking ejaculations of the orchestra, punctuated now and then by gentle chanting by the choir.

It was gorgeous, unforgettable Oriental drama.

*

During the next several years I paid periodic visits to Phnom Penh for talks with King Sihanouk and his principal counsellors, as well as with the local French colonial officials. A significant moment in the Cambodians' long history had arrived. For nearly a century their country had been a French Protectorate, and throughout it they lived quite contentedly under the benevolent if Imperial guidance of friendly, cultured administrators from Paris. Associated with them in this subordination were their neighbours in the other Indo-Chinese lands: Laos, Tonking, Annam and Cochin-China, the last three joined in a united territory called Vietnam. Recent events, however, had changed their attitude to this state of affairs. During the World War French rule continued, but was subordinate to Japanese military power, which asserted itself over all South East Asia. French prestige suffered a blow from which it could not recover, and in Vietnam a nationalist movement that had started some years earlier woke into fresh life, passionately eager for independence from any foreign rule. After the restoration of more effective French government in 1946, Vietminh forces in the north began a violent revolt, and for the next several years maintained brilliantly conducted guerilla warfare against the French and their South Vietnamese supporters.

In next-door Cambodia peace prevailed; but there, too, yearnings for self-government grew among politicians and intellectuals. This was all part of the great Asian Revolution against foreign Imperialism – whether French, British, Dutch or anything else – which surged across that continent after the war and started capsizing colonial administrations and carrying indigenous governments into power in one land after another. By the time of my first visit to Phnom Penh in 1948 India, Pakistan, Burma, Ceylon and the Philippines had become independent sovereign states, and events were moving towards the same conclusion in Indonesia, Malaya and elsewhere. The Cambodians became infected by a similar nationalist spirit. Although a numerically small people counting only about three millions, they were proud of their distinguished history and culture, and so an agitation for a recovery of freedom stirred among them. Their king – the proudest of all the modern Khmers – felt this urge strongly in his young head and heart.

Several years earlier he had ascended the throne by the hallowed constitutional procedures which for centuries settled the succession to it. On the death of his predecessor a group of royal councillors met to choose the new ruler. They could pick whoever they judged most suitable among the surviving male members of the reigning house within a certain degree of consanguinity to the late monarch. When they foregathered in 1941 they took a remarkable decision. Passing over the claims of Sihanouk's scholarly father, two able uncles and other experienced older relatives, they cast their votes for this youth of eighteen years. I do not know what considerations influenced them. The prospect ahead looked troublesome and pregnant with change; various fresh political ideas were starting to intrude into Cambodia from the rest of Asia; and the nation's next leader must be capable of adapting himself to all sorts of unforeseen situations. Exceptional qualities would be required in him. Indeed, as things turned out, he must possess a talent for guiding a Revolution. Possibly some such thoughts affected the decision of the selectors when they rejected the elderly, conservative candidates and chose a juvenile instead. Whatever their reasons, Sihanouk became the new sovereign.

During the early years of his reign some people questioned the wisdom of this choice. They thought him a charming young man, but perhaps too light-hearted. He had many diverse attractive gifts, some of them not necessarily required in a prudent ruler. For instance, he was an author of sentimental poetry and a composer of gay music. In the palace drawing-room stood a grand piano on which His Majesty strummed his latest concocted tunes. He was a skilled performer, too, on another formidable musical implement, the saxophone. Indeed, he was also the conductor of a modern Western-type dance band, every member of which happened to be a prince of the royal blood. So with his own baton he would direct his own playing on his own wind-instrument of his own musical compositions accompanied by his own orchestra. And when he grew tired of puffing a saxophone he laid it aside and crooned a song of his own authorship.

Later he took to another occupation, the directing of cinema films based on his own scripts which were shot by his own team of camera-men and in which he sometimes himself played a leading role. All these activities were partly frivolous recreations, and partly serious pastimes. He was a zealous upholder of the traditional arts and crafts of his people, but he wished their skills to move with the times, and to express up-to-date ways of life as well as preserving relics of a past culture. A patron of the long-established village drama, he therefore encouraged its rustic actors to perform plays representing modern as well as antique themes. A generous benefactor, too, of the Royal

Corps-de-Ballet, he commanded its ballerinas to dance acts representing contemporary events as well as classical episodes. Incidentally, one charming child dancer in that troupe was his eldest daughter Princess Buppha Dhevi, who later became its talented *première ballerina.*

His zeal for equestrian sport was likewise indulged in for reasons of both pleasure and duty. He loved horse-riding as an exhilarating exercise in which he personally excelled, but valued it also as an occupation that helped to develop manly qualities in Cambodia's military officers. One of his enthusiasms was for the Royal Khmer Army, towards which he displayed not just the condescending, formal patronage of a monarch for soldiers wearing the King's uniform, but the serious concern of a Head of State who sensed that the times could be dangerous, that his country might become threatened, and that its armed forces must be in a state of efficient readiness to defend their nation's existence. Sometimes he spent weeks on manoeuvres with his troops, and later he became for a while their active as well as titular Commander-in-Chief.

In addition to all these various preoccupations he naturally took a considerable part in government, and sometimes could not avoid getting drawn into internal politics. Inevitably the public life of his people revolved largely round him, the heir to the supreme power exercised by most of his predecessors. During the period of French rule that suzerainty had been maintained more in theory than in practice; but the colonial era was now passing, and customary royal authority could be resumed. In high state affairs he therefore became the pre-eminent personality in the kingdom.

Thus on his young shoulders lay the sometimes almost intolerable burden of rule. Modern Cambodia was in some ways very different from ancient Kambuja. It was a much smaller, much less influential country. Yet in other ways it remained important, for it occupied a significant position in South East Asia. Lying not far from the borders of China – where in 1948 Mao Tse-tung's regime was about to spread its authority over the entire mainland – alongside Vietnam where the Vietminh were successfully maintaining their guerilla warfare against the French, and with Laos and pro-American Thailand as its other neighbours, the little land was a frontier area wedged between the Communist and the Free worlds. A territory of distinct political strategic importance, therefore, it could become subject to pressures from both sides in the cold war, and might find great difficulty in either achieving or maintaining national independence. But its king was determined to attain both those aims.

Observers who in the first few years of his reign thought his delight in cheerful pleasures a sign of an engaging but irresponsible nature, misread his character. Those interests were the hobbies of an exuberant and gifted youth compelled to assume prematurely the cares of government. They stayed with him, helping to keep him young in spirit long after his elevation to power; but as he gained knowledge of his new tasks his intelligence steadily ripened. His flair for politics gradually opened from bud to flower.

The development of his ideas on national and international problems can be traced in countless speeches, proclamations and actions through the following years. First and foremost a Cambodian patriot, he felt passionately eager to serve the well-being of his fellow countrymen. Thus he became one of numerous contemporary Asian leaders striving for the national independence of their peoples, with the extraordinary contrast in his case that whereas the others – like Gandhi, Nehru, Ho Chi Minh and Sukarno – were mellow elders, he was an immature youth, and whereas they were commoners who rose from the ranks of democratic political movements, he was a born King-God.

This circumstance made the issue in Cambodia less simple than in other countries. The rising, typically twentieth century political urge there was not just a longing of nationalists to free their country from a foreign yoke. Among many local intellectuals sentiment was revolutionary in other ways too, radical elements wishing to release their compatriots from an allegedly out-of-date, reactionary form of society which included among its encumbrances the institution of monarchy itself. These zealots were opposed to every vestige of archaic feudalism, and the fact that for some generations the royal family had appeared willing tools of French Imperialism made the position of the king all the more precarious. After the World War ended Republicans increased in numbers in Phnom Penh, and were inclined to give King Sihanouk the same short shrift as had been accorded to crowned heads in many other lands round the world.

In that uncertain situation he was guided by his natural capacities to feel sincerely, form clear opinions, and act courageously. One reason why he survived was his spontaneous sympathy with most of the aims of the Cambodian radicals, though not with them all. He had no wish to end French rule simply to restore the earlier Kambujan regime and become a selfish despot. He was determined to discard various features in the old system which weighed oppressively on the population, and to introduce economic, social and political reforms which would give them a more free and fuller life. Indeed, he was socialistically inclined. The only major aim on which he differed from similarly ardent liberal spirits was their desire to abolish the monarchy. His views on that were the opposite: feeling proudly that through Cambodian history the kings had often been good leaders of the nation to whom their subjects looked for wise guidance, he resolved that the latest Khmer king should himself lead the necessary reformation. In fact he was a remarkable combination of a modern socialist revolutionary and an antiquated conservative royalist.

During the earliest years of his reign these thoughts were latent. Young and inexperienced, he had to establish his own as well as other people's confidence in himself. In any case the current situation was uncertain; the moment was not ripe for decisive action to gain national freedom from either the Japanese or, later, the French. Moreover, after the restoration of France's suzerainty he felt that its overthrow should be a gradual, not a sudden process. The French should be humoured, not alienated. Independent Cambodia would be a small state living in a troubled world, and would need the help of larger friendly peoples. Its situation in a frontier area between strong Communist and anti-Communist nations exposed it to certain risks. He and his fellow-countrymen desired national independence, but as a result of long political tutelage by a Western power they were inclined to be democrats whose freedom should be expressed in parliamentary-style institutions. They did not want to jump out of the frying-pan of French colonial rule into the fire of Chinese communist domination. So they needed the amicable sympathy of some more powerful nation which could lend them aid in case of need. France, so well known and understood by the Cambodians – the cultured, civilised France which in some ways had done so much for Cambodia in recent generations – would be their first choice as an ally, provided that the French would adapt themselves to a new relationship of partnership with them instead of overlordship.

For a few years King Sihanouk therefore temporised. He did not press a demand for quick complete independence, asking only for a succession of preliminary concessions from Paris. So he kept reaching compromises with the French. The more extreme, impatient nationalists lost confidence in him, and republican sentiment among the left-wing intelligentsia gathered strength. Partly as a result of this, communist ideas also began to spread in some quarters.

Meanwhile a dangerous situation was developing across the border. The Vietminh movement, posing as purely nationalist, had fallen under communist leadership, and made formidable progress in Vietnam. Now it threatened to extend its activities into Laos and Cambodia. Suddenly in 1953 units of its guerilla forces invaded both those small lands under the guise of liberators seeking to expel French Imperialism. The position in Cambodia became critical; all sorts of unpleasant possibilities loomed. One manifestation of an ugly mood was the murder of the local French Resident, who was stabbed to death by his previously loyal, trusted valet as he lay asleep in bed in Phnom Penh.

As soon as the Vietminh invaded the country King Sihanouk took personal command of his troops; and, side by side with French comrades-in-arms under over-all French control, they fought to eject the intruders. However, Sihanouk himself was now growing impatient at the slowness of political progress in Cambodia, and had already stepped-up his demands from the government in Paris. Feeling that the time had arrived for decisive action, he asked for early complete independence. He was showing himself to be the champion of his people's emancipation both from lingering old Western colonialism and from threatening new Communist imperialism.

When the French hesitated, he revealed his determination in an extraordinary way. A hitherto mostly hidden trait in his temperament suddenly appeared. An emotional, impulsive streak exploded. Feeling frustrated, he jumped into a car one dark night, sped hundreds of miles across the Thai frontier to Bangkok, and settled in a hotel there. Declaring himself a voluntary exile from his country, he announced that he would not return unless the French conceded full national sovereignty to its people.

Friends and foes alike were astonished by his conduct, many of them thinking it as politically injudicious as it was regally unorthodox. Professional diplomats judged it stupidly amateurish, whilst intellectual nationalists called it puerile. I confess that I for one felt it imprudently risky. Almost everyone assumed that Sihanouk had miscalculated, and that such behaviour could only result in his losing personal prestige without gaining any advantage for his subjects.

But they were proved wrong. The French were shocked into making a considerable concession. That jaunt to Thailand forced the issue. It lasted only a few days during which swift communications flew between Paris, Phnom Penh and Bangkok, arranging a compromise solution. Although this did not grant immediately Sihanouk's whole demand, it went a long way towards doing so, and enabled him to return to his kingdom as a hero. After a few more intense diplomatic efforts he gained his full purpose. French statesmanship adjusted itself to the situation, and the authorities in the Quai d'Orsay made a historic declaration of their readiness to negotiate forthwith an agreement establishing Cambodia as an independent sovereign state.

*

King Sihanouk's sincerity as both a Khmer patriot and a friend of France enabled him to understand how Cambodian and French interests could be mutually reconciled; and his flair for judging shrewdly when to act, and for acting then with zeal, helped greatly to achieve effective results. But those qualities by themselves would not have been enough. He buttressed them by conduct which made him the clear and undeniable voice of a nation. Had he not based his authority on massive popular support, left-wing sections among the local nationalists might have aroused criticism of him for his policy of continuing friendship with old Imperial France, whilst the French might have felt able to resist his request for absolute independence.

A vital part of his genius was his capacity to root his political strength in virtually unanimous acclaim by the people. He achieved this by going out to meet the humble peasantry and urban workers, mixing cordially with them, showing himself to be their supreme friend, and rallying them to every cause that he espoused. Thus their traditional loyalty to him as the monarch was reinforced by their affection for him as a person. He became their national idol.

I often had opportunities to observe how he exercised his popular leadership. I remember, for instance, an occasion when I visited Cambodia soon after the country gained independence in 1954. He happened to be away from Phnom Penh at the time, travelling through a province where day after day he met the local population, discussed rural problems with their headmen, and made speeches to vast crowds. At the end of his tour he planned to spend a few days relaxing in a villa he owned at a seaside resort called Kep; and he sent me a message inviting me to come and stay with him there.

When I arrived early one morning he awaited me at the front door, and held out both hands in glad friendship as I stepped from my car. Over cups of coffee he said he would like me to view the beautiful surrounding countryside, and proposed that we might drive through rustic scenery to a mountain on whose summit we could eat a picnic lunch and enjoy grand views of the Gulf of Siam.

I agreed with pleasure, and he promptly asked whether I could be ready to start in half-an-hour. Remarking that the sunshine would be hot, he added that if I would like to wear an open-necked shirt and slacks he would do the same. And would I be so bold as to trust myself to being driven by him in his new sports car? With a grin he said that the vehicle was equipped with two or three novel mechanical devices which had been invented by him, and which seemed to work all right; so he hoped we should arrive safely at our destination.

I accepted all these propositions. When I had changed my clothes and returned downstairs, my illustrious chauffeur was already sitting at the wheel of his car. As I jumped into the seat beside him he hooted a horn, and a lorry-load of police on the road ahead jerked into motion. A royal foot was pressed on an obedient accelerator, and we were off.

As we drove along a highway bordering the ocean, and afterwards turned inland across a plain covered with padi-fields, the King talked of recent political developments in Indo-China. He described the instability of the situation in Vietnam, condemned the Vietminh invasions of Cambodia and Laos, and sketched the problems of relations between his newly free kingdom and its pristine overlord France. He spoke candidly, eloquently and occasionally excitedly about his perplexities in the present and his hopes for the future. I expressed my opinions with equal frankness, and in the course of a three hours' journey we surveyed widely the contemporary state of affairs.

But our conversation was frequently interrupted by diversions beyond the car's windows. News of the King's expedition had evidently travelled ahead of us, and everywhere we went the country folk were eager to catch a glimpse of him. At the sight of the police van preceding us by a hundred yards they ran from their fields to the roadside to stare. Near every farm hut its family stood expectantly, in every hamlet a cluster of peasants lined our way, and in the market towns crowds of citizens were assembled. As they peered into the car to see their sovereign lord they clasped their hands devoutly, and many of them sank to their knees with arms upraised in homage and faces lit with adoration.

The King's responses were equally remarkable. He greeted with friendly words every individual and group whom we passed. As we approached each one he slowed our car's pace almost to a halt, waved a hand gaily through the window, and shouted a few sentences to the delighted spectators. Even if we were meeting only a single rustic standing at the edge of a field, he did this. He of course addressed them in Khmer, and I could not understand a word of what he said beyond an occasional un-Khmer phrase which sounded extraordinarily like 'Malcolm MacDonald'. On those occasions he told me he was telling the people that I was his companion in the car, and that Great Britain was a staunch friend of Cambodia.

'They'll be very pleased,' he commented with a smile.

Often the men and women called sentences back to him, and he responded with further remarks. He had asked about the state of their crops, the well-being of their children, or some other family problem, and they were answering him. His attitude to them was self-assured, but genial and not superior. It was unaffected, kindly, and extremely friendly. Except for the significance of those upraised, clasped hands of his subjects, he and they might have been familiar acquaintances passing the time of day.

Occasionally he was amused by the astonishment expressed in some villager's eyes, as if the fellow could not believe what he was seeing.

'He can hardly realise it's me in this sports-shirt,' he remarked. 'He expected to see me in royal uniform with a crown on my head!'

So he greeted many thousands of his subjects scattered in individual families, small groups and larger crowds at frequent intervals along a route extending over sixty miles. At length we came to the foot of our destined mountain, left the cultivated plain, and started to climb a steep, zig-zag track ascending through jungly forest. No living creatures now surrounded us except wild birds and beasts. The branches of densely growing trees on either hand met overhead like the vault of a green tunnel, and we saw no more distant landscape until eventually we emerged into open territory along a highland ridge three thousand feet above sea level.

After a while we arrived at our appointed picnic spot lying near the edge of a majestic precipice which fell sheer to cultivated fields far below. The view from it was breathtakingly beautiful. A wide plain of farmlands stretched to a coastline indented with capes and bays; off its shore lay the calm, sunlit ocean pierced here and there by islands: and beyond them appeared an almost infinite horizon of sea and sky.

We were joined at lunch by two dozen of the King's friends and courtiers who had followed us from Kep. Our meal was served in the half-ruined, roofless hall of a royal hunting lodge which had been blown to bits recently by an invading Vietminh guerilla band. Our shattered surroundings made no difference, however, to the grandeur of the feast. Butlers and waiters had preceded us there, and laid an array of china, glass, cutlery and silver on a banqueting table under the blue sky. We sat guzzling roast duck and other delicacies washed down by vintage wines. It was the most regal picnic I have ever attended.

Again, news of the King's arrival had spread by jungle telegraph all over the mountain top, and as we gossiped over coffee at the end of lunch numerous foresters and other labourers with their families gathered in a courtyard to salute him. After a while he went to speak with them. As soon as he appeared they fell on their knees and raised their clasped hands towards him. He strolled to them, calling words of friendly greeting. Going to each one in turn, he laid a hand gently on his or her shoulder, and asked them their names, occupations and family news.

Recollecting how these yokels regarded him as not simply their king but a semi-divinity, I realised what unspeakable joy they must feel at his kindly touch. He spoke to them as man to man, with a humanity and understanding which banished all shyness in them. Nor was this attitude feigned, an affectation to gain their favour. I could sense his true esteem for these people. His was the conduct of an individual who loved his fellows, and cared about their well-being. He regarded the whole Khmer nation as one family united by a common heritage, character and interest. Certainly he viewed himself as the father in the family, with the authority which belongs to such a position. But if he was the head of the community, this made him also its chief servant.

*

After gaining independence the Cambodians faced various difficult problems touching economic, social and political affairs inside their homeland. Some of these were matters of controversy, and none more so than the question of what form the nation's new constitution should take. King Sihanouk held strong views on the subject. A democrat in spirit, he nevertheless felt it would be imprudent to establish at once in practice a fully developed parliamentary democracy on the Western model among an illiterate, inexperienced population accustomed to benevolent autocratic rule. Indeed, a recent Cambodian constitution had attempted something of the kind, with certain unfortunate results. He judged that his subjects needed gradual training in the exercise of uninhibited political liberties, and that this should be achieved by successive stages of constitutional progress. As a first step in the process he proposed an arrangement by which every local council throughout the land should be elected by voters on a popular franchise, whilst the National Assembly would for a while be indirectly elected. Some politicians inside the country and propagandists outside it vigorously opposed this allegedly reactionary notion. They roused an agitation among the intellectual élite which threatened serious trouble.

Suddenly, without warning, King Sihanouk abdicated. On waking one morning his fellow countrymen were stunned to learn that he had voluntarily, and apparently impulsively, resigned his crown. He announced that he did this because the opposition had thwarted his constitutional plan. Sceptics shook their heads critically, declaring this to be further evidence that he was an unstable and irresponsible character incapable of the sustained application required for guiding their nation through the difficulties of its newly independent existence. Once more they were proved wrong. Sihanouk's admittedly astonishing action indicated that he was prepared to go to any length to create circumstances in which he could continue as the effective leader of his people.

His father and mother became the King and Queen, and he left Phnom Penh so that his presence in the capital would not embarrass them during the early days of their reign. Withdrawing to a villa in distant Siem Reap alongside the ruins of the ancient capital at Angkor, he hoped to consider in quiet leisure there his and his country's future. However, that retreat did not enable him to escape from the attentions of Ministers, party leaders and other personages concerned with state affairs. He remained the most significant as well as popular man in the land, and no one could decide with assurance what his own conduct should be until he knew what Prince Sihanouk – as he had now again become – proposed to do next. Many notables therefore poured into his home in Siem Reap, and for the first time in six centuries that famous neighbourhood became again the centre of political activity in the realm.

Shortly afterwards his father asked him to lead Cambodia's delegation to the important 1955 conference of non-aligned Asian and African nations held at Bandoeng in Indonesia. On his way there he stayed with me for two days in Singapore, and for another day on his return journey.

In conversation I asked him whether his apparently spur-of-the-moment decision to abdicate was in fact long premeditated.

He replied that he had indeed considered the possibility for some time, but that he only decided the moment for it had arrived when he was frustrated in his wish to alter the constitution.

'The nature of Cambodia's problems has changed,' he said. Expanding on this theme, he explained that until recently the Cambodians' most urgent need lay in the field of international affairs. They wanted independence from France, and as king he could lead the nation in striving for that. But after they achieved it their main problems shifted into the field of internal affairs. Administrative reforms, economic development, and advances in social welfare were required – and it was difficult for him as king to lead in those matters. The occupant of the throne should not intervene too much in domestic political questions; he should stay above politics. So Sihanouk's personal power became limited. 'I felt restricted,' he said, 'and decided to abdicate so that I could play my full part in helping my countrymen to progress in modern ways.'

He explained much else. Among other things he asserted that he would not get involved in quarrelsome party politics, or become the leader of any one of the rival parties. As an ex-king and continuing member of the royal family, it would be wrong for him to do so. He hoped his influence could be at the disposal of all the constitutional parties. Indeed, in his view there should now be a cessation of party warfare for a while, so that a government of national unity could be formed. He told me that he was working behind the scenes to accomplish this.

He spoke of his plans for the development of agriculture, public health and education, and invited me to visit Cambodia as his guest so that I could see some of his new schemes getting under way. We agreed that I should go there two weeks later, immediately after his return from Bandoeng.

'Do you like water ski-ing?' he suddenly asked, with his characteristic enthusiasm for robust physical sports. 'I'd like to take you water ski-ing on the West Baray at Angkor.'

'That's a wonderful idea, sir,' I answered. 'I love ski-ing.'

I did not add that I was referring to snow ski-ing, and that I had never been on water-skis in my life. I wished to treat his suggestion as a royal command, and not to disappoint him. Moreover, the prospect of water ski-ing on the West Baray, a large artificial lake created almost a thousand years earlier by a Khmer Emperor as a reservoir for Angkor's water supply, seemed too romantic to be resisted.

*

He had brought his seven-year-old daughter, Princess Sorya, as a companion on his journey to Bandoeng.

To amuse her one evening, I stood on my head and then walked on my hands round a room.

She was not particularly impressed.

'Papa,' she remarked, drawing his attention to my antic, 'I've got a monkey that can do that.'

*

Contemplating the proposed exercise at the West Baray a few days later, I thought it would be prudent to take a lesson in water-ski-ing before my command performance there; so one afternoon I borrowed a pair of skis and went to the sea-shore near Singapore to try my luck on the ocean waves. Several years earlier I had snow-skied in Canada's wintry mountains, and fortunately I found that the two techniques were not unduly dissimilar. At the first attempt I rose on my skis and slithered safely over the rippling Straits of Johore.

When I arrived in Siem Reap my host arranged an interesting programme of activities for my few days' stay. He took me to see a half-finished irrigation project, a new land settlement scheme, a recently opened school for peasant children, a freshly established hospital, and a similar convalescent home for Buddhist monks, all items in a development plan which he had initiated throughout the district. The school-teachers, doctors, nurses, engineers and other professional people running them were city-bred experts who had never before ventured into the countryside, and who were now, under his inspiration, enthusiastic workers in that hitherto neglected region.

The prince was evidently familiar with the details of their tasks, and discussed with them their current problems. At the monks' home he made a devout speech, in the school he took temporary charge of classes of children, and at the irrigation project he grabbed a shovel and cleared away piles of rubble. Everywhere he chatted with the workers about his hopes for Cambodia's well-being, and thanked them for the useful parts they were performing in the building of its better future. He made them proudly conscious that he and they were partners in a grand adventure.

One morning he let me play truant from such activities, so that I could go and renew my acquaintance with Angkor's ancient monuments whilst he attended a conference of political leaders who had come from Phnom Penh to seek his counsel. After several hours of ramblings among temples and palaces I rejoined him and his visitors at an open-air lunch on a terrace overlooking a lake. The company at the meal was remarkable. It consisted of a score of leading members of half-a-dozen rival political parties, a selection of the most prominent men in the nation's public life. A few weeks earlier some of them had scarcely been on speaking terms with one another; but now they munched sandwiches and drank beer together under the conciliatory presidency of their royal mentor. They seemed to be in care-free mood; their conversation was light-hearted and gay, and only occasionally did a few grow serious and argue solemnly about some point connected with the main purpose of their gathering. They had met to consider the possibility of adopting Sihanouk's proposal that party squabblings should cease, and that a government of national unity should be formed. The goodwill which they showed each other was an encouraging augury for the success of their deliberations.

Tall jungle trees shaded the terrace where we sat, shielding us from the fiercest heat of a mid-day tropical sun. A flight of antique stone steps flanked by sculptured lions descended to a pleasure pool on which centuries ago Khmer Emperors and their courtiers had conferred as they floated in boats across it. Now untamed forest surrounded the water where cultivated gardens had previously spread. The prospect was as peaceful as it was wild and beautiful, and in its quietude I sensed the presence of ghosts from those earlier times. The terrace seemed to be a meeting place for past and present Cambodian history, where a living descendant of the old Emperors strove once more to guide wisely the Khmer people's destiny.

Sure enough, a few days later the group of guests at that picnic announced unanimous agreement to combine their separate parties in a united organisation to be called the Socialist Community. Several months later the community captured every seat, against small but obstinate opposition groups, in independent Cambodia's first general election for its National Assembly.

*

Whilst we lunched beside the lake that afternoon a crowd of rustics gathered at the woodland's edge to stare at us. Rumour had spread through the neighbourhood that Prince Sihanouk was there; and, as always, he was a magnet irresistibly attracting the populace. Foresters, temple guards and other local workers flocked with their wives and children to catch a glimpse of him. Squatting on their haunches on the ground beyond our terrace, they started a jibber-jabber of speculation about the purpose of this extraordinary occasion.

After a while the prince interrupted his duties as host to the statesmen, and went to speak with those humbler folk. As he approached them they fell on their knees with hands upheld in gestures of worship. He put them at ease at once by cracking a joke which made them guffaw with laughter. Then he started asking them questions. This or that man or woman in the crowd answered him. He put more questions, and the interview became a general conversation in which everyone felt free to join. Sometimes His Royal Highness made little speeches, whilst they listened intently and occasionally muttered some guttural comment. Judging by the periodically changing tones of his voice he seemed to be lecturing, chiding, twitting and encouraging them in turns. Every now and then they burst into throaty laughter at some sally which he made. They lost all sense of shyness. As he talked, old crones chewed wads of betel-nut, young mothers suckled babies at their breasts, men threw remarks into the conversation, and children stared in wonder at this sample of Divine Royalty. But some of their elders never for a moment lowered their hands raised in pious devotion to him.

When he eventually left them to rejoin his guests the whole crowd shouted their affectionate gratitude to him. I realised that this young prince had discovered the true secret of good government – that it should be by love. A government must of course possess various qualities, such as strength and wisdom and authority; but all those together are not enough. Unless rulers are inspired by true affection for the people under their care, they will lack the instinctive understanding, the natural communion with the multitude, which alone enables them to satisfy their needs.

*

Later that afternoon the prince, the politicians and I went to the West Baray for our water ski-ing. His Royal Highness and I were to be the performers, whilst the others came as a slightly sceptical and highly amused audience. During the last few centuries the huge artificial lake where we would disport – which originally stretched across a few square miles – had shrunk somewhat in size; but it was still a vast sheet of water with plenty of depth to drown rash intruders.

Whilst boatmen tested the engines of the motor-launch that would tow us, we sipped tea in a pavilion overlooking the lake. A hot sun shone from a cloudless blue sky, and many wild ducks, grebes and cormorants swam on the water in happy ignorance of the rude invasion of their territory which was about to occur.

When all was ready Prince Sihanouk got into bathing trunks, waded into the shallows, fitted skis on his feet, and crouched in readiness as the launch manoeuvred into position to pull him forward. At a signal the boat gathered speed, he was dragged for a few moments with dubious splashings towards deep water, and then suddenly rose like a sea-god from the waves, standing serenely erect and skimming safely over the lake's surface. A cry of loyal delight broke from us spectators on the beach, whilst flotillas of cormorants dived in fright and flocks of wildfowl flew in panic in all directions.

The prince made two wide circles round the Baray with splendid dash and unfaltering grace. Then it was my turn to try. As luck would have it, the skis proved equal to their difficult task of bearing me on the waters, and no mishap occurred to spoil the thrill of my first swift slither across the great tank of the Khmer kings. The courtiers on the shore took the hint that this must be an easy exercise, and two or three of them got into bathing-suits and shuffled on to skis. After numerous collapses and duckings, however, they revised their opinion of the sport, and contented themselves with judicious sun-bathing on dry land.

Prince Sihanouk repeated his successful run half-a-dozen times. The lake was as calm as a mirror, and gliding over its glassy, sunlit surface was great fun. Like him, I took several turns. It was exhilarating sport, rushing at top speed over the boundless liquid skating-rink, swinging in wide arcs first in this direction and then in that, slaloming nonchalantly through shorter, sharper twists from side to side, tossing on choppy wavelets as I passed diagonally across the launch's wash, and at the end of each run alighting with swaggering poise within a few feet of the admiring spectators on the shore. As I repeated these antics with apparent impunity my self-confidence grew, and I decided to demonstrate an accomplishment which even Prince Sihanouk had not displayed. That was of course a piece of unpardonable *lèse-majesté*.

As I sped over the lake I shifted my weight on to one ski, shook the second ski off my other foot, and continued the journey balancing with both legs planted on a single narrow slip of wood. For a while I remained upright, and a cry of astonishment rose from the beach. Leaning slantways across my ski so that it swerved swiftly and sharply away from the direct line of the boat's advance, I shot outwards in a wide semi-circle of super-slalom motion. I had never before attempted this athletic feat, for it cannot be performed on snow: but having watched it done by others on water, I assumed – with high conceit – that I could faultlessly accomplish it. Sure enough, I continued careering onward and outward, and felt very conscious of the fine figure that I cut. But I had miscalculated the correct rate and dimension of the swerve, and raced onward too fast. My speed exceeded that of the boat, the rope connecting me with it therefore went momentarily slack, my pace promptly slowed, and my ski began to sink! In the few seconds before the rope became taut again – to pull me safely forward once more – I failed to adjust my balance, and capsized on the ski. The lake waters leaped in high splashes all around me; and as I submerged, the columns of flying spray seemed to assume the shadowy forms of departed Khmer Emperors. I thought I heard them hiss, 'That'll teach you not to take outrageous liberties with our reservoir.'

*

A crucial question that the leaders of independent Cambodia had to decide was what their foreign policy should be. The situation in South East Asia made this a delicate problem. The two rival power blocs in the world were beginning to introduce their cold war into the region, each seeking to make it a sphere of influence for itself against the other.

I personally felt strongly opposed to the injection of the cold war into South East Asia. All its peoples in their various lands were charming, characterful and cultured folk who should be left in peace to pursue their own chosen ways of life. Of course the rich members in both the Western and the Communist blocs could show a sympathetic interest in those small nations' well-being by providing financial, technical or other kinds of aid for their economic and social development; but they should not seek to create opposing military camps in the area, each endeavouring to recruit the local peoples as subordinate allies, and so provoking rivalries which could generate not merely a cold war but also hot wars among them. This could inflict misery and death on their populations.

In the middle 1950s my familiar contacts with Far Eastern affairs made me believe that it would be possible to establish a wholly non-aligned South East Asia, and to guarantee its maintenance by an international treaty approved by all those peoples themselves and signed by the British, French, American, Russian and Chinese governments as well. I thought this would be in the interests of not only the small nations in the region, but also the external super-states, including the Western powers. Of course it would not mean that ideological affinities between some nations inside and outside the area could not continue to exist. The Vietminh movement in North Vietnam, for example, had become so potent that possibly a united independent Vietnam would eventually be ruled by a Communist administration. But in my judgment any such regime would become as truly non-aligned a member of the 'third world' as Yugoslavia was in Europe. Again, Thailand, Malaya and Singapore would wish to keep much closer associations (including co-operation in defence matters) with the Western than the Communist governments; but their foreign policies could nevertheless be basically non-aligned.

In 1955 – when I was on leave before assuming a new post in India – I put this idea of an internationally guaranteed neutral South East Asia to Foster Dulles, the American Secretary of State, in private conversations in Washington.

'We don't want a neutral South East Asia,' he replied.

'What do we want?' I asked.

'A Western-aligned, anti-Communist South East Asia,' he answered.

I expressed the opinion that this was impossible to achieve; any forceful attempt by Western powers to create it would meet resistance from Communist sympathisers and other radical groups not only in Vietnam but elsewhere, which would inevitably gain them external support from China and Russia, and tend to increase rather than decrease Communist influence in the region. I urged that the most effective way of countering that influence would be by substantial assistance to the local peoples' economic progress.

Dulles contested this, asserting that active American and other Western military alliances with friendly governments would win over every people in the area as our allies. I do not suggest that American policy was wholly to blame for the tragedies which have occurred in Vietnam, Laos, Cambodia and elsewhere as a result of this attitude. Communist authorities have also been guilty of wrongful interferences in the internal affairs of certain local nations, and so have contributed to persistent cold and hot wars there. But Dulles' outlook on various Asian problems bears a grim responsibility for the set-backs which American and other Western interests have suffered since.

*

Sihanouk's prime concern was for the well-being of his fellow Cambodians. Having gained their national independence, he wished them to enjoy it in security and peace. To achieve this, he decided that the right policy for his country in international affairs was one of non-alignment. He sought to maintain friendly relations with the Western and Communist powers alike, hoping that as a result neither side would interfere in the internal affairs of his nation. Indeed, he wished to gain the positive understanding and goodwill of both groups, as well as of Cambodia's immediate neighbours. This aim would be difficult to achieve at the centre of a South East Asia where the cold war kept increasingly intruding. Not only in Vietnam, but also in Burma and Laos civil wars broke out between rival Communist and anti-Communist factions, with varying degrees of military support from outside for each belligerent party.

Moreover, Cambodia itself was to some extent associated with the West. Its close relationship with France might arouse resentment on the part of the Communist powers, especially as the French gave his country valuable aid not only towards economic and social development, but also for its military defence. Sihanouk was determined to continue receiving this help. To counter possible criticism in Peking and Moscow he was therefore emphatic in his declarations of a neutralist policy. As a practical expression of his desire for peaceful co-existence with nations in both blocs, his government exchanged ambassadors with the principal Communist states and accepted substantial financial and technical aid from them also. Taking a long view of the prospect, he was particularly anxious to get on good neighbourly terms with the government in Peking because China was potentially the greatest foreign power existing close by little Cambodia. In the present or the future the Chinese could take decisive action to weaken if not destroy Cambodian independence, should they so desire. This undeniable fact did not cause him to kow-tow to the government in Peking. On the contrary, in addition to other non-Communist attitudes, such as his co-operative association with France, he made no attempt to hide his aversion to any extension of Communism inside Cambodia. He denounced in speech and opposed in action the activities of the native Communist faction called the 'Red Khmers', and made clear the hostility he would feel against any foreign attempt to help them.

The Chinese government accepted this. They recognised that French military aid to Cambodia was for wholly defensive purposes, in no way inspired by any intention to commit aggression against China. All that the Peking authorities insisted on was that Sihanouk's government should not entertain any military alliance with the Americans which would enable those inveterate foes of Red China to use Cambodia as a base for military attack against it or its nearby allies. In other words, provided he preserved a policy of true non-alignment, they were ready to accept his stated position, and to raise no objection against his anti-Communist policy in Cambodia's internal affairs.

Unfortunately the Americans were not so wise. After establishing military alliances with the South Vietnamese, the Thais and a faction of the Laotians, they resented the Cambodian government's neutralist policy, and tried to stimulate in Cambodia an anti-Sihanouk movement which would swing the country against his non-aligned attitude. It would appear that the C.I.A. engaged in subversive plots aimed at ousting him from power, and at establishing a pro-American administration in his place. This was one of several not only morally wrong but also politically stupid activities initiated by that secret agency in various parts of South East Asia, sometimes without the knowledge (as well as against the advice) of American ambassadors on the spot. In Cambodia this clandestine conspiracy became known to Sihanouk, who bitterly resented it. The delicate situation that ensued was aggravated further by his impulsive nature, which made him utter every now and then in public speeches angry criticisms of American foreign policy.

His suspicion of the Americans was increased by another circumstance. For historic reasons relations between Cambodia and its closest neighbours on either side, Thailand and South Vietnam, were not good. Through the centuries frontier disputes had arisen between them, and in the 1950s and 1960s these again raised their ugly heads. Sihanouk laid claim to certain areas across each border, and there were signs that the Thai government wished to acquire a region in western Cambodia, whilst the South Vietnamese were ambitious to secure ownership of some Cambodian islands off the south coast. The fact that the United States was an ally of both those other countries, and that for long it refused to dissociate itself publicly from their territorial aspirations, made Sihanouk suspect that the Americans privately supported them. All this produced an unhappy state of affairs which caused rifts in American/Cambodian friendliness, sometimes resulting in breaches of diplomatic contact between them. The Thais and South Vietnamese did not help by their constant hostility to Sihanouk's neutralist policy, and by the selfish influence they exerted on the Americans against him. Naturally in these circumstances diplomatic relations between the governments in Phnom Penh on one side and Bangkok and Saigon on the other got disrupted.

I must not write more here on the historic and other reasons for this quarrelling, except to comment that none of them caused Sihanouk to change his sincere desire for non-alignment. They did make him continue indulging in occasional harangues against the Americans – as well as the Thais and Vietnamese – which strengthened the case of his detractors in Washington. He was sometimes equally outspoken in criticisms of Chinese policy when he had reason to believe that Peking was interfering in Cambodia's internal affairs; but the Chinese were much more prudent than the Americans in their response to these attacks, and in their general conduct of policy towards him. They gave him fewer occasions for such denunciations. Incidentally, if the outbursts of this leader of a small country against the governments of great powers were signs of imprudence, they also demonstrated his courage. He was prepared to do everything he could to defend his people against anyone.

So he managed to keep walking along a tight-rope of neutralist policy in spite of various attempts to knock him off it on one side or the other. Sometimes he wobbled in this direction or that; nevertheless he retained his balance. It was an extremely difficult act, but a correct one in the interests of his compatriots.

If he had bent too much to the side of the Vietminh and the Chinese, he would have given the South Vietnamese and Americans an excuse to invade his country; and if he had leaned too far over on the other side, he would have invited similar action by their opponents. In either case his homeland would have become a battlefield for those external forces fighting their ferocious cold and hot war against each other. Instead he maintained peace, security and unity for the Cambodian population, whilst disunity and insecurity afflicted the peoples in some nearby lands. It was a remarkable achievement.

Sometimes through that period he became the actual Prime Minister of the current government, and always he was the most powerful personal influence in Cambodian political life. When his father died and the throne became vacant he resisted suggestions that he should once more be King. Instead he accepted the title of Chief of State, whilst his mother was called Queen Mother. In his new office he continued to exert without hindrance his pre-eminent authority.

*

I returned periodically for talks with him in Phnom Penh not only so long as I remained Britain's Commissioner General in South East Asia, but throughout the next fourteen years when I filled successive posts in India, Europe and Africa. Sometimes we also met in France or Switzerland. My visits to him were always a mixture of the serious and the gay. On one occasion, for instance, when half-a-dozen Chinese friends from Singapore accompanied me on a holiday jaunt to Angkor to view its ruins, he entertained us as his guests for three days in the Private Palace in Phnom Penh on our return journey. One evening after a dinner party in our honour attended by a charming group of royal courtiers we all trooped to a nearby pavilion, where His Majesty became the conductor of an orchestra whilst the rest of us glided on 'light, fantastic toes' round its ballroom. Sometimes to the waving of his baton and at other times to the blaring of his saxophone, the band played joyous dance tunes of the day, including some of his own compositions. Periodically he cast aside his wand or instrument, stepped to a microphone and crooned in a pleasing, night-clubby voice the words of his own sentimental ditties. Every now and then he approached one or another lady in the company, bowed to her, and danced a waltz, fox-trot or two-step with her.

His energy never flagged for a moment; nor did his geniality. No host could be more engaging than he.

*

He and I always discussed at length the current Asian situation in general and Cambodian prospects in particular. We spoke confidentially, expressing our views with mutually friendly trust. Occasionally when some recent incident had upset cordial relations between Britain and Cambodia we were able to smooth out the difficulties and restore an amicable state of affairs.

During one of our conversations I ventured to speak frankly about his own character. After referring to his admirable qualities as a statesman and leader of his people, I remarked that it might be helpful if I mentioned, with the candour that is one of the privileges of true friendship, a defect in him which I thought sometimes damaging to Cambodia's interests.

He said he would welcome such criticism from me.

I then spoke of his occasionally too impetuous, over-emotional reaction to events, expressing the view that he was sometimes apt to talk aloud before he had thought, and to act hotly before he had considered coolly every aspect of a situation. This sometimes made him leap into excessive as well as inexpedient public denunciations of (for example) American policy which gave great offence to the authorities in Washington, causing them to suspect that he was shifting from a non-aligned to an anti-Western attitude. This was an immense pity because it placed unnecessary strains on his personal and official relations with the United States, and helped his critics there. I urged him to restrain his tongue at such times, and to speak more moderately, and only after careful thought.

He listened courteously to my impertinent little lecture, nodding his head in accord now and then.

When I fell silent he said, 'You're right. That's a fault in me, and I should try to correct it.' Then he commented that the defect was typical not only of himself but also many of his fellow-countrymen, past and present. Through the generations Kambujans had always been inclined to react too emotionally to events that upset them in either private or public affairs, and to act impulsively as a consequence. Then he laughed and added, 'I'm aware of the fault in myself; but one difficulty is, I've discovered that it often pays for me to display it!'

With a twinkle in his eyes he asked me whether I remembered the occasion when he had suddenly jumped into a car, driven across Cambodia's frontier into Thailand, exiled himself in Bangkok, and declared that he would not return to his country until the French made a clear statement of their intention to grant national independence.

I said I remembered the episode well.

He remarked that at the time I had probably thought his conduct foolish.

I confirmed the accuracy of this guess.

He grinned and said, 'I was inclined to think the same. When I woke up in a Bangkok hotel the next morning and realised what I'd done, I felt very worried, and wondered why I'd acted so impulsively. But things turned out all right!' And he reminded me that within a few days the French had given way, conceding sufficiently to his demand to enable him to return triumphantly to Phnom Penh.

'Sometimes the same sort of consequence of my hasty actions has happened since,' he observed.

'Not always,' I commented.

'No, not always,' he readily agreed.

In those talks he spoke freely about his problems and policies. He was coherent and voluble. In earlier years his knowledge of English had been very limited, and he spoke it little. Khmer was of course his mother tongue, and French his adopted tongue;

and he conversed fluently in both. It was a mark of his desire to communicate easily with American, British and Commonwealth representatives that later he took trouble to learn English so thoroughly that he became proficient in it.

Among other matters he described to me his attitude to the Chinese. Although he greatly admired them, he was in some ways critical and suspicious of them. Throughout history they had regarded themselves as a superior race, the only civilised people in a world otherwise inhabited by 'barbarians'. They had looked condescendingly on all non-Chinese, viewing them as inferiors who should acknowledge 'the Middle Kingdom's' suzerainty. And there was no denying that when those hundreds of millions of capable, well disciplined Chinese formed a united, self-confident nation – as they showed signs of becoming again under their Communist rulers – they could be a supremely strong power who (if they wished) could assert their influence inexorably over small next-door populations – as the Tibetans had recently learned. They were the only super-state in the Far East, a fact of life which the tiny nations in South East Asia could not ignore. Whilst being ready to stand up for themselves, those weaker peoples must try to be on good terms with their mighty neighbour. Nor was this too difficult, for another long-established trait in the Chinese was their preoccupation with their own affairs, and their readiness to let nearby peoples pursue their customary ways of life without interference – provided those peoples did not allow foes of China to exploit their territories as possible bases for attacks against China. It was South Vietnam's harbouring of American forces which made the Peking authorities give substantial support to the Vietminh.

Sihanouk therefore took particular care to maintain friendly relations with the Communist leaders in Peking. Nevertheless he continued to let them know with characteristic frankness that he was averse to any introduction of Communism in Cambodia. The wise Chou En-lai showed respect for this attitude, and guided his government's relations with Phnom Penh accordingly.

The Vietminh Communists were not so prudent. Powerful practical reasons caused this: partly because they had ambitions to turn Laos into a satellite state, but mostly because transit routes through Laos would be helpful to their guerilla forces travelling to battle fronts in South Vietnam, they had established the Ho Chi Minh trail through an area of eastern Laos, and collaborated with the Communist-inclined Pathet Lao. Later they intruded for similar purposes into a little inhabited Cambodian region near the Vietnam border, whilst also intriguing with the Red Khmers. Sihanouk protested strongly to the North Vietnamese against these activities inside Cambodia, and when his objections produced little result he sought Peking's help. But the Chinese government's influence in Hanoi was limited. Improper Vietminh activities in a corner of Cambodia continued, though on a much lesser scale than would have been the case but for Sihanouk's opposition. Their restriction was also partly a result of the work of an International Control Commission established by the Geneva Conferences to help sustain the Laotian and Cambodian governments' neutrality regarding the Vietnam war.

The Thai and South Vietnamese leaders remained extremely critical of Sihanouk's non-aligned policy, and even neutralist Ministers in Laos felt he was insincere in his opposition to Communist influences in their lands. They therefore kept denouncing him to the Americans and other Western powers.

In my talks with Sihanouk he expressed his deep regret at their persistent hostility. He wished for friendly understanding and co-operation between the Cambodian, Laotian and Thai peoples in particular, since they were neighbours whose interests in many ways coincided. Enlarging on this theme, he emphasised that all three held certain profound beliefs in common: they were Buddhists in faith, traditional monarchists in constitutional outlook, and non-Communist in their internal political affairs. They should therefore tolerate the difference in their foreign policies, and establish good diplomatic relations. But (he said bitterly) the governments in Bangkok and Vientiane as well as

Saigon refused to do this on the basis which was essential to Cambodia's continued security, and which he made a condition for exchanges of ambassadors with every other government round the world. That condition was publicly declared respect for Cambodia's existing frontiers. Russia, China and other Communist states including North Vietnam and France, Britain and many Western nations including eventually the United States of America, had all made declarations to this effect. But the South Vietnamese and Thais adamantly refused to give any such undertaking, whilst the Laotians tried to impose an inappropriate counter-condition which was unacceptable to the Cambodians.

I do not suggest that the fault for these unfortunate disagreements lay wholly with those other governments. Sihanouk also made certain mistakes in his conduct of diplomacy. Nevertheless his success in achieving his main purpose was remarkable. In spite of all the difficulties, he sustained through more than fifteen years after Independence his country's non-aligned policy, and so preserved peace and unity among its citizens amidst the strife and turbulence which afflicted some neighbouring peoples. The Americans gradually came to recognise the sincerity and merit of his non-alignment, and resumed diplomatic relations with his government. For their part, the two major Communist powers continued to respect his attitudes. It looked as if his compatriots might enjoy indefinitely the blessings of his rule.

Certainly whenever I visited Cambodia I saw evidence of his immense, unchanging popularity among the masses there. One circumstance did worry me. To accommodate him, his wife Princess Monique and their personal staff wherever they went on his frequent tours here, there and everywhere throughout the land, he acquired a number of royal residences. Most of those dwellings were modest in size, but they were rather luxuriously furnished. His ownership of them displayed a plutocratically regal standard of living which to many modern-minded people might appear excessive. However, I reconciled my democratic prejudice to it by assuming that the immense difference between his and the peasants' simple manner of life would cause no offence to those subjects of a Chief of State who was, to them, not merely a beloved human being but something of a King-God.

*

Unfortunately developments in the Vietnam war gradually increased difficulties for him. As I have mentioned, the Vietminh were not so respectful of his neutralist foreign policy as were the Chinese and Russians. In the late 1960s they expanded the secret military hide-outs in a corner of Cambodia alongside South Vietnam where their guerilla bands sometimes took refuge and at other times launched attacks against the enemy across the frontier. Naturally the Americans and South Vietnamese protested, urging Sihanouk either to take effective action himself to stop it, or else to let them do so. He objected strongly to the Communists' growing use of Cambodian territory, and asked the authorities in Hanoi to withdraw their troops. When they refused he appealed to the Peking and Moscow governments to exert pressure on their North Vietnamese friends; but the two Communist powers either could not or would not compel the Vietminh to abandon those guerilla bases. Since Sihanouk's own armed forces were too weak to drive them out, he gave the Americans permission to bomb the military installations. At the same time he insisted that no American or South Vietnamese land army should enter Cambodia, for this would inevitably provoke the Vietminh to reinforce their units, and so spread the war further into Cambodia.

This was the situation when I went to spend two days in Phnom Penh as his guest in December, 1969. His regard for the British as friends of his country was demonstrated in a remarkable way when I arrived. I had now retired from government service, and my visit to Cambodia was entirely private and personal. Nevertheless, when I landed at the airport

I found to my surprise that a Cabinet Minister was there to meet me on the Prince's behalf, a guard-of-honour with a military band stood on musical parade for my inspection, crowds of school-children were marshalled to give me a cordial welcome, and an array of Union Jacks and Cambodian flags fluttered side by side from long rows of flagpoles.

As always, Sihanouk and I discussed thoroughly the current situation in South East Asia. With his usual sincerity he expressed views about it, and about the policy which the Western governments should pursue to help maintain a cordon of non-aligned countries, including Cambodia, between the Communist and the Free Worlds in Asia. I believe his ideas would on the whole have been acceptable to the French, British, Chinese and Russians, and should have been acceptable to the Americans, for they could have served the interests of all the nations concerned both inside and outside South East Asia. I shall not record his suggestions or other expressions of view here, for he spoke to me in confidence. Incidentally the genuineness of his non-aligned attitude was illustrated by the fact that whilst right-wing critics in Phnom Penh at the time accused him of being pro-Communist, the local left-wingers charged him with being pro-American.

After dinner on my last evening in Phnom Penh he showed me and other friends his latest film, called *Joie de Vivre*. It was a competently directed, pleasingly acted, light-hearted romance almost wholly devoted to sentimental aspects of human life; and it threw a brilliant beam of light on that side of its creator's character. Afterwards he and I bade each other 'adieu' until our next meeting.

Three months later, whilst he was away on a visit to France, his government was overthrown by a military *coup d'état*, and he was dismissed from office. I shall not comment on the episode, during which it seemed to me that everyone, including the Prince, made mistakes. I need only say that his disappearance from the scene, and the greatly increased military intrusion into it of foreigners such as the Vietminh, the South Vietnamese and the Americans, was a tragedy for the charming, peace-loving Cambodian people.

*

Whatever other causes may have contributed to Sihanouk's downfall, I think a fault in his statecraft played its part. His relationship with the masses of his fellow-countrymen was just about as perfect as could be. Among the peasantry and other humble citizens he mixed with cordial, laughing familiarity wherever he went. He showed his deep care for their well-being with a wonderful humanity which I have never seen surpassed by any leader anywhere else round the world. He loved them, and they returned his affection with a deep devotion that had to be seen to be believed.

His relations with some individuals in the élite ruling class, however, were less friendly. With many political leaders he stayed on good terms: they agreed with his ideas in public affairs, admired his qualities as the pre-eminent Cambodian statesman at a crucial moment in their national history, and supported him loyally in successive governments. He responded to their trust in him with confidence in them, and he and they were excellent colleagues. But other politicians were less amenable to his ways. They resented the almost absolute power which his combination of royal prestige and popular appeal enabled him to exert. One cause of their disaffection was, no doubt, jealousy; his authority curbed their own personal ambitions. On his side he may not have tried sufficiently to win their support by taking them into his confidence, consulting them on vital matters, and treating them as significant leaders in national affairs. The inborn streak of an Oriental potentate perhaps made him too impatient of opposition, too assertive of his own ideas, and too imperious in taking decisions. So his double personality – the mixture of a democratic twentieth century statesman and an autocratic tenth century King-God – had its drawbacks. And it may well be that as the years passed he became too self-confident and insensitive, tending to treat some eminent colleagues as subordinates who should do his bidding, restricting their initiative, limiting their power, and hurting their pride. In any case opposition developed in influential quarters, and played into the hands of whatever indigenous or foreign influences plotted the *coup d'état* in March, 1970.

Nevertheless, despite his human faults, he was probably the most independent, courageous and wise statesman in South East Asia during the difficult quarter century immediately following the Second World War. In spite of his impetuosity he was more protractedly consistent in maintaining a coherent policy, in spite of his emotionalism he was cooler in his long-term calculations, and in spite of his autocracy he was a more dedicated servant of his people than any other leader in the region. That is saying a lot, because several of them in different countries – such as Tunku Abdul Rahman in Malaysia and Lee Kuan Yew in Singapore – were statesmen with fine heads and hearts.

At the comparatively early age of less than fifty Sihanouk is now exiled from his country, deprived of his responsibilities, a prisoner of events beyond his control. Has he disappeared from power for ever, or will he return once more to be a ruler in Cambodia? For the moment we cannot tell; but I for one would not be wholly surprised if he reappeared as the most important character in the Cambodian scene. Yet one trait in his character may prevent this: he is so independent in outlook and behaviour that he would never become subservient to either a Western or a Communist master.

Certainly if he were to return to Cambodia, an overwhelming majority of his fellow-countrymen would feel supremely happy. Whatever may be his ultimate fate, his place in history is assured as probably the last and undoubtedly one of the best of the royal rulers of the Khmers.

Jawaharlal Nehru

Nehru, whose looks 'had the aristocratic refinement of the Kashmiri Brahmin which he was', with his sister, Mrs Pandit, and the author.

I MET Pandit Jawaharlal Nehru for the first time in January 1948, a few months after he assumed office as Prime Minister of newly independent India. I was staying with Lord and Lady Mountbatten, the former of whom had recently ceased to be the last Viceroy and become the first Governor-General in Delhi. On the evening of my arrival Nehru came to dinner. As he left the stately ex-Viceregal Lodge afterwards he invited the Mountbattens and me to lunch with him the next day. The Governor-General, however, was already committed to entertaining numerous Maharajahs at that meal; so Edwina Mountbatten and I went by ourselves to the Prime Minister's house.

No one else had been invited. We sat on the lawn of a spacious garden in the shade of gloriously flowering bougainvillaea bushes, enjoying a picnic in the perfect sunshine of a Delhi winter's day. Nehru was at his most charming; and although our conversation roamed over many serious topics, it stayed informal and relaxed.

At one moment during the talk Edwina turned to the Prime Minister and remarked, 'Malcolm can do something you can't do, Jawaharlal.'

'What's that?' asked Nehru, with a slight frown at such an impertinent suggestion.

'He can walk on his hands,' she answered.

Nehru looked surprised. 'I'd like to see him do it,' he said in a tone of scepticism.

I rose and strolled thirty or forty yards away, then turned, raised myself upside-down on my hands, and sauntered topsy-turvy back across the lawn to Nehru's side. Halting within a few inches of him, I restored myself to an upright position.

He laughed, and looked quite impressed. In retort he wagered me that he could stand on his head longer than I could on mine. I did not dispute the claim, for I knew that he stayed in that posture for considerable periods every morning before breakfast as part of his regular Yoga-style exercises. But I commented that I should greatly like to see him in physical reverse. He promptly took off his Gandhi cap, placed his head on the ground, and with the agility of a schoolboy turned his neat, almost sixty-years-old figure the wrong way up. I stood on my hands and walked round him half-a-dozen times. At that we called our acrobatic contest a dead-heat.

He asked me whether I practised Yoga. I said I did not; to which he answered that the exercise would help me to keep bodily fit, mentally alert and spiritually serene. When I enquired precisely what I should do, he sat cross-legged like a Buddha on the grass and demonstrated a few examples of the physical jerks he recommended.

One of the unforgettable features about Nehru was his delicately handsome face. Now, however, those good looks became warped, for his visage assumed a succession of grotesque aspects as he displayed to Edwina and me the disciplined control of this and that set of muscles which Yogi exercises encouraged. He quivered his eyebrows, rolled his eyeballs, trembled his cheeks and twisted his mouth into various violent grimaces. Then, with his countenance immobile, he transferred the contortions to other parts of his body, such as alternate contractions and bulgings of his stomach in a series of monstrous in-and-out motions. So the expression on his face was at one moment diabolical and at the next sublime.

That was the start of my friendship with the mighty – and for many years in India the virtually Almighty – Jawaharlal Nehru.

*

I have already mentioned his remarkably handsome face. At first glance he seemed small, his trim, always neatly costumed figure standing only five and a half feet tall; but any momentary impression of insignificance was immediately dispelled by the arresting distinction of that countenance. Another such magnetic face which I remember belonged to his older kindred spirit, the poet Rabindranath Tagore – although the two were different in detail, Nehru's clean-shaven cheeks and chin contrasting with Tagore's massively flowing prophet's beard. Nehru's looks had the aristocratic refinement of a Kashmiri Brahmin – which he was – with a softness of skin that to his dying day left it smoothly unmarred by wrinkles. His features revealed both strength and gentleness, accompanied by a delicate sensuousness indicated in his full, sometimes pouting lips, classically modelled nose with sensitive nostrils, and bright, contemplative eyes. Frequently those eyes looked sad, seeming to gaze upon all the sorrowful problems of the human race.

I have enjoyed the privilege of knowing several of the greatest men alive during the last half-century, in both the Occident and the Orient; and none of them was a more fascinating study than this noble Indian. In none of the others, for instance, were human frailties more evident – which is saying quite a lot, for naturally all of them had their failings, some of them rather gross. Nehru's faults were so apparent, and sometimes so petty and exasperating, that occasionally one was tempted to wonder whether he could really be a great man at all. But much more often his lofty wisdom and extraordinary influence all round the world were so compelling that one knew he must be ranked among the most significant giants of modern times. In any case his defects usually only became apparent at close quarters; they were apt to be lost to view at a greater distance, as if his faults were mainly private and his virtues public. This circumstance made me once remark of him that he was a unique object in any landscape; whereas every other feature in a scene looked big close at hand and grew smaller the further you drew away from it, he appeared smaller the nearer you approached, and larger at a distance. Nevertheless, at close quarters, too, he could be tremendous; his charm and friendliness as well as his distinguished personality were often captivating. Yet at other times, in other moods, he displayed none of his graces, being aloof, cold and even surly.

One of his weaknesses was a liability to occasional violent fits of temper. His ire could be suddenly aroused, and as quickly extinguished. I remember a day when he, his daughter Indira and her two schoolboy sons arrived at Delhi airport on his return to India from some triumphant visit overseas. A multitude of his fellow-countrymen awaited the arrival of their beloved leader. When he and his family alighted from the aircraft a group of eminent citizens approached him to hang garlands of flowers round his neck. Then some of the crowd broke through a cordon of police, and rushed to give him an enthusiastic welcome home. They surrounded his party, halting its walk towards a reception lounge and jostling his daughter and grandsons in attempts to shake hands with them and him. In a flash Nehru lost his temper and began hitting out at the seething company, bashing them on their heads and bodies as if they were a mob bent on attack instead of a jubilantly friendly throng come to pay him homage. It was a strange revelation of a streak of the Oriental autocrat in his make-up.

Some of his faults were the defects of his qualities. Thus he was sometimes naïvely trustful of unreliable people because he himself was so honest in his relations with them that he could not believe they were less honest in their dealings with him. Again, his occasional inconsistency in words or deeds was a characteristic which seems to me to mark some representative Indians, springing perhaps from certain contradictions in Hindu mythology which they imbibe in their childhood, and to which I shall refer later. His flashes of vanity, too, were reflections of the instinctive superiority complex of a Kashmiri Brahmin. Yet at the same time that vanity was partnered by a conflicting humility which made him resent adulation, tolerate generously most people who disagreed with him, and quite often confess his own errors in public.

Indeed, in some ways he was a mixture not only of human

strengths and weaknesses but even of personalities. Many acquired Occidental traits were combined with inherited Oriental elements in his character. This was largely due to his upbringing during his early, impressionable years. In boyhood he spent much time in Anglo-Saxon or Celtic company at his father's house in Allahabad, where British friends were frequent visitors; and afterwards he became first a pupil at Harrow, then an undergraduate at Cambridge, and later a law student in the Inner Temple. As a result he imbibed many British ideas and tastes in social, cultural and political matters. He himself wrote in his 'Autobiography' that he was 'a queer mixture of the East and the West, out of place everywhere, at home nowhere'. This was an over-modest portrayal, for his familiarity with the customs and notions of both hemispheres made him in fact out of place nowhere and at home everywhere. A facet of his greatness was that he became one of the first true Citizens of the World – a sort of universal man somewhat ahead of his own time.

On another occasion he observed that in his likes and dislikes he was 'perhaps more an Englishman than an Indian . . . as much prejudiced in favour of England and the English as it is possible for an Indian to be'. This un-Indian trait was apparent in his efforts to break down various deep-rooted Hindu concepts such as the caste system. It was evident, too, in the democratic political ideas which he adopted from Britain, and which he put into practice in India throughout his seventeen years as Prime Minister. Indeed, it is tempting to try to be too clever, and to quip that he was the last of India's British Viceroys rather than the first of its native Prime Ministers – and to the extent that there is an element of truth in this comment one should hasten to add that he was the greatest of all the Viceroys. But the description is superficial. The mental outlook which Nehru acquired from his early English environment was more than outweighed by the profound nature inbred in him from his Indian ancestry. He was essentially an Oriental personage – even an Oriental potentate. And of course the motives inspiring his attitude towards all India's problems were – unlike those of the Viceroys – fundamentally Indian instead of British.

Nevertheless he always retained an affection for England; and one result of this was his decision in 1947 that independent India should not break all its political ties with Britain, but should on the contrary maintain a special association with her as a fellow-member in the Commonwealth of free and equal nations which was emerging from the old dependent Empire. This was an act of great importance. Had he determined that his country must leave the Commonwealth because the organisation might appear to be a neo-colonialist relic, it is doubtful whether any other non-white peoples in Asia, Africa, the Caribbean or elsewhere could afterwards have felt it expedient to retain this association with Britain after they attained their independence. India's resolution to become a member of the Commonwealth set a precedent which has since enabled more than a score of other ex-dependent countries to follow suit. Thus Nehru played a decisive role in the creation of this widespread multi-racial partnership of nations which can do a great deal to help solve gradually and peacefully some of the difficult, delicate and indeed dangerous inter-racial problems which now afflict mankind.

The most important political idea which he acquired in England was that Parliamentary Democracy on the British model is the best system of government yet devised: and even after thirty years of vehement agitation against British rule – including nine years lingering in gaol – he adopted it wholesale for independent India. Every five years throughout his over-lordship some 200,000,000 electors scattered across the vast land queued-up at polling booths to cast their votes by secret ballot for representatives in the national Parliament and many Provincial legislatures. However, if the practice of this system was a result of his education in an English environment, his Indian heredity partially countered its influence in an inexorable way. Although he was the head of a government responsible in all its actions to a popularly elected National Assembly, and although he himself was occasionally quickly responsive to shifting moods in the electorate, he asserted his authority in both the Cabinet and Parliament with all the forcefulness of an autocratic Oriental Emperor. He laid down the law, over-rode opposition, and issued orders to Ministerial colleagues (whom he quite often treated as subordinates) with the traditional wilfulness, and sometimes the accompanying rough temper, of a dictator. As I happen to believe that most Asian peoples at the present stage of their political development need and expect to be governed by partly authoritarian methods, I make this observation not in criticism, but with understanding approval. It was Nehru's blending of the ancient Eastern tradition of autocracy with the contemporary, Western-inspired fashion of democracy that enabled India to progress more or less tranquilly through all her difficulties during most of the first two critical decades after Independence.

He was therefore a complex mixture of qualities; and I cannot pretend to be particularly competent to offer an exact analysis of his character. In his latter years at least – when I knew him – it was difficult for any newcomer to break deeply through his reserve. Some high diplomats in Delhi were pleased to delude themselves (and their governments) into supposing that they were favourites of Nehru who shared his confidences, influenced his thinking, and interpreted him with intimate perception. Unless I am mistaken, this was (to quote an old phrase) 'all my eye and Betty Martin'. Nehru was often affable and gracious, and sometimes he took an Ambassadorial arm in a manner very flattering to the limb's owner; but the gesture usually meant nothing more than that the Indian Prime Minister could be the most courteous person on earth when he chose to adopt that attitude. To me he was invariably charming and usually candid, but rarely if ever totally confiding. Although I often had long discussions with him, was always free to express my opinions without inhibition, and could sometimes give him information which he had not received before, I doubt whether anything I said ever affected his own thoughts more than marginally. He knew his own mind on every subject that interested him; his judgments were formed by long, deep introspective thinking; he felt confidence in his own rightness on virtually all matters; and so he did not need anyone else's help in reaching conclusions or deciding policies.

Reserved in his innermost being, therefore, and to most individuals rather indifferent, he did not give his affection easily – except to children, who did not intrude on his jealously guarded personal privacy, nor seek to unravel his secret soul in order to report its contents to London, Moscow, Washington, Peking or anywhere else. Towards young boys and girls he often showed true warmth, and it was charming to see him chatting and laughing with parties of them. This is not to say he was incapable of heartfelt affection for adults. On the contrary, a capacity for love was an essential part of this coolly intellectual and yet emotional man; but during his later years at least he permitted the flame to leap sparingly in relation to individuals. In the past he had given deep devotion to his great mentor, Mahatma Gandhi, and to some other comrades in the Indian national struggle; but after their deaths it is doubtful whether he felt particular fondness for any Indian contemporary except his gifted daughter Indira. Among non-Indians the only people in recent times whom he welcomed as intimate friends were the two Mountbattens; and it is impossible to exaggerate the benefits which that brilliant pair as a consequence bestowed on British-Indian amity.

Although he was frequently surrounded by a crowd of colleagues, counsellors and visitors, he therefore often seemed a lonely, almost solitary figure. No sadhu meditating in a cave among the foothills of the Himalayas could be more aloof in spirit. But the affection which he extended to few individuals he showered instead on humanity in general, and on the humble masses of India in particular. They were the people nearest to his heart.

At all hours of the day he was accessible to a ceaseless flow of visitors. This was partly a continuation of ancient Indian custom; throughout history many Indian rulers had dutifully made themselves available to all their subjects, both humble and exalted, who wished to plead with them personally on this or that problem. Most of Nehru's Ministerial colleagues were likewise accessible to their constituents and other voters; it was a means by which the governors kept in touch with the governed. But in Nehru's case the demands made on him by streams of important and unimportant callers alike were much more taxing; he was not only the supreme ruler of his own people but a leader of world-wide renown whom travellers from everywhere round the globe desired to meet in person. Many foreign visitors to Delhi who had no justification for intruding on the Prime Minister sought talks with him – and far too often he granted their request. They wasted his time, unnecessarily filling hours when he should have been free to engage in serious work. As a result he continued doing that work into the small hours of every morning. His readiness to accord such interviews to all and sundry was part of his extraordinary humanity.

I have already mentioned that the people who commanded his affection were the masses of his fellow countrymen, the workers and peasants and their families scattered in hundreds of millions across the sub-continent. Periodically the strength of this affection showed itself in a remarkable way, which incidentally also demonstrated his astonishing vigour of body and mind. No man ever worked harder or more continuously day after day, month in and month out, year after year – and sometimes he became extremely weary. Most men would then have retired for a few days' rest in the peace and quiet of their homes. Nehru did the opposite. He sought refreshment in a bout of hectic activities which would have completed the exhaustion – and even caused the breakdown – of any ordinary mortal. Leaving Delhi, and setting forth on a few days of political touring in some other region of India, he addressed every morning, afternoon and evening a succession of public meetings in villages, towns and cities. In between those gatherings he hobnobbed with talkative deputations of his compatriots, often continuing to do so late into the night. And always he returned from those expeditions to Delhi rested and refreshed! This result was a remarkable tribute to both his and his followers' qualities. As regards him, it showed that, unlike many political leaders who express their devotion to 'the masses', but who in fact merely use them as a means to further their own personal advancement, he really cared about them, loved them, and enjoyed mixing with them. And as regards the common folk, it indicated that they possessed sterling if simple qualities which gave their chieftain constant solace and inspiration.

They of course returned his affection a million fold. Wherever he journeyed in India they crowded his meetings in thousands, tens of thousands and sometimes hundreds of thousands, often walking many miles across the countryside to attend. Throughout his speeches – which often were lengthy – they hung on his every word, usually listening silently. This was impressive, because he was not a gifted popular orator, still less a rabble rouser of the Sukarno type. His style of speaking was more that of a university lecturer – thoughtful, academic and even philosophical, containing many observations which might be above the heads of most of the throng sitting or standing in front of him. Again, their quiet, concentrated attention was all the more remarkable because often many in his audience scarcely understood a word that he uttered – he spoke in a tongue different from the local dialect which was their only means of expression. But they loved him and idolised him as the leader of their nation; and they watched with heartfelt devotion his every expression and gesture. For them just the sight of him was a privilege, a joy, an inspiration.

*

I learned most of these things about Nehru by observing him at fairly close quarters during my five years as British High Commissioner in India between 1955 and 1960. During that time many interesting events occurred inside and outside the sub-continent, and I watched him deal with them. Throughout the period he was at the height of his power, and his authority among his countrymen continued unchallenged. Indeed, with few exceptions, they regarded his wisdom as superlative, never for a moment questioning it.

I suspect that during my long stay in India I influenced him in only one matter. Soon after I settled in Delhi I started paying visits to the National Museum for instruction about old Indian sculptures, bronzes, miniature paintings and other such beautiful works. I also went to local antique and handicraft shops to buy examples of both ancient and modern Indian art which would give pleasing touches of local colour to my wife Audrey's and my new home. One of my passions – to the point almost of a vice! – has always been collecting specimens of native arts and crafts wherever I lived in Europe, North America, Asia or Africa.

A temptation for which I fell in Delhi was the purchase of traditional old brass temple lamps for use in our dining-room of an evening. Part of their handsome structure was a saucer-like bowl near the top of their tall stems, round the edges of which several thick, bare wicks soaking in oil burned naked flames like those of candles, but larger and fiercer. The lamps were like super-candlesticks, majestic in their gleaming, flickering lights. Within a few weeks I acquired several such pieces, and at dinner parties they gave flamboyant illumination to the room, with all the modern electric bulbs switched off.

At one of the first parties which Audrey and I gave, Nehru was the guest of honour. About fifty people were present, and they dined at six round tables distributed through the room, each lit by one of those lamps. Several guests commented on the brilliance of our idea in so using these Hindu temple relics, which smacked of Indian history and culture.

I decided to acquire a few more of them, to increase their use in the house; and before going to my office next morning I visited three of the shops where I knew such treasures could be purchased. To my astonishment none had any lamps left. When I expressed my surprise to the shop-keepers, each of them replied that if I had come the previous afternoon I could have bought two or three admirable specimens – 'but they were all bought early this morning,' they added.

'How come?' I asked.

'The Prime Minister's private secretary telephoned us as soon as we opened, and asked us to send every piece we had to his house for his inspection – and he's bought every one.'

A few evenings later Nehru invited Audrey and me to dinner with him, and when we entered his dining-room his eyes shone with pleasure as he pointed to the lamps flaming on a table in the otherwise unlit chamber.

An appreciation of beauty was a trait lying deep within his make-up; but he was so engaged with official work that he enjoyed little leisure to indulge it, and still less to cultivate it to the point of becoming himself a learned connoisseur. However, the taste was there, and one of his merits as the Head of Government in India was not only his support for traditional native arts like dancing and music, but also his encouragement of contemporary artists. In his house admirable examples of modern painting and sculpture hung on the walls and stood on pieces of furniture. His daughter Indira, who in those days had more time to visit exhibitions of such works, was partly responsible for this discriminating patronage.

*

Incidentally, when the Indians threw off British rule and gained Independence one of the legacies of departing Imperialism was a collection of paintings hanging on the walls of the Viceregal Lodge in Delhi. They were portraits of the Viceroys who had lived either there or in earlier official residences of those overlords, many of them dressed in their ostentatious 'pukka sahib' uniforms. On the achievement of Independence most Congress leaders naturally assumed that these pictures would be taken off the walls and sent back to England, if not thrown out of the windows on to bonfires.

I was told that Nehru resisted the proposal. His colleagues

and supporters were astonished, and protested, pleading with him for the portraits' removal.

'What shall we put in their places?' he asked.

'Nothing,' they replied.

'Then the vast rooms will look very bare,' commented their leader.

'That's better than having them filled with those awful relics of Imperialism,' came the answer.

Nehru smiled and remarked, 'You can't change history by taking a lot of pictures off walls.'

And there, so far as I know, the portraits still remain.

I remember an occasion some years later when they caused astonished comment in certain high international quarters. This was during a State visit to India by the Head of the Union of Soviet Socialist Republics accompanied by the then masterful Nikita Kruschev. One evening a sumptuous banquet was held in honour of the guests in the large dining-room of old Viceregal Lodge, now the residence of the President of India and re-named Rashtrapati Bhavan. The host was President Rajendra Prasad; Pandit Nehru and the other surviving leaders of the struggle against British Imperialism were present; and at the table also sat many members of the Diplomatic Corps. Looking down on the assembly were a group of past Viceroys – those portraits on the walls – all appearing extremely smart and in some cases rather snooty in their much bemedalled scarlet, white and gold uniforms. I watched Kruschev gazing up at them, pointing a questioning finger at this or that picture to enquire whom it represented, and almost popping his eyes out with flabbergasted surprise when he received the answers.

During a later visit to Delhi by Chou En-lai, the Prime Minister of China, a banquet was given in his honour in the same room. But he did not betray the same awareness of the portraits. If he happened to look at any of them, it was with an expressionless, enigmatic glance, as though they were strange but unimportant ghosts.

*

The problems of government in India were – and are – so vast and so difficult that they would baffle, and perhaps defeat any but the highest statesmanship. The difficulties are obvious – although they are too little understood in many parts of the outside world. During Nehru's Premiership the country's population already counted more than 400,000,000 men, women and children, a large majority of them illiterate, undernourished and poverty-stricken. In cities like Calcutta and Bombay countless numbers were – as they still are – homeless, sleeping every night on bare street pavements. Moreover, although India's teeming multitudes of peasants and urban dwellers have qualities of endurance, patience and friendliness which are a strong foundation for law and order throughout the sub-continent, most of them are sustained by a religion which makes them fecklessly other-worldly rather than practical citizens on this Earth. Not only was India backward economically when its leaders won Independence, but also its predominantly Hindu society was in some ways medievally conservative. Of course, Hinduism has its innate strengths as well as its frailties, otherwise the new nation would soon have collapsed; but it preaches that for every individual his or her present life is only one link in a long chain of many existences, and that it is of little importance compared with their future lives. Indeed, a calm acceptance of poverty is a virtue which could earn them promotion in later incarnations. So this faith reconciled the Hindu masses to their contemporary sufferings, deprived them of that 'divine discontent' which makes other peoples strive eagerly to improve their lots, and so acted as a brake on efforts by their leaders to achieve their material uplift.

These were some of the difficulties which Nehru and his colleagues faced when in 1947 they assumed responsibility for India's government; and to them he added the extra hazard of tackling national problems by democratic methods instead of the authoritarian means which were more customary in Asia – and which, incidentally, the British themselves adopted during most of their generations of Imperial sovereignty. In some ways the resultant periodic outbreak of elections based on universal suffrage, the existence of argumentative legislatures in every state capital as well as at the national centre, the widespread publication of irresponsible as well as responsible newspapers, the holding of mass meetings, propaganda processions and similar agitations, and all the other trappings of Western democracy helped Nehru's cabinet because its power was manifestly based on popular consent; but in other ways the ceaseless delays, debates and quarrellings which ensued threatened to set damaging curbs on progress. In addition the system gave countless opportunities to the ancient Oriental (and not only Oriental) vices of corruption and nepotism to prejudice efficiency. But all those difficulties were tackled confidently by Nehru, partnered during the first years of Independence by his able colleague, Sardar Patel. He imposed his forceful leadership at the summit of the system, and was supported by the moral integrity of the group of Congress leaders surrounding him, as well as by the capable team of Indian Civil Service administrators trained by the British in earlier years. One of the things which I learned during my years in Delhi was that no race of people anywhere round the Earth have better brains than the educated Indians.

Nehru's first notable achievement was therefore to give decisive direction from the top. Yet his benevolent autocracy would have been misplaced if he had exercised it foolishly, to further wrong causes. His finest contribution to India's internal affairs was the liberal wisdom of many of his policies. Driven by the restless stimulus of their chief, his government achieved some improvement in material conditions through much of the agricultural countryside, began large-scale industrialisation of the nation, introduced schemes of social welfare which promoted the health and education of the masses, emancipated in large measure the hitherto purdah-confined women, reduced discrepancies between the various castes (in particular significantly uplifting the 'Untouchables'), attacked other ancient, deep-rooted social customs which were barriers to progress, established a secular state where Hindus, Muslims, Christians and others were equal citizens, and led the nation along the road of modern technological and scientific advance. Success in some of these directions was more impressive than in others; for example it was greater in political and social affairs than in some economic fields such as agricultural development. In certain cases initial mistakes were made which had afterwards to be corrected; and, characteristically, Nehru was primarily responsible for many of the mistakes as well as for many of the successes. But the net result was that an economic and social Revolution got under way in India comparable in scale to those occurring, for example, in Russia and China. And it was promoted by democratic means which avoided the political suppressions and occasional cruelties of Communist regimes. Indeed, the 400,000,000 Indians gave a demonstration of the practical and benevolent – if slower – workings of a Parliamentary system unsurpassed in magnitude anywhere else round the world.

Nehru was the driving force of this peaceful Indian Revolution. His radical, scientific and in many ways enlightened mind conceived many of its developments, whilst his political zeal impelled it forward. He was not only a cool thinker, but also a warmly passionate actor, with fire in his belly. And the mighty national effort inspired by him was achieved among a vast population divided by different races, languages, castes, creeds and local loyalties. One of his notable successes was the maintenance of the political unity of India in spite of various forces which could have disrupted it. Some of his reforms may not long outlast his lifetime: for example, certain changes which were offensive to conservative Hindu custom may be modified if that conservatism strongly reasserts itself. But in most matters, such as the industrialisation of India, his influence will probably be as enduring as that of a Stalin.

The priority which he gave to this industrialisation revealed one of the differences between him and his earlier master, Gandhi. In some ways the Mahatma was much more conservative than his younger disciple. He was wedded to the ancient, traditional ways of life which had characterised humble Indian village society throughout centuries. If he instead of Nehru had become Prime Minister in 1947, he would have relied much more on cottage industries like hand-loom weaving for maintaining the country's economy, and would have spurned many of the vast plans for steel plants, railway workshops, textile mills and mechanised factories which Nehru stimulated. Gandhi was opposed to the hectic pursuit of material wealth which characterises the contemporary world, and had little use for the sophisticated scientific technology which has made the 'developed' countries so much richer than the 'developing' ones. Nehru on the other hand – partly as a result of his Western education – was an enthusiastic advocate of these twentieth century techniques, and strove to enable India to take her place beside other nations in attaining by every up-to-date device progressively higher standards of physical well-being.

That is why Nehru can be more justly described than Gandhi as 'the Father of modern India'. Although Gandhi was the main driving force in winning India's independence, Nehru was the inspirer of the shape which independent India afterwards assumed. The results of the fact that he instead of Gandhi became India's leader show how individuals as well as collective events can, to some extent, influence the course of history.

His purpose in striving for India's economic development was not primarily to make his nation a first-class power, but to raise the standard of living of its masses. They were the people whom he most cared about; and his first, unswerving loyalty was to them. His affection for them was the chief stimulant of the socialism in which he believed, the spark which lit the fire of the partly private-capitalist but mostly public-enterprise industrial society that we now see in India. Perhaps he devoted too much attention to the industrialisation of his country, and too little to the modernisation of its basic economic foundation, agriculture. That error is now being corrected by its present government.

*

Nehru's influence on India's foreign policy was of course as profound as on its internal policies. He was determined that his country should not become allied to either side in the bitter cold war between the Western and the Eastern blocs which was then raging, and in which the United States of America and Russia were the rival leaders. He believed in a united, co-operative world where all nations lived together in peaceful co-existence regardless of divergences of colour, creed and ideology; and he thought such comprehensive international amity the only means by which the human race could progress towards the higher material and cultural civilisation which the discoveries of modern science placed within its grasp. He felt that if unrestricted 'hot' war broke out, the sophisticated weapons which the two sides could now hurl at one another would cause the destruction of huge sections of mankind. This was to him an unthinkable conclusion to Humanity's long and on the whole slowly progressive history; and he considered both parties in the cold war equally foolish in indulging in dangerous polemics. Apprehensive that in the international atmosphere existing in the 1950s a real risk of military conflict loomed, he knew that if it occurred with the Indian nation allied to one side or the other, then India would be among the lands destroyed – and all his work, all his ambitions for his compatriots would be smashed with it. The only way to save India's population was therefore to avoid any such alliance.

For these reasons he conceived and proclaimed the policy of non-alignment in the cold war, which made India largely free from dangerous entanglements. It also put his government in a position to exert equal influence on both sides, in efforts to persuade them to relax tension, reach compromise agreements on vital questions, and so establish a foundation for true peaceful co-existence.

Incidentally the policy secured another substantial advantage for India, since it gained the authorities in Delhi far greater financial, economic and technical aid from foreign countries than would otherwise have been the case. The two opposing groups in the cold war were naturally eager to win India's favour – and so America and her allies on one side, and Russia and her satellites on the other competed to give Nehru's administration every possible assistance in its successive Five Year Plans for economic and social development. By remaining nonetheless firmly non-aligned India continued to enjoy this double heap of profitable blessings.

So Nehru was the author of the significant attitude of non-alignment which soon infected many other countries far beyond India's own frontiers. Almost all the new nations in Asia and Africa, as well as some other regions, adopted it when they attained independence. Its acceptance by them resulted in a great growth of India's influence among them in the formulation of policies on various international issues. Whilst Nehru remained in his prime as the leader of the physically huge and – so it seemed – morally pure new India, that influence continued to thrive. Later, and especially after his death, it seriously declined. This was an extraordinary illustration of the prestige which one Titanic individual can lend to a whole nation.

The policy of non-alignment bore occasional sour fruits; but generally it worked for reasonableness and sanity in the world. However, its frailties, as well as Nehru's disappearance, contributed to the later reduction in India's international influence. As he himself was to learn shortly before he passed from the scene, his policy was based partly on wishful thinking. He was an idealist too apt to believe that the leaders of other nations shared his ideals. He closed his eyes to some of the harsh realities – the continuing nationalist selfishnesses, rivalries and ambitions – in the supposedly new and more enlightened world, a world apparently not yet ripe for truly sagacious internationalism.

Another weakness in his policy was that it did not always appear entirely impartial between the two blocs. Sometimes it seemed tinged with a bias against the Western democracies and in favour of the Eastern communists. Insofar as this was true, the prejudice sprang partly from a hang-over of hostility in the Indians' minds against the recent Imperialism of Western

Powers, whose colonial rule still persisted through the 1950s in some Asian and many African countries. But it derived also from resentment against policies pursued by the United States of America under the guidance, or misguidance, of John Foster Dulles. In the eyes of that somewhat unperceptive Secretary of State everything everywhere seemed to be either black or white; there was no grey in the international political scene. If a government was not 100% anti-Communist, he considered it to be pro-Communist; if it was not allied to the United States, it was hostile to that great power. He therefore vilified Indian non-alignment, opposed it in various directions, and created an anti-American and anti-Western feeling in high and low places alike in India. As a result Nehru's government was inclined to put the worst interpretation on American and some other Western actions, and by contrast to give Russia's and China's deeds, however suspicious, the benefit of the doubt. This occasionally led Nehru into mistakes. For example, although he promptly denounced Britain's attack on Suez in 1956, he hesitated to criticise Russia's simultaneous, equally wrong suppression of the nationalist uprising against Communist dictatorship in Hungary. He appeared to wish to find excuses for the Soviet's action. As a consequence he was accused of accepting two standards of behaviour for different groups of nations – one for the West and another for the East.

In later years his and his countrymen's prejudice against America was corrected. This occurred especially after President Kennedy came into office and gave a new look to American foreign policy. Kennedy understood the motive, wisdom and value of Indian non-alignment; and from that moment friendly co-operation between India and the United States grew. It was further strengthened when fighting between China and India broke out along their common frontier in 1962, when the Americans immediately offered useful military aid to India. I shall revert later to that episode. First I should write something about the Suez incident.

*

At six o'clock one morning in October, 1956 a telephone beside my bed began to ring. Awakened, I lifted its receiver and heard my Deputy High Commissioner, a wise man called Arthur Clarke, tell me that in the small hours he had received a Top Secret telegram from London containing a personal message from Sir Anthony Eden (then our Prime Minister) which I should deliver to Pandit Nehru as early as possible that day. I asked Clarke to bring it to me immediately, jumped out of bed, dressed and went downstairs to meet him.

He arrived holding several sheets of typed paper in his hands. Pointing to them, he remarked, 'Whom the gods wish to destroy they first make mad!'

Then he gave me the documents. They contained an announcement that British and French military forces were on the point of taking action in the Suez Canal zone to enforce its maintenance as an international waterway. Accompanying the text of a personal message from Eden informing Nehru of this event were instructions about the arguments I should use in oral explanation of the reasons for it.

I thought the prospective action against Egypt very wrong, and believed it would prove a disastrous error. But as Britain's High Commissioner I was of course duty bound not only to inform the Indian authorities of my government's policy on all matters of concern to them, but also to defend it with whatever reasoning might impress them.

I telephoned Nehru's house, and he agreed to see me at once.

As he read the message I saw a look of shock growing on his face; and my statement of the reasons for the British military intervention did not impress him. I answered a few questions that he asked – and then he voiced in no uncertain terms his very critical opinion of the development. He spoke calmly and thoughtfully, more like a philosopher analysing a problem and expressing his judgment on it than a politician denouncing a policy with which he vehemently disagreed. Yet, his view was at the same time emphatic: he considered Eden's decision wrong from many points of view. I had to conceal my agreement with most of what he said, and to state firmly the counter arguments which I knew my Prime Minister would wish me to make. But in my unhappiness at the situation I felt glad that Nehru was presenting so clearly the case against the British government's action, for it would be my not displeasing duty to report his remarks at once by telegram to London. I hoped that the case made so forcefully by India's leader would exert some influence on the thinking of Ministers in Downing Street.

For the next few days I became a busy diplomatic postman delivering messages between the British and Indian authorities. Several times I went for talks with Nehru, to explain to him personally my government's view of this or that element in the situation, and to hear his comments. Always his observations were calm and courteously friendly, but uncompromising in their opposition to the policy being pursued. One phrase he invariably used impressed me. When referring to the British action in Egypt he never described it as 'Britain's policy' or 'the British government's policy', but always as 'Eden's policy'. I felt that his knowledge of the British people and their Parliamentary representatives made him guess that opinion in Britain was very divided, that a majority of them were dubious about the affair, and that their Prime Minister was the individual primarily responsible for a gross error of judgment. This speculation was of course receiving support from various newspaper reports and BBC commentaries. So he did not allow the episode to make him violently critical of the British nation; his disapproval was directed mostly against one man. And he always expressed it more in sorrow than in anger.

Meanwhile the military intrusion into the Suez area by British and French forces increased. I felt more and more frustrated at having to defend it to the Indians, but this continued to be my duty so long as I remained a diplomatic representative of the British government. It was also my responsibility to report back to London the reactions of the Delhi authorities; and I did this as energetically and accurately as I performed the former obligation. Nor did I send to Whitehall only reiterations of the arguments which Nehru put to me, but also sought out and talked with other important personages in Delhi to whose opinions I hoped my masters in England might pay heed. For instance, I despatched an account of a conversation I held with the President of the Congress Party, who was in close touch with widespread Indian opinion. In my cabled commentaries on the Indian attitude I did not seek to hide my own personal views.

However, my series of messages seemed to produce no effect; and after a week I felt that I could no longer remain a loyal servant of my chiefs in Downing Street. I must resign my post as High Commissioner, and slip as quietly as possible into obscurity. One evening after a busy day's work I therefore drafted a personal telegram of resignation to the Secretary of State for Dominion Affairs. I realised that I should warn Arthur Clarke of my intention, for I was seeking immediate release from my job, which meant that he must be ready to assume acting responsibility, probably within a matter of hours. So I asked him to come for a secret talk with me; and I read my draft telegram to him. I told him that I proposed to sleep on it, not because there was any chance of my changing my mind, but because on re-reading the draft with fresh eyes early the next morning I might improve one or two of the phrases in which I expressed my reasons for resigning. I would then send the final text to London in time to be on the Dominion Secretary's breakfast table, where the clock ticked several hours behind ours in Delhi.

Clarke said that he could not disagree with my opinions or my proposed action. Unlike himself, I was not a regular member of the Diplomatic Service who should stay at his post regardless of his private judgment on this or that policy; as a less tied representative I was more free to act according to my conscience on such a major issue as the Suez crisis.

I hastened home, packed some essential papers which I should take to London when I departed, and went to bed.

Early the next morning the telephone at my bedside began to

ring. I lifted its receiver and heard Clarke's voice at the other end of the line. He told me that he was happy to say that I need not send my telegram, since an official message had just arrived from London asking us to tell the Indians that our Government's policy on Suez was being altered, and that our troops in Egypt would observe a cease-fire forthwith.

Some months later I was informed by a public servant who held an important post on the Prime Minister's staff in 10 Downing Street throughout the Suez crisis that three considerations persuaded the Cabinet to reverse their policy. The first was criticism by the Americans and others in the United Nations, the second was a Russian threat of violent retaliation, and the third was my succession of telegrams from Delhi reporting the Indians' bitter opposition. I do not know whether this estimate was correct, but the individual concerned was very much in the know.

If his analysis was right, Nehru had not pleaded in vain.

*

The charge that Nehru sometimes accepted a double standard for different governments' behaviour in international affairs became particularly effective when occasionally it touched India's own conduct. Thus, many people thought the pacific Nehru guilty of hypocrisy when he employed military force in 1947 to compel an unwilling Hyderabad to join the Indian Union; and almost the entire world held him guilty of it when Indian troops invaded and annexed Goa in 1961. The latter was a particularly flagrant violation of the principles of the *Panch Shila* of which he was an author and champion – even taking into account the stubborn refusal of the colonialist regime in Portugal to face the facts of the mid-twentieth century. For many years Nehru himself had opposed any such aggressive move, and I for one believe he agreed to it with extreme reluctance in the end. Perhaps the explanation was that he was then beginning to slip in physical and intellectual powers, and that he allowed his better judgment to be overruled by pressures from less peace-loving influences inside and outside his cabinet.

Of course this capacity for occasionally saying one thing and doing the opposite, and for preaching one principle and practising the reverse, is not confined to Indians. It is shared by many other peoples round the globe. Yet perhaps at the period of which I am writing no race displayed a greater facility than some Indians in performing such contradictions. I do not know what may have been the correct explanation of this trait, and was inclined to think it might reflect a profound, anciently inherited influence of the Hindu religion on their national character. In the crowded pantheon of Hindu gods and goddesses many individuals are angels whilst several others are devils; but they are all deities, or more or less sacred individuals whose conduct is presumably excusable. So any action by a human being, however good or bad, can be justified by reference to the example of one or another of those holy creatures. I do not pretend to understand Hinduism, and my judgment on this phenomenon may be stupidly superficial; but I can think of no other explanation of the ease with which noble-minded Indians like Nehru could occasionally reconcile obvious contradictions between their good words and their more dubious deeds.

The most oft-quoted of such alleged contrary attitudes was Nehru's government's policy regarding Kashmir. This is not the place to examine in detail that obstinate controversy between India and Pakistan. Mistakes were naturally made on both sides; and the initial error may perhaps have been committed when, partly on the whim of the local Hindu Maharajah of a predominantly Muslim population living alongside Pakistan, Kashmir became associated with India rather than Pakistan at the time of partition. The root of the trouble afterwards was the intense antipathy between Hindus and Muslims, both of whom held passionately to their very different and in some ways irreconcilable religious beliefs. Possibly Nehru's motives in taking the firm stand he did against self-determination for the Kashmiris in practice, whilst agreeing that they should enjoy it in principle, sprang from several contributory causes such as his personal identification with Kashmir as a member of an ancient local family, his resentment against Pakistan on account of its leaders' insistence on partition, and other considerations. But his main reason was the honourable one that he had established a secular state in India in which Hindus, Muslims, Parsees, Christians and members of other faiths enjoyed absolute equality of rights, and that the transfer of Kashmir from India to Pakistan would appear as a confession that its Muslim population could not be guaranteed security in India.

I think his Kashmir policy was partly wrong, for his apparent opposition to self-determination when it did not suit him whilst being a passionate advocate of it in all other circumstances, did more damage to his and India's reputation than could have been inflicted by that degree of qualification of the established fact that India was a non-discriminatory secular state. Nevertheless, the problem was not simple. Many observers bitterly criticised him for not agreeing to hold a plebiscite in Kashmir to test the wishes of its people. But soon after my arrival in Delhi in 1955 I realised that a plebiscite would do irreparable harm not only in Kashmir itself, but also further afield throughout both India and Pakistan; and I so advised the government in London. An electoral campaign in favour of a transfer of the province to Pakistan would have been conducted with high emotion by its advocates, not on reasonable grounds of any economic, social or political advantages which might come to the local inhabitants from the change, but on the passionate religious argument that it was improper for a Muslim population to live in a predominantly Hindu country. They would have attacked the Hindu faith – and the champions of Hinduism would naturally have retorted in kind. So rival religious fanaticisms – which everyone knew from bitter experience lay just beneath the surface in both India and Pakistan – would have been whipped up. A wave of killings would have started, and the bloodshed could not have been confined to Kashmir. It would have spread inexorably against multitudes of Muslims living elsewhere in India, and masses of Hindus living in Pakistan. Nehru's grand concept of a secular state would have crashed in ruins; and the blow could have been mortal not only to a peacefully progressive India, but also to any chance of friendship between the two neighbouring nations.

Nehru was therefore right to oppose a plebiscite. But he was wrong not to be more tirelessly earnest in seeking other ways of negotiating a mutually acceptable agreement on the subject with the Pakistani leaders. One difficulty was, of course, that they were just as rigidly uncompromising as he was on this issue. Neither he nor they had much room for manoeuvre; yet he was the one man in India with sufficient authority to impose on his people a compromise settlement.

*

I have already written that Nehru's policy in international affairs was influenced partly by a tendency to indulge in wishful thinking. A significant example of this was his confident satisfaction at his co-authorship with the Chinese Prime Minister, Chou En-lai, of the famous agreement which pledged India and China to abide by the *Panch Shila* or 'Five Principles of Peaceful Co-existence' in their mutual relations. Under it the two huge nations promised to observe non-interference in each other's internal affairs, non-aggression against one another, and the settlement by negotiation of any disputes that might arise between them. In addition they undertook that those principles would guide them in their dealings with all other countries round the Earth. Nehru trusted the Chinese completely – or almost completely – and he became the leading champion of Communist China's right to membership of the United Nations Organisation. He also did everything he could to persuade others that the Peking Government should enjoy liberty to deal with its own national problems in whatever way it thought best in the interests of its people.

He therefore became deeply concerned when, not long

afterwards, in apparent breach of the *Panch Shila*, a Chinese army in Tibet imposed complete Red Chinese rule on its population. Hitherto that little state perched on 'the roof of the world' had been a buffer area between India and China. In several ways Nehru showed his sympathy for the Tibetans, in spite of their (to his way of thinking) very out-of-date society. Later his concern grew first to anxiety and then to alarm when he learned that Chinese military forces were intruding further south than Tibet, and occupying a remote uninhabited region in Ladakh which the Indian Government claimed to be part of India. His worry swelled to anger when he heard that they were building an allegedly commercial but could-be strategic road there. I cannot write in detail here about the formidable dispute between India and China which then flared up. The Chinese counter-claimed that successive governments in Peking had never recognised Indian sovereignty over the area and that, on the contrary, they had always regarded it as part of Tibet – which in Chinese eyes had itself throughout history fallen under the ultimate suzerainty of China. There was a good deal to be said on both sides; the dispute arose from an honest difference of opinion between the two nations of which Nehru should have been aware, but to which he chose for long to close his eyes. If he had been more actively concerned about it earlier, he could probably have negotiated a mutually satisfactory compromise agreement on the whole Indian-Chinese frontier problem with Chou En-lai, who (I know from talks with him at the time in Peking) was prepared to do so.

Now Nehru suspected sharp practice by his Chinese neighbours. To him their action made their *Panch Shila* treaty a scrap of dishonoured paper. He suffered an awful disillusionment, and his disappointment was all the greater because he had expected that the newly freed nations of Asia would set an example to the rest of mankind in peaceful co-existence. The prospect of conflict between the two most important of them profoundly shocked him. But cold, mutually recriminatory communications between the authorities in Delhi and Peking failed to settle the quarrel pacifically – and a vicious frontier war broke out between their armed forces. In the eyes of all Indians the Chinese became guilty of aggression – another breach of the supposedly sacred Five Principles. The emotional atmosphere which prevailed made Nehru himself revert to being a fervent nationalist. He called for unity among the Indian people against the Chinese enemy, ordered his army into battle along every disputed part of the frontier, and declared that India would never surrender an inch of its territory. His government bought arms from Britain, America and Russia alike, to try to make the nation's defence effective. Incidentally, this caused a setback to his ambitious plans for India's economic development, because huge sums of money allotted to industrialisation and agricultural reforms were diverted to the purchase of military equipment. Even so, the effort failed to save the Indian army from a humiliating defeat at the hands of the Chinese.

In this dispute Nehru gained Russian support, for Russia had its own frontier problems with China, and did not wish to see the Chinese succeed in extending their territorial boundaries. That Soviet support was important for Nehru in several ways. Among them, it helped to salvage his crucial policy of non-alignment between the two cold war blocs. Nevertheless, an important element in the policy lay in ruins.

*

The shattering war with China opened the eyes of more people than Nehru himself to a weakness in his foreign policy. Many of his hitherto unquestioning supporters inside and outside Parliament all over India realised that he had made a dangerous misjudgment in international affairs. Until then the supposedly infallible wisdom of their leader had been accepted by virtually all his compatriots, with scarcely a whisper of doubt from any but a few more or less insignificant voices. This unanimous adulation was surprising to newcomers like myself from the old democratic West to the new democratic East, for in Occidental countries even the most popular statesmen were always exposed to criticism. And impressive though this trust in a benevolent Oriental autocrat might be, it was unhealthy. Much of the time it made him over-confident, and all the time it made his supporters and even potential critics over-submissive. One of the most valuable elements in a democratic government – the right to criticise the authorities freely within the law – was in practice all but non-existent so far as India's Prime Minister was concerned, until the last two or three years of his life. Then, following India's humiliation by China, it suddenly asserted itself. The damaging effect of this on Nehru's own feelings was probably considerable. Although he no doubt blamed the Chinese for an undeserved let-down, his hitherto unshaken confidence in his personal judgments on people and problems must have received a crippling knock. And the criticism of his wisdom which began to spread widely among his fellow-countrymen perhaps hurt him deeply. Even though his trait of humility would make him at certain times accept this as right and proper, his pride must have been profoundly upset. And the change came when he was already ageing, when it was more difficult for him than for a younger man to adjust himself to a new situation.

I had left India two years earlier at the end of my term as High Commissioner; so I was not able to observe in person the effects on him of these troublesome developments. But I think they probably hastened a decline in his physical and mental fitness which had already shown signs of starting. Until recently his stamina had been astonishing. When I left Delhi towards the end of 1960 he had already been Prime Minister for more than thirteen years, striving ceaselessly for the progress of India and the peace of the world. He worked about eighteen hours every day including week-ends, month after month and year after year, with scarcely ever a holiday. He was already more than seventy years old – yet his body looked as trim as an athlete's, his step was light and energetic, and his mind stayed delightfully fresh. Probably he counted on his fine physique to keep him alive and kicking as India's leader for another decade; and I suspect that when, in 1962, it suddenly betrayed its human frailty in the form of a kidney ailment, he suffered an awful psychological shock. I happened to be passing through Delhi at the time, and went to visit him in his sick room. He had been ill for two or three weeks, but his doctor judged he was making an excellent recovery. Sitting on his bed without blankets or sheets, and clad only in pyjamas in the summer heat, he looked rather like a naughty boy confined to his room as a penance for some mischievous deed. He was gaily talkative, and appeared rested and revived. Yet I detected in his eyes a look of disillusionment, of defeat – even of doom. He had hoped he was blessed with eternal youth, for his mind and spirit possessed this quality; but he had discovered with dismay that his body was that of an old man. I think he never really recovered from the shock, and the unhappy conflict with China soon afterwards speeded his decline.

I saw him only once again, shortly after the debacle with the Chinese. The occasion was a small luncheon party in his house attended by four or five close friends. The rest of us maintained a mixture of cheery and serious conversation, but he sat almost completely silent throughout the meal – rather as if he were a ghost appearing in our midst.

*

I recall remarks made to me by the headman of a village about a score of miles from Delhi. When I could escape from official work and enjoy some leisure at week-ends, I indulged in my hobby of bird-watching in fields and woodland surrounding its cluster of dwellings. By invitation from that *zaildar* or headman, as soon as I completed my observations of Nature I used to sit drinking tea and talking with him in his house, and invariably a crowd of villagers would squat in the room around us. They asked me questions on all sorts of subjects, listened eagerly to my answers, made with uninhibited candour their own comments on my remarks, and then put further queries to me.

Those talks were typical samples of the garrulous curiosity of the Indian workpeople and peasantry, who have unappeasable appetites for information on any and every topic under the sun.

In the middle of one such conversation the *zaildar* said to me, 'When are you British coming back to India to rule us?'

I answered 'Never', and enquired why such a strange notion entered his head.

He replied that the rural folk like himself and his neighbours had felt happier in the days of British administration because they then enjoyed much closer contacts with the government's district officers and other local officials, who often visited them to sit discussing their problems with them. This practice had become less common after those men were replaced by Indian successors.

I felt embarrassed, and switched my audience's minds to another aspect of the same subject by remarking, 'Did the Viceroy often come and talk with you in those times?'

'Oh no!' my host answered. 'Of course, we never saw him.'

'But you often see Pandit Nehru at public meetings, and listen to him telling you about his government's policies.'

Enthusiastic assent came from everyone in the room, with vigorous noddings of heads in recognition of the fact that the supreme leader of their country himself now paid much more personal heed to them. Our discussion turned to the qualities displayed by Nehru. The villagers' admiration and affection for him poured forth in a torrent of words expressing feelings lodged deeply in their hearts.

*

A most moving tribute to his greatness as a leader was the sense of irreparable loss demonstrated by hundreds of millions of Indians of every race, caste and creed when he died. The photographs of his funeral procession showed unprecedented multitudes of stunned, grieving, adoring, weeping, hopeless mourners. And the close-up pictures of his corpse lying on a couch as it passed through the thronged streets revealed his youthful face still unblemished forty-eight hours after death – as if he were merely dozing and would awake before the cortège reached his funeral pyre, and rise to chide the populace for being so foolish as to think he would die and desert them.

That soft-skinned, almost completely unwrinkled death mask was the face of a true Immortal.

Jomo Kenyatta

Kenyatta with the author and Haile Selassie — 'he put on no superior airs, and rather disliked pomp and ceremony.'

'Kenyatta's dark-skinned, shrewd-eyed, characterful and bearded face beneath a tribal cap was impressive.'

By the time I reached the almost over-ripe age of sixty-one I had become familiar with countless countries scattered across almost every region of the world; but, except for an occasional brief transit stop in Cairo, had never set eyes on any part of the so-called 'Dark Continent'. I presumed I would have to wait until my next life on Earth for the experience, and hoped that I might then enjoy it, perhaps by being re-born as a giraffe in the National Park outside Nairobi, a springbok leaping through the Kalahari desert in Botswana, or a hippopotamus wallowing in the river below the Murchison Falls in Uganda. I felt sad that I should have to wait until that reincarnation.

Then suddenly Duncan Sandys – who was Secretary of State for the Colonies at the time – proposed that I should go to Africa without further delay as a member of a different animal species which was in fact quickly becoming extinct. He suggested that I should assume office as Governor of Kenya. At first I resisted the notion, for it seemed to me that my almost complete ignorance of African affairs and peoples made me a bad choice for what appeared to be a particularly delicate task. I argued with Sandys that there must be better qualified men with considerable experience of African problems available for the post; but with characteristic stubbornness he brushed my contention aside, urging that if I would not accept his offer at once, at least I should not reject it outright. He asked me to consider it carefully before letting him have my final answer – which he hoped would be in the affirmative. So we left the matter open for a while.

I did feel genuinely concerned lest my inexperience of contemporary Africa would make me a poor Head of Government in the current Kenyan situation. On the other hand the difficulties which would face me were of course a tempting challenge, and the idea of living and working at last in Africa also greatly attracted me. Another reflection intrigued me. For a few years past a strange premonition had occasionally flitted through my mind – a hunch that I was doomed to meet my death by being torn to pieces by an angry black African mob. I used to wonder why this intuition of a fate similar to that of General Gordon in Khartoum should intrude into my consciousness – but now Duncan Sandys' proposal began to make sense of it. I somehow felt drawn to the idea of testing whether the presentiment was evidence of the profound truth of such instincts, or was just a figment of my romantic imagination.

On further reflection I accepted Sandys' suggestion. When I did so I expected to stay in Kenya for less than two years, because the authorities in London planned that by then the Kenyans would gain national Independence, with no further use for an anachronism like a Governor. As things turned out, however, I lingered there for seven years, changing my function successively from Governor to Governor-General, and then to High Commissioner in Nairobi, and afterwards to Special Representative in East and Central Africa, and finally to Special Representative in Africa. So for quite a long time I watched at close quarters the unfolding of history in Kenya as well as in many other lands strewn across the continent; and I enjoyed almost every minute of the experience.

*

Although I had never previously set foot in Africa south of the Sahara, and for the last twenty-three years had been so continuously pre-occupied with the affairs of Britain, Europe, North America and Asia that I got no time to give a thought to African problems, during the 1930s I was concerned with them in Whitehall during my two terms as Secretary of State for the Colonies. Through the interval of almost a quarter century the facts of political life in Africa had changed in some revolutionary ways. Many developments had occurred with which I was out of touch, although they had mostly moved towards the ultimate aim which authorities at the time told me I was the first Colonial Secretary to define unequivocally – national independence for all our African dependencies. The pace of advance towards that objective had been enormously accelerated, and it was indeed already achieved in several countries. Now, to everyone's surprise, many people's delight and other people's horror, it was approaching realisation in Kenya.

I flew to Nairobi at the beginning of January, 1963. Before leaving London I had no time to read more than a few official documents about the contemporary situation in Kenya, for I spent only ten days in England following a long tour through the Far East. So I arrived with little knowledge of the problems and personalities that would confront me. During my brief stop-over in Whitehall I did ask the government's expert advisers a few questions on current affairs, and among the topics on which I showed curiosity was the personality of the famous – or rather infamous – Jomo Kenyatta. Not all the answers that I received were consistent, but most of them were sufficiently so for me to gain a clear impression that I would meet in him a wicked old man who was fortunately far past his prime, who was quickly declining in physical and mental powers, and whose influence was being progressively subordinated to that of younger and abler political colleagues. He might still have a certain temporary importance because his name was something to conjure with among the African masses – but this too, I was informed, would linger but briefly, since he was a heavy drinker who was rapidly boozing himself to death.

It is true that one or two people whom I questioned were more cautious in their judgment, confessing that few Europeans either inside or outside Kenya really knew much about Kenyatta. They explained that a decade ago the British authorities had banished him to a remote semi-desert, that they had not bothered to keep in serious contact with him since, and that for long they had virtually dismissed him from their thoughts, trusting they could forget all about him in connection with future Kenyan affairs.

I felt glad that I should arrive in Africa before he passed finally from the scene, so that I could gain an at least brief first-hand acquaintance with an individual who was obviously, in one way or another, a fabulous personality.

*

Audrey and I landed in Nairobi one sunny morning. The Acting Governor met us at the foot of the steps descending from our aircraft. He was accompanied by Ronald Ngala and Jomo Kenyatta, who were the leaders of the two rival political parties represented in the Council of Ministers. Kenyatta's dark-skinned, shrewd-eyed, characterful and bearded face beneath a decorative tribal cap was impressive – indeed rather leonine. A large fly-whisk which he gripped in one hand and waved at me in friendly greeting somehow emphasised that I was entering a new world very different from all the other continents where I had previously lived. Incidentally, he was almost inseparable from that whisk, and a journalist wrote in a perceptive phrase at the time that he held it as if it were the sceptre of a king.

That evening I invited all the African, Asian and European members of the Council of Ministers to come for drinks with me at an informal party in Government House, so that we could begin to get to know each other not only as official colleagues but as friends. Incidentally I was told later that this was the first occasion when the African and Asian leaders had been admitted to such an intimate social gathering in that splendid residence, which was the home of the Excellency wielding supreme power on behalf of all the black, brown and white Kenyans, but which had apparently been regarded hitherto as a more or less exclusive preserve for the white minority.

All the dozen-and-a-half Ministers came, and we had a relaxed, gay party which laid the foundation for our agreeable co-operation throughout the next important year.

At its beginning I asked Kenyatta what he would like to drink.

'Coca-Cola,' he answered.

I felt surprised, and wondered whether I had heard him correctly.

'You can have anything you like,' I remarked. 'There's champagne, gin, whisky and everything else.'

He repeated that he wanted only a glass of Coca-Cola. All the others present took more potent refreshment; but he abided by his resolve.

*

For the next three months the group of African, Asian and European members in the Council of Ministers worked energetically under my chairmanship on the draft of a Constitution for first a self-governing and afterwards an independent Kenya. I should explain that the council was a coalition body in which two rival political parties joined in an uneasy partnership – the Kenya African Democratic Union (or KADU) led by Ngala, and the Kenya African National Union (or KANU) led by Kenyatta. The division between them sprang less from ideological divergencies than tribal quarrellings. As regards political aims, and especially the aim of early Independence, they were in accord; but traditional suspicion and conflict between the major Kikuyu and Luo tribes (who mostly supported KANU) and numerous smaller tribes like the Masai, Abaluhya and various Kalenjin peoples (who sustained KADU) were deep and bitter, causing them to hold conflicting opinions about certain provisions which should (or should not) be written into the constitution for the protection of the minority tribes. Each party was represented in the Council by an equal number of Ministers, most of them black Africans. But also among them were a few brown Asians and white European settlers, which added to the complications.

Our toil was hard and long. Immediately after my arrival in Nairobi, when I had felt the pulse of the political situation, I decided that the work must be speeded-up so that the African leaders should not become frustrated by undue delays. The Council's discussions were progressing too slowly. I found that its members met for only a single morning each week to consider one by one the numerous controversial details of the proposed constitution, and that on this basis our efforts could not be finished for many months. I therefore suggested that we should meet three days every week, and that on each of those days we should hold three sessions – morning, afternoon and evening, with short breaks for lunch and before dinner. To help make the atmosphere relaxed and genial as well as efficient, I proposed to give the Ministers tea during the afternoon sitting and a buffet supper with drinks before the evening meeting, both served at our table in the Government House conference room where we held our discussions. My British advisers praised this good intention, but were sceptical whether the African members would wish to work so hard. They also feared lest some of them would become drunk if I served strong liquors at nights. In the event both those apprehensions proved unjustified. All the Africans welcomed the intensification of our labours, and were unflagging in their attendance at every session. As for the risk of drunkenness, only once did a solitary Minister imbibe too much, and I received the unanimous support of all his sober colleagues when I ruled him out of order every time that he opened his mouth to utter a sozzled contribution to our debate. After three attempts he became discouraged, laid his head on his outspread arms on the table, and fell asleep, not disturbing our further discussions by so much as a snore.

Otherwise whisky, gin and liqueurs were consumed in reasonable quantities by most of those present. But Kenyatta never took anything except an occasional cup of tea or glass of Coca-Cola.

So on three days every week we sat from 10 o'clock in the morning until 11 o'clock at night talking and disputing. Quite often there were passionate arguments. Kenyatta, then aged over seventy, sat through all those meetings early and late. He did not take a greater part in the talk than most other Ministers, and intervened less often than several of them. Two or three of his younger colleagues such as Tom Mboya and James Gichuru exerted more influence than he did on the settlement of many important questions, and he was clearly guided a great deal by their advice. Sometimes he seemed undecided on policy, and occasionally even not interested in a detailed matter under examination. He appeared to carry less weight in his KANU party counsels than did the able pair whom I have mentioned. Nevertheless, when he did speak it was with clarity and authority. In addition he was invariably reasonable, and prepared for sensible compromises with the rival KADU politicians. His sagacity was impressive, if it did not seem to be outstanding.

Even at 11 o'clock at night, after a full day's labour, the septuagenarian was wide awake. His eyelids never flickered with drowsiness, as I had sometimes seen those of elderly Cabinet Ministers in other countries do in similar circumstances. Although he sometimes stayed quiet and untalkative for hours on end, he was always alert. That quietness, and his tendency to follow the advice of colleagues, made me feel that it was probably true that age was sapping his energies, and that his physical and mental powers were on the decline – yet his shrewd-eyed alertness made me wonder whether this was really so. As for drinking himself to death, there was not the slightest sign of that. I had never known any judge who stayed more sober.

Those Council meetings were a liberal education for me about the Africans. I learned many things from their lively arguments, banter, quarrels and subsequent accords. It was then, for example, that I first became acquainted with the glorious African sense of humour. A spontaneous and sometimes uproarious wit rippled through much of our discussions, more natural and engaging than any I had met among other peoples. It was a civilised virtue, and often it saved a threatening situation. In the middle of a crisis, when the KANU and KADU Ministers were clashing in what appeared to be irreconcilable disagreement and I began to think that our negotiations were about to break down, someone would make a joke – and immediately everybody round the table burst into peals of almost childlike laughter. The crisis was over. Both sides recovered their sense of proportion, someone yielded a point, accord was reached – and we passed to the next item on our agenda.

Kenyatta's capacity for joking and leg-pulling was as robust as the best of them, and he laughed just as heartily at a jest against himself as at one levelled against anybody else.

Another characteristic which I learned to respect was the African leaders' common sense. They did not adopt rigid, emotional attitudes on affairs. They stood firmly by their beliefs in matters of principle, but kept flexible minds on questions of detail, ever ready to respond to reason or to facts. Nor did most of them harbour grievances, bearing old grudges which prejudiced their judgment on current problems. They remembered the injustices that they and their people had suffered, and showed active resentment against any fresh slight, actual or imagined; but they did not allow those feelings to influence unduly their decisions on policy.

This did not mean that they would not sometimes express over-emotional and unreasonable sentiments in their public speeches, as distinct from the pragmatism which marked their private negotiations. They of course had to keep a watch on their relations with their followers, so as to maintain their influence over those multitudes outside our council chamber, and to prevent extremist political rivals from stealing their leadership. This sometimes forced them to make concessions to less responsible nationalist opinion in their platform orations. Several times at the end of our weekly deliberations, when they were about to leave Nairobi to face the voters in their constituencies at week-end meetings, one or another of them would say to me, 'Don't be worried by the wild things I'll be reported in the newspapers as saying in a speech tomorrow. I've got to satisfy to some extent my supporters' political emotions. But when I return on Monday you'll find me just as ready to accept reasonable compromises as I've been today.' And they were always as good as those words.

Among other things, in the light (or rather shadow) of the recent bitter hostility between the African nationalists and many of the white settlers in Kenya, it was remarkable how ready they were to consider with friendly fairness the claims of European as well as Asian residents to proper treatment as partners in the independent Kenya which we were trying to bring into being. Again, in all those constructive attitudes Kenyatta's good example was conspicuous.

People's impression of him during those months was partially formed by his conduct of affairs outside our Council room. The two rival parties were preparing for a General Election which would take place immediately after we in Nairobi (in consultation with the government in London) had settled the terms of the proposed Constitution. KANU was therefore going through all the customary pre-election preparations of a political host which hopes for victory at the polls – the selection of Parliamentary candidates, the drafting of an election manifesto, the co-ordination of various sectional interests, the perfecting of local constituency organisations, and related activities. Those problems were bedevilled not only by the usual personal rivalries, but also by inter-tribal jealousies between Kikuyu, Luo and other supporters. We outsiders got the impression that the party chairman was not master of the situation, and that although his voice probably still carried pre-eminent authority, it was being seriously challenged. Quite often he appeared to be forced to postpone awkward decisions, or to make muddled compromises. Some people supposedly in the know whispered that his usefulness as a popular rallying figure would not long survive the election. As for the KADU opposition, all its leaders and candidates were outspoken in their criticism of Jomo Kenyatta. In fact he did not seem to be the sort of national chief who could powerfully unite a people in their hour of national need.

Nevertheless, in my own judgment formed gradually during my few weeks' knowledge of him, he was the wisest and perhaps strongest as well as most popular potential Prime Minister of the independent nation-to-be. I felt – though I could not yet be sure – that the opinion about him given to me in Whitehall was seriously mistaken. I did not think anyone else available would be as good. Moreover, another important consideration weighed heavily in my mind: he was the political chief of the largest, ablest and most dynamic tribe in Kenya, the Kikuyu. Its typically human mixture of good and less good qualities made it capable of either bringing real benefits or causing grave mischief to the new nation, according to its mood at the time when Independence was attained. I reckoned that if its KANU party were defeated in the elections, or gained an insufficient number of seats to give it effective power in government – thus forcing it to make uncongenial concessions to some other political group – it would feel frustrated, and as a result perhaps grow irresponsible and fall under the influence of less sagacious leaders than Kenyatta and his principal lieutenants. This latter possibility existed because in addition to the two major parties, KANU and KADU, a separate, splinter group had been formed by tribalist Kamba politicians who hoped to win sufficient seats in their home region to give them a decisive balance of power in the new House of Representatives.

I felt that if, on the other hand, the Kikuyu-dominated KANU gained a clear majority in Parliament, and so was free to exercise its authority without undue restraint, it would not be upset by a sense of frustration, and the qualities of ability and wisdom in the Kikuyus' make-up would then grow at the expense of their more irresponsible traits.

Hitherto the authorities in London had taken an opposite view. They not only suspected Kenyatta of increasing feebleness, but also the Kikuyu as a whole of innate viciousness (as expressed in the Mau-Mau episode) which would make an unrestricted KANU Administration very undesirable from the point of view both of friendly relations between Britain and Kenya, and of reasonably peaceful government in Kenya itself. They realised, however, that if the voters in the General Election were free to express their views without interference, a majority would almost certainly opt for Kenyatta's KANU party. When I arrived in Nairobi I discovered that the British Colonial officials (with the consent of Whitehall) were therefore doing everything they discreetly could in marginal constituencies to ensure that KANU candidates would be defeated, so that as a result KADU would either gain a clear majority in the new Legislature or else be able to count on the support of the Kamba splinter group. In that case Kenyatta and his KANU colleagues would either have to join a coalition administration under a KADU Prime Minister, or else go into Opposition.

I thought this not only immoral but also imprudent, and within a short while I changed the policy, insisting that British officials should leave the Kenyan people entirely free to make whatever decision they wished through the ballot boxes.

I naturally never told Kenyatta or any of his colleagues of my reversal of the British attitude towards them, not wishing to prejudice them against the authorities in England. They and the KADU Ministers did learn of another change in London's policy which I initiated. When I arrived in Kenya the proposed time-table for constitutional progress towards Independence was that a General Election should be held in the autumn of 1963, internal self-government should follow immediately, this interim stage would continue for another year, and – if local affairs then appeared to be proceeding peacefully – Independence should be granted by the end of 1964. After the Council of Ministers agreed to my acceleration of our negotiations on the future constitution I decided that – as some of the principal African politicians were urging – the period of transition could be considerably shortened. This seemed to me desirable because the longer Independence was delayed, the greater would grow the risk of impatience among the Nationalists reaching a point where their leaders must either become more extremist or else surrender power to less responsible rivals. I therefore proposed that the Election should be held in May 1963, internal self-government inaugurated on June the 1st, and Independence attained during December of the same year. With considerable courage Duncan Sandys – who would be held responsible, and severely criticised in Britain if this perhaps rash hastening proved a mistake – agreed to the change.

Such a speed-up at short notice required that many radical changes in the machinery of government which were necessary to fit the swiftly altering circumstances must be contrived with almost unbelievable rapidity. Indeed, something like a miracle was needed to accomplish them – but my team of British colonial officers led by the able Deputy Governor, Sir Eric Griffiths-Jones, performed the miracle. They were as capable a group of government servants as I have known at any time in any country.

*

By early March the Council of Ministers reached unanimous agreement on every clause in the constitution-to-be except a few of the most difficult and significant ones. In any case we could not make final decisions on these without the approval of the Secretary of State; so for the final lap of our marathon discussions Sandys flew to Nairobi to assist us in our work. Throughout the debate on all sorts of important and controversial matters during the previous two months he had been consistently helpful and constructive. His statesmanship was conspicuous, and I felt confident that he would lend decisive aid in settling satisfactorily all the outstanding matters. Nevertheless I was anxious on one point. I knew that certain of his personal foibles in negotiation might sometimes cause offence to the Kenyans, unintentionally increase difficulties, and even conceivably throw an afterwards unextractable spanner into the works. So I decided to describe confidentially but candidly to the Council of Ministers my chief's faults as well as his great qualities, to ask them not to be surprised if on occasions the former were displayed, and to ignore them, paying full heed instead to his grand abilities. At the close of our final preparatory meeting prior to his arrival twenty-four hours later I therefore gave them a friendly but frank appreciation of his character.

They listened fascinated. When I finished speaking they sat silent for several moments. Then one of them remarked, 'That's very helpful, and we'll do as you suggest. Please tell Mr Sandys equally candidly about our awful African faults, and ask him to take no notice of them either!'

There was a burst of laughter, much nodding of heads – and on that note our work ended.

Sandys' visit was a complete success. Final accords were reached on every outstanding question, the agreed draft Constitution was sent to the printers for publication, and the General Election began. It was close fought, with all the customary charges and counter-charges, arguments and counter-arguments, promises and counter-promises hurled at one another by the contesting parties. In the last week of May a few million voters went to the polls. When the ballot papers were counted KANU had won a substantial majority in the House of Representatives and a very narrow one in the Senate of the new two-chambered Parliament. So the KADU leaders were to pass into opposition whilst Kenyatta became Prime Minister in a wholly KANU government.

*

A day or two before the formal introduction of the Constitution and the swearing-in of the new cabinet we held a last meeting of the old Council of Ministers to settle some final details concerning the transition. At its opening Ngala made a charming little speech of felicitation to Kenyatta on his victory, and at its close I congratulated both parties on the excellent work they had achieved in partnership during the last few months. In response they kindly thanked me for my help; but I remarked that they should not speak too soon. Although Kenya's internal self-government was about to dawn, and my constitutional powers as Governor would become severely restricted, I should still remain for a while their Imperialist chief who might interfere unduly in the exercise of their responsibilities. 'If I do that,' I added, 'and you decide to put me in detention, I hope you'll incarcerate me in a certain very attractive house in a pleasant countryside which I saw recently on some travels in northern Kenya. I would settle happily there.'

Kenyatta said with a smile that they would consider this, and asked me where the place was. I described the bungalow in remote Maralal where he had been confined during the last months of his nine years' banishment.

Guffaws of mirth greeted my proposition, and no one laughed louder than the old ex-detainee himself.

*

I would now cease to preside over the meetings of Ministers, for the Prime Minister would take the chair in his cabinet, which was to enjoy unrestricted freedom of policy-making on virtually all the domestic affairs of Kenya. Under the new arrangement I retained only limited powers in certain matters touching internal security, whilst at the same time keeping complete control over questions of national defence and international relations. I could exercise my authority in all those matters without any consultation with Ministers, and regardless of whatever opinions they held – as was customary in the cases of Governors throughout Britain's colonial territories at that stage of their constitutional progress.

But I decided not to exert this prerogative. I was anxious not only to maintain close confidential co-operation between myself and the Kenyans in all matters of vital importance, but to demonstrate publicly my trust in Kenyatta's statesmanlike ability. And I wished to stimulate his own self-confidence as well as his national prestige. I therefore told him in conversation that I should like to share fully with him as Prime Minister all my reserved powers in both internal and external affairs, taking no decisions whatever regarding any of them except after consultation and agreement with him. He of course gladly accepted this, and I announced the decision on the day that he assumed his new supreme office.

*

At a simple but dignified ceremony conducted on June the 1st in front of vast multitudes of cheering people under a bright sun in the streets of Nairobi, I swore Kenyatta and the members of his cabinet into office. A new era in the story of Kenya began.

At once a remarkable thing occurred. On that very day Kenyatta's character seemed to grow, taking on additional dimensions, as if it had previously been an unopened bud which now suddenly burst into flower. He became energetic, indeed dynamic; he became decisive; he became masterful. He showed himself not just the nominal chief, but the effective leader of the government. His was the most powerful influence in the cabinet, proposing and, if he thought necessary, imposing policy concerning major questions. When disagreements arose he insisted that, after proper consultation, his Ministerial colleagues should accept his final considered view; and they conformed to his wish. This was impressive evidence of the force of his personality, for among them were several men of considerable ability and character.

The remarkable blossoming of his qualities surprised not only comparative strangers to him like myself, but also many old friends who had worked closely with him throughout many years. On separate occasions Gichuru and Mboya both said to me with evident astonishment, 'We didn't know the old man had it in him.'

He drew his pre-eminent authority from two sources. First, his popularity with the people was unrivalled. They regarded him with such admiration and affection that he was the only national hero in Kenya. Secondly, he now showed that within himself he possessed a self-confidence, strength of will and mellow wisdom which made him dominate his capable team of Ministers.

Why had his superb qualities of leadership not appeared earlier, during his membership of the coalition government? Perhaps there was a mixture of reasons. For instance, he had been released only recently from nine years of banishment in remote parts of the country, and during that long exile was unable to keep in close contact with political developments in Nairobi and other populated regions of Kenya. Changing events had altered many features of the political scene since he was familiar with it, and he found himself out of touch not only with the realities of the contemporary situation but even with the evolution of opinion in the Nationalist movement of which he was the father. As a result he felt for a while confused and uncertain, and took time to adjust his thinking to the new circumstances. Only gradually did he form his own fresh judgments which enabled him to assert opinions decisively.

Again, in the coalition government neither he nor his party commanded a majority. They were mere partners with their KADU rivals, and as a consequence he personally had to share authority with the KADU leader, Ngala. Moreover, three of my British civil servants also held important posts in the Ministerial team. Nor did Ministers wield true executive power, for technically they were simply advisers to myself as the colonial Governor who presided over their Council meetings. Constitutionally I was free either to accept or reject their collective advice. This was not a situation in which Kenyatta felt wholly at ease, nor in which he was at liberty to assert himself as leader. He accepted it in a friendly and co-operative spirit as a temporary expedient – and bided his time.

Then, when the electors gave his party a Parliamentary majority empowering him to form the cabinet that would rule self-governing Kenya, almost all those limitations on his freedom disappeared, and he was able to give uninhibited expression to his nature, his gifts, and indeed his genius.

The resulting assertion of his will to rule was fortunately supported by high statesmanship. He revealed a ripe sagacity which guided all his policies, displaying itself in various ways. For instance, he combined a tendency to personal authoritarianism with a democratic readiness to seek the views of others, listen to them carefully, be influenced by them when desirable, and always carry colleagues with him in the formulation of policies. Consulting his cabinet on every significant matter, he thus made all important government decisions expressions of collective Ministerial responsibility. At the same time he was accessible to innumerable humbler people who wished to discuss various questions with him. Nor did he attempt to limit freedom of speech, permitting criticism of the government in Parliament, public meetings, and the press. Among others he gave the KADU Opposition full rein in the expression of their opinions.

Although himself a Kikuyu very conscious of the pre-eminent part which his tribe could play in the government of Kenya, he was anxious for all the other tribes to have a proper share in the enterprise. He was in fact a Kenyan first and a Kikuyu afterwards, recognising that the greatest threat to a united and prosperous Kenya would be a continuation of traditional suspicions and quarrellings between its various clannish groups. So he preached earnestly and eloquently co-operation between them in their common interests, and saw to it that his regime practised what he preached. He sought as far as was practicable to appoint adequate representatives of all the important tribes not only in his Ministry but throughout the civil service, the police, the armed forces and other organisations helping to promote national well-being. Nevertheless, partly to ensure the highest possible standard of ability in administration, but partly also no doubt because of a streak of tribal prejudice, he did allot many important posts to members of the most capable tribe in the country, his own Kikuyu.

His efforts to create widespread national unity went further than attempts to eliminate old inter-tribal rivalries. Although no other leader in Africa was a more passionate African nationalist, he recognised the important, and indeed essential, roles which the large European and Asian communities could play in the development of a prosperous Kenya. This recognition was helped by the sensible way in which most of the leaders of the white settlers adapted their views to 'the winds of change' blowing through Africa and accepted the right of the black majority to exercise democratic rule in an Independent state. In return Kenyatta was determined that these settlers should be treated fairly, and from the moment of his assumption of the Premiership he sought to assure them that no discrimination would be shown against them. Knowing the bitter hostility which most of them felt towards him personally, he lost no time in talking in a sympathetic way to them. Within a few days of his government's assumption of office he addressed a large meeting at Nakuru in the former 'White Highlands'. It was a dramatic occasion. Many members of the audience came reluctantly, sceptically, even resentfully, feeling angry that they should have to listen to a speech by a man whom most of them still regarded as their arch enemy, and indeed as the devil incarnate. However, they felt it prudent not to stay away, and so attended in glum mood. Then the unexpected happened. Within a few minutes of the start of his speech he got them laughing with him, and afterwards cheering him; and at the end of it they expressed their astonished conversion by giving him a long standing ovation.

One of the qualities in Kenyatta's make-up which this speech revealed was his magnanimity. For many years he had been imprisoned by the British authorities; they had done all in their power to defeat him and destroy his work – and he knew that the crowd of farmers sitting in front of him at Nakuru were among his bitterest foes who had tried to frustrate everything he stood for. They had failed, and he had just achieved triumphant victory. But he never referred to that fact by even one jubilant sentence which might hurt or humiliate them. On the contrary, he greeted them as Kenyan friends and partners. He said, 'There is no society of angels, whether it is white, brown or black. We are all human beings, and as such we are bound to make mistakes. If I have done a wrong to you, it is for you to forgive me; and if you have done something wrong to me, it is for me to forgive you. The Africans cannot say the Europeans have done all the wrong; and the Europeans cannot say the Africans have done all the wrong. . . . You have something to forget, just as I have. Many of you are just as Kenyan as myself.' And of his imprisonment he declared, 'This has been worrying many of you; but let me tell you Jomo Kenyatta has no intention of retaliating or looking backwards. We are going to forget the past, and look forward to the future. I have suffered imprisonment and detention; but that is gone, and I am not going to remember it. Let us join hands and work for the benefit of Kenya, not for the benefit of one particular community. . . .' So he assured them that he appreciated the valuable contribution which their work was making toward Kenya's well-being, that his Government wished them to continue making it, and that they could feel secure in their lives and properties so long as they gave loyal support to the new nation.

Magnanimity is perhaps the rarest, and it is certainly one of the finest qualities in statesmanship. Possibly only Gandhi and Nehru in modern times have shown a personal magnanimity the equal of Kenyatta's.

As it happened, I gave a party at Government House the following evening for the members of the old Council of Ministers which had been disbanded a few days earlier. The KANU and KADU representatives all attended, and there was a lot of chaffing as well as serious talk. Kenyatta's speech at Nakuru had been reported in the morning papers, with special emphasis on his appeal to blacks and whites alike to 'Forgive and forget' the past wrongs they had done each other. In conversation with him at my party some of his own lieutenants in the new cabinet, as well as others, expressed disagreement with part of his remarks, asserting that he had gone too far in assuring the European settlers that their earlier, often viciously racialist hostility to African majority rule would now be forgotten. But Kenyatta vigorously defended his theme, and converted the critics by the persuasive wisdom with which he argued the case.

One significant action in his effort to create a multi-racial as well as multi-tribal nation was his appointment of certain white politicians to high posts. The most important of these was the inclusion of a European Minister in the cabinet; and for the next seven years Bruce Mackenzie continued to sit alongside his black colleagues, until ill-health compelled him to resign. It would be impossible to exaggerate the value of that able white farmer's contribution to the Kenyans' unity and progress during this crucial period. His appointment was perhaps not surprising, for throughout many previous years he, like a handful of other British settlers, had consistently and courageously advocated a steady advance to Independence with majority rule in the colony, suffering as a result much unpopularity and ill-treatment from most of his fellow-whites. Even more eloquent of Kenyatta's sincere wish to heal old wounds in the Kenyan body politic was his nomination to important posts of some white political leaders who until recently had been among the most uncompromising opponents of majority rule. One of these became the Speaker of the House of Representatives (and a very wise, popular Speaker at that), another was confirmed as Chairman of the Board of Governors of the National Museum, and other similar instances occurred.

*

Under Kenyatta's inspiration, from the moment that the new Ministers assumed their responsibilities they pursued sensible policies. Many long-resident Europeans, including high government officials, felt astonished by Kenyatta's statesmanlike attitudes, and were not convinced by them. They questioned his sincerity, and suggested that his actions were cunning temporary expedients to lull the non-Kikuyu tribes, white settlers, foreign governments and other gullible people into a false sense of security. Those gloomy prophets foretold that, when in due course he became Prime Minister in a fully sovereign state and so was freed from the last shackles of Colonial overlordship, his mood would change. The old Mau-Mau devil in him would then reassert itself. . . . However (if I may anticipate for a moment) when six months later Kenya did become Independent no such duplicity was ever revealed. On the contrary, Kenyatta continued to show the same enlightened attitude not only in words but also in deeds.

Some critics thereupon argued that this moderation was the mark of a man grown aged whose physical, mental and emotional powers were becoming rapidly feeble. A fire no longer burned in his belly. Moreover, they added, he had now achieved everything – and more than everything – that he personally ever hoped for. Kenya was free, and he was its Prime Minister. Had he really expected this? Most commentators answered the question emphatically in the negative, and contended that he had become a 'satisfied power' with no further ambitions. He felt no need for continued agitation, merely wanting peace and quiet in his contented old age.

There is evidence, however, that his friendly moderation was no new frame of mind which suddenly affected him in his moment of triumph. It influenced and guided him, too, in his earlier years of striving and even apparent defeat. One of his devoted lieutenants who used to join in discussions with him during his banishment in the uncongenial north told me an interesting fact when I spoke with him about Kenyatta. I had commented that the Prime Minister's plea that everyone should 'Forget and forgive' the past hostilities between Africans and Europeans was a gesture of remarkably magnanimous wisdom.

'That's nothing new,' my companion replied. 'He used to preach "forget and forgive" when he was locked up. He often told the rest of us that we were too bitter against the British, and too extreme in wishing to rid Kenya of all the white settlers. He argued that if the British would accept majority African rule we must then be ready to renew friendship with them, and enable many of them to stay in Kenya helping it to develop as a prosperous country.'

I must add another comment. Far from appearing to be an old man whose enthusiasms and powers were gradually failing, throughout his first several years as Prime Minister and afterwards President he behaved with the energy, zeal and resolution of a leader in his prime. His physical and mental capacities showed remarkable freshness and alertness; and he put many men half his age to shame. Incidentally, his two youngest children were both born when he was well past the age of three-score years and ten.

Let me draw attention to another trait in his character. I have already mentioned that before I first arrived in Nairobi I had been warned that he was drinking himself to death. On discreet enquiry I learned that this had in fact seemed true during the last period of his exile in a semi-desert; he drank intoxicating liquors in gross excess, and was gravely impairing his general fitness. No doubt there were mixed reasons for this: the hot climate induced a considerable thirst, the lack of interesting work caused boredom, and the apparent destruction of any hope of realising his political ambitions sometimes threw him into fits of depression which inclined him to drown his sorrows. Then of a sudden his hopes were restored, and his sorrow disappeared. At once he resolved to cure himself of his bad habit, so that he could dedicate himself afresh to the service of his countrymen. From then onwards he quenched his thirst only with such liquids as Coca-Cola and tea. That abrupt change must have required stern self-discipline which in itself is a notable quality.

*

Kenyan affairs progressed peacefully, and the population moved steadily towards Independence. That great event was achieved on December the 12th, 1963, amid tumultuous rejoicing throughout the country. Kenyatta's sagacity as a statesman, as well as his awareness of the paramount need for inter-tribal and inter-racial co-operation in the new-born nation, was illustrated by a change which he then made in a small but significant matter. Hitherto the oft-shouted slogan which expressed the aim of all true Kenyans was the Swahili word 'Uhuru!', meaning 'Freedom!'. As the day for the attainment of this aspiration drew near their leader naturally expressed in speeches his joy at the impending event; and at the end of each oration he called on his audience to shout loudly 'Uhuru! Uhuru! Uhuru! . . .' But he also began to explain that Independence was not a final end in itself; it was only a means towards an even more valuable end.

This was the ever greater well-being of the whole Kenyan people. They were ridding themselves of one enemy – colonialism – and must now start attacking and overthrowing other enemies such as ignorance, poverty and disease. He emphasised to the crowds who hung on to his every word that Independence would not automatically dispose of those foes; they could only be overcome by hard work by the whole population in agriculture, industry and every other sphere of national life.

To mobilise this effort he proclaimed on the day of Independence a new slogan. In place of the popular cry of 'Uhuru!' would be substituted the clarion call 'Harambee!', which being interpreted means 'Let's all pull together'. This choice of phrase was a stroke of genius. 'Harambee!' was the refrain in a song chanted by gangs of African labourers when they were pulling a heavily-laden cart or engaging in some other strenuous collective manual toil. Thus it was a summons to co-operative effort which sprang directly from the African soil; and at their leader's command the crowd at the Independence celebration yelled over and over again, 'Harambee! Harambee! Harambee!' At once it became accepted as a definition of the new nation-building mood which should inspire everyone on the morrow of Independence. Adopted as the national motto, it was emblazoned beneath Kenya's fresh coat-of-arms, and continued thereafter to echo like a trumpet call at all public gatherings.

*

Government House was re-christened State House, and I continued to live in it as Governor-General instead of Governor. So I still observed from close and friendly quarters not only the development of Kenyatta's policies, but also the unfolding of his character.

One of the marks of his greatness was his simplicity. He had a strong sense of personal and official authority; yet he put on no superior airs, and rather disliked pomp and ceremony. He remained an unspoilt mortal conscious that in common with all other human beings he had his faults as well as his fine qualities. At all times he was accessible to others, both exalted and humble – and of those two types he inclined to prefer the latter. With the ordinary people he mixed easily as one of themselves, always treating them as human equals. This sincere attitude was one of the secrets of his popularity. Yet at the same time he had no false modesty; he knew full well his unique importance in Kenya and his unrivalled prestige in Africa; and he felt a sense of mission to lead his followers from their past bondage to freedom and well-being.

One of his potent weapons as a political leader was his power as a public speaker. Probably he had no superior in the art of what is sometimes called mob oratory. With a crowd of thousands or tens of thousands of people his spoken words could work magic. But he did not achieve the miracle by resorting to histrionic stunts or irresponsible appeals to the multitude's cheaper passions. He addressed them in simple words and idioms which they understood, with frequent touches of humour and occasional flashes of poetic eloquence; but he appealed to their reason much more than to their emotions, and sometimes mixed candid criticism of them with calls to their grander qualities. He spoke straight from his heart to their hearts.

He was not always so successful as a Parliamentary speaker. This was perhaps partly because, unlike many other eminent Nationalist leaders in ex-British dependencies in Africa, Asia and elsewhere, he received little or no training in the work of a Legislature. His long exile from Nairobi deprived him of that experience until late in life. In his early, more impressionable political years he never got a chance to learn the techniques of parliamentary debate or the disciplines of legislative council procedures; and when he eventually entered the House of Representatives the chamber's size seemed too confined for his soaring style of oratory. I remember an evening when he was making an after-dinner speech at a rather formal banquet over which I presided, and at which about eighty members of the Commonwealth Parliamentary Association were present. His audience was listening with appreciation to his remarks; but somehow he did not himself seem quite at ease. Suddenly he interrupted his argument to exclaim with a laugh, 'Oh, I'm no good at talking to a tame audience like this. I want thousands of people in front of me!'

As regards his magnanimity, let me quote more examples of this virtue. During my time as Governor-General the world-famous anthropologist Louis B. Leakey made some important discoveries in Kenya which added further evidence in support of his thesis that the creature called *Homo Sapiens* first began to evolve millions of years ago in East Africa. I used to enjoy fascinating talks with him on the subject. One day I asked him whether he had told Kenyatta about his latest finds.

He replied 'No', and said that he would much like to do so, but dared not suggest it since he was afraid Jomo Kenyatta would refuse to meet him. When I asked why, he explained that he had taken a certain part in the trial when Kenyatta was condemned to years of banishment which would probably make the now victorious Premier regard him as an enemy to be contemptuously ignored.

I expressed the view that Kenyatta was too noble a character to adopt such an attitude, and that he would be keenly interested to hear at first hand from Leakey himself the facts about his significant discoveries. Leakey was very pleased, and agreed to come to lunch one day with Kenyatta and myself at State House – if I could arrange this with the Prime Minister.

When I next saw Kenyatta I put the proposal to him, and he accepted with alacrity. He expressed high admiration for Leakey, and spoke with considerable knowledge about his work. He remarked that, when Leakey first published his opinion about the origins of Man, almost all the authorities received it with scepticism or outright disbelief, and he recalled that among those critics had been his own tutor at London University, the distinguished Professor Malinowski – who incidentally advised Kenyatta in the writing of his book about the Kikuyu people called 'Facing Mount Kenya'. Kenyatta added that Leakey's later work had proved him to be in the main right, and his learned opponents wrong.

A few days later the two men came to lunch with me. Leakey arrived several minutes before the Prime Minister, and I could see that he felt rather nervous about how their first meeting since the trial at Kapenguria would go. Then Kenyatta appeared. Striding across the floor of the drawing-room with a friendly smile on his face and a hand outstretched, he gave Leakey the warmest possible greeting. They broke into conversation in Kikuyu, laughing together with uninhibited camaraderie. I do not know what they said to one another, for only later did they start to speak in English, bringing me into their conversation. I never attended a more interesting, scholarly and cordial lunch party.

I recalled the incident a year later when I was High Commissioner in Nairobi and went to see Kenyatta one morning about some official problem. After we finished our business we gossiped on other topics. He mentioned casually that an hour earlier he had sworn-in a certain English member of the East African Court of Appeal as Acting Chief Justice in Kenya during the absence on holiday of the incumbent of that office. I expressed some surprise, asking whether the lawyer concerned was not the judge who a dozen years before had dismissed Kenyatta's appeal against condemnation to banishment, and who had therefore finally thrown him into that nearly fatal exile.

Kenyatta grinned and replied, 'Yes.' He commented that the fellow had been doing his duty conscientiously at the time, that his judgment had probably been correct on the evidence presented, and that if he himself had been presiding on the bench he 'would probably have reached the same verdict' – not aware that some of the evidence was false.

'He's a good lawyer, and he'll be a good Acting Chief Justice,' he concluded.

I could give several other instances of his personal practice of the policy of 'Forget and forgive'; but I need not overburden this essay with them. In that connection, however, let me add another thought on Kenyatta's character. In all my dealings with him I learned that he possessed not only a wise head but also a warm heart. On many occasions – such as when the exercise of my, and later his, prerogative of mercy for prisoners condemned to death had been invoked – he revealed his deep concern for the welfare of all sorts of people, and his aversion to any form of violence. I know no more than any newspaper reader about events in Kenya during the dozen troubled years prior to 1963, for after my arrival I was so continuously busy helping to deal with the problems of the present and the future that I had no leisure to research into the past. Consequently I have little intimate knowledge of the truth behind the controversies regarding Kenyatta's conduct during that earlier time. I shall hazard two comments. First, in my judgment it is extremely unlikely that he ever approved of – still less was responsible for – the atrocities committed by Mau Mau gangs against Europeans and Africans. Second, his possibly unjust imprisonment may have been a blessing in disguise because it preserved him from the assassin's panga which might have chopped him to bits if he had remained at liberty and tried to exert a moderating influence on events. It is a strange thought that Providence perhaps intervened in the odd shape of an Imperialist Governor to lock him up in safety.

I can only write with confidence about the man whom I knew through several later years; and I feel as sure as I can be that a person with his bigness of head and heart must have disapproved of the extreme methods used by the Mau Mau, even though he agreed with their aim of Kenyan independence. The dilemma in which he found himself at the time probably arose because he lost control over the wildest elements in the Nationalist movement and, whilst seeking to curb them in private he could not come out in public condemnation of their activities. In any case he was arrested and exiled before the most vicious Mau Mau period developed, and so became helpless to intervene in any way.

His famous speech to the European farmers at Nakuru in

which he urged that both whites and blacks should forgive and forget the 'wrongs' they had done each other in the past implied condemnation of the Mau Mau cruelties. I do not for a moment suggest that he is a pacifist opposed in all circumstances to the use of violence. On the contrary, he is a realist who is prepared to justify it in unavoidable, last-resort circumstances.... Or do I under-estimate an evil trait in his character? I confess that occasionally I have seen not only a mischievous but even a wicked glint flash into his eyes – which sometimes made me wonder! Is there a mixture of devil and angel in the make-up of this fascinating human being?

*

A few days before Kenya became a Republic and Kenyatta assumed office as its President he achieved another triumph in his attempts to create a united nation. He persuaded the KADU members in Parliament to leave the Opposition benches, cross the floor, and join the KANU party supporting his government. Indeed, some of them became Ministers.

Very privately and personally I had suggested this to him sometime earlier. He at once told me that he favoured the idea, but mentioned certain practical difficulties which would make it injudicious to hasten the change too quickly. Nevertheless he asked me to throw out the suggestion informally in confidential conversation with one or two leaders of the Opposition. When I did so they also reacted sympathetically, but attached a condition to their acceptance which I knew would be impossible for Kenyatta. I told him of it, encouraged him to persevere nonetheless in his plan, and judged it expedient for me myself to drop out of the discussions, leaving the Kenyan leaders to decide what was proper in this important domestic issue. For weeks I watched from the wings Kenyatta's shrewd handling of the exchanges, which thanks largely to his prestige as well as his political skill produced a successful result on the very eve of the establishment of the Republic.

I then made a silly misjudgment. As a result of the impending dissolution of the Opposition and the creation of a broad National Government, a reshuffle in the cabinet became necessary. Kenyatta told me in confidence of the changes he planned to make in the Ministerial team. Of course, I made no attempt to influence his decisions, which in any case seemed to me to be good; but I did suggest that it would be prudent for him to inform some of those concerned of their proposed shifts in office a day or two before the public announcement. Then if – as I suspected would be the case – some of them objected so strongly that they might resign from the Government, he would have time to make whatever adjustments he thought desirable. I had it in mind that in similar circumstances a British Prime Minister would almost certainly take this precaution. However, Kenyatta answered that he would do no such thing; his Ministers could read of the changes when they were announced in the newspapers.

I felt nervous for the next few days; but I need not have worried. When the new cabinet list was published every Minister accepted their moves without even a whisper of discontent. Then I realised that I had been too British in my apprehensions! African politicians would not react in a similar way to their British counterparts – and Kenyatta's confidence that they would accept his decisions showed his understanding of his colleagues.

*

The wise policies which he and they pursued included the development of agriculture and industry, the appeasing of land hunger among the African population, an expansion of urban as well as rural employment, the extension of children's education, the training of youth in national works, and a steady but not too fast Africanisation of the public services. In various directions the results were impressive. This is not the place to describe them in detail, for I am not sketching the conduct of Kenya's government but the character of its leader. I should mention in passing, however, that many of the problems which his Administration tackled were very difficult. Unemployment was high, land hunger ravenous, economic resources limited, the people largely illiterate, and a population explosion threatened to aggravate the situation. One disconcerting fact was that many peasants and workers expected a substantial improvement in their lot within a few days of Independence. They were simple folk who believed the facile promises made by some irresponsible political leaders that on the morrow of *Uhuru* the landless would gain farms, the unemployed would get jobs, the children would receive free schooling, and others who dreamed various dreams would see them all come true. So among sections of the masses a sense of disillusionment grew when this did not happen overnight. The main reason why they did not respond to extremists' appeals to express their feelings violently, but instead stayed co-operative with the government, was their affectionate respect for Jomo Kenyatta. They heeded his calls for patience, hard work, and 'Harambee'.

Perhaps I should add that it was believed in some quarters that the sensible attitudes adopted by the newly independent African government owed much to my private guidance. Many people assumed that Kenyatta and his colleagues continued to seek my counsel on important problems, only taking decisions in personal agreement with me. This was not the case. On the contrary, after they gained self-government the cabinet rarely consulted me, taking their own decisions in all questions great and small, and treating me, their Governor and later Governor-General, as a constitutional Head of State. This was further evidence of Kenyatta's self-confidence. Moreover, his government was manned not only by a great chief but also a capable team of Ministers, whose opinions were based on a much deeper knowledge of local Kenyan conditions than I possessed. Undoubtedly Kenyatta was considerably influenced by the views of such able lieutenants as Gichuru, Mboya and some others.

For my part, I made no attempt to intrude into policy-making, nor to question any of the Ministers' decisions when they were reported to me. I gave no grounds for any suggestion that they were continuing to act in accordance with my views, for I realised what harm it would do them if they could be charged with becoming 'stooges of the British Imperialists'. I knew that if Ministers really wanted my advice on any matter, they would seek it discreetly, confident that I would give it in a manner unembarrassing to them. But in fact they scarcely ever sought it. Kenyatta, however, kept me regularly informed of every important development in national affairs; and in personal conversations he told me frankly his views on personalities and problems in the Kenyan scene.

I filled much of my idle time by writing a book about wild animal and bird life in East Africa called 'Treasure of Kenya'.

*

On the first anniversary of Independence Kenya became a Republic. I ceased to be Governor-General, and Kenyatta was proclaimed President. A short while earlier Ministers in London had asked me whether I would be willing, after a period of leave, to return to Nairobi as Britain's High Commissioner; and when the Kenyan cabinet agreed to this unorthodox proposal I accepted with pleasure.

On my last day as Governor-General the Kenyans gave Audrey and me a most kindly send-off at the airport. Vast crowds gathered there to wave us goodbye; Cabinet Ministers, the Diplomatic Corps and other official groups were lined up to play their customary parts on such occasions; a military Guard of Honour stood on parade for my farewell inspection; and troupes of native dancers with bands of traditional musicians were assembled to add gaiety to the demonstration. When the ceremonial was completed I presumed that Audrey and I would immediately climb into our aeroplane. I therefore felt embarrassed when I saw Kenyatta remount a small platform from which we had taken the guard's salute, and heard him start to make a speech. After some friendly remarks he expressed his government's pleasure that we were not departing for ever, since I would come back to Nairobi a few weeks later as High Commissioner. He hoped I would then have less hectic work to do than during the last two busy years, so that I should have leisure to enjoy the attractions of Kenya, including indulgence in my favourite hobby of bird-watching. Wishing Audrey and me a happy holiday and a safe return, he held out his hand to pull me on the platform to receive the plaudits of the multitude.

This caught me unawares. Having received no warning that Kenyatta would make a speech, I had not prepared any words of thanks. I spoke a few impromptu sentences of appreciation of his too generous remarks. Then I added that I certainly intended to do a lot of bird-watching after my return to Kenya, for I looked forward to watching 'the wisest old bird in Africa, Jomo Kenyatta', continuing his superb leadership of the Kenyan nation.

We mounted the aircraft to hilarious laughter and prolonged applause.

*

Kenyatta settled his own methods of work. After he became President, for instance, he did not live in his official home, the palatial State House in Nairobi, but stayed at his family farm-house in the Gatundu countryside about thirty miles away. Early each morning on week-days he motored into the capital, held a succession of meetings and interviews in his office in State House until the late afternoon, and then returned to Gatundu. He never attended diplomatic cocktail parties or other official receptions or dinners except when he himself was host at a banquet in honour of some visiting celebrity. Often such gatherings add unnecessarily to the fatigue of hard-worked Presidents or Prime Ministers, and Kenyatta had the good sense not to fritter away his energies at them. During the evenings and throughout week-ends he received many visitors in his home at Gatundu, including not only Ministers and Members of Parliament, but also common folk from various parts of Kenya who wished to talk with him about their local problems. Otherwise he relaxed, retiring to bed early each night, sleeping soundly, and rising at crack of dawn the next morning. For two or three hours he then strolled around out of doors, supervising work in his garden and on his farm. He revelled in that rural life, which refreshed him at the start of each day before he motored to Nairobi to resume official duties. But often he telephoned one of his Ministers around 6 a.m. to seek information on some current problem, regardless of their habits as later sleepers!

Rarely did he read cabinet papers or other such documents, preferring to be given oral summaries of their contents by some intelligent member of his inner circle of counsellors, and then to discuss them with Ministers concerned before making up his mind on policy. Another means by which he saved himself much time and trouble was by delegating responsibility on problems of less than top importance. This avoided his becoming involved in too much detail and being hopelessly over-worked; and it carried the additional advantage of showing confidence in his colleagues, and enabling them to gain experience in the exercise of high responsibilities. Yet they were usually looking over their shoulder to ensure that he approved their actions, for they knew that if he disagreed he could object emphatically! He was the boss – 'Mzee' Kenyatta, the 'wise old man'.

Sometimes on difficult issues he appeared undecided and even lethargic, postponing decisions. Impatient younger colleagues were then inclined to criticise him, suggesting that he was slipping into the careless laziness of an elder who had passed his energetic prime. But often his indecision was deliberate. In his judgment the time had not yet arrived for action; he must delay whilst all the elements in a situation fell into the right relationship for the step which he privately contemplated. In several delicate matters he showed himself an extremely patient and astute judge of timing. His shrewdness in dealing with personalities as well as problems was outstanding, and an important element in his success as the leader of a nation.

His handling of his difficult yet attractive, if crafty, Ministerial partner Oginga Odinga, was an example of this. Soon after Odinga became Home Minister in the government formed in mid-1963 his intrigues to make himself heir apparent, and even to supplant his chief, began to cause resentment among other important members of the cabinet. They knew he was a more left-wing Nationalist than themselves, and suspected that he worked in secret, paid alliance with Chinese and Russian Communists, becoming disloyal to the whole government as well as to its leader. They urged the Prime Minister to challenge his activities and dismiss him from the Administration. For a long time Kenyatta rejected their pleas, leaving Odinga free to pursue his subversive operations. He even continued to show some favouritism towards the conspirator.

In private talks with me he revealed his inner mind on the subject. At first he thought other Ministers were being unjust in their accusations against their colleague, whom Kenyatta regarded as a loyal friend and true Kenyan patriot. He felt grateful towards Odinga, who had been one of his most helpful supporters in the Nationalist movement during his long exile. Gradually, however, intelligence that he received about Odinga's contacts with foreign Communist authorities, and about his covert and increasingly successful efforts to buy support for himself among KANU politicians inside and outside Parliament, made Kenyatta change his mind, regard the Home Minister with suspicion, and recognise his hostility to the government. Nevertheless, although influential colleagues continued to plead for Odinga's dismissal, he still took no such step.

In our conversations he gave me two reasons. First, he did not wish to take an initiative which might play into Odinga's hands by making KANU supporters generally feel that he (Kenyatta) was to blame for their rift, so swinging sympathy to the other's side. He must wait for an issue on which most sensible men would see that Odinga, not he, was in the wrong. Second, so long as Odinga remained a member of the cabinet, not only would he have to act with a certain restraint but also his intrigues could be kept under observation by Kenyatta and his expert advisers, whereas if the cunning fellow disappeared from the government such scrutiny would become more difficult. So Kenyatta bided his time, awaiting the right moment for whatever action might be required.

I told him that I agreed with his tactics, for I too thought the Ministers who were urging Odinga's prompt dismissal were being over-hasty. I felt considerable regard for Odinga, who had many excellent qualities; and although I thought some of his conduct misguided, I hoped that the sagacious Kenyatta might still be able to persuade him into wiser ways. In any case it was better for the Prime Minister (in his own words) to 'give Odinga enough rope to hang himself' – if that was to be his ultimate political fate – rather than that Kenyatta should appear to be an over-eager executioner. My private support may have strengthened the Premier's confidence in his own judgment, but even if I had disagreed with him I am sure he would not have altered his mind.

I need not go into further detail. The situation dragged on; Odinga continued his subversive activities with increasingly fruitful results, and also with growing indiscretion as his self-assurance swelled. Eventually it appeared that he was about to win a decisive victory; and his Ministerial critics grew desperate. Then Kenyatta struck his first warning blow at Odinga – and struck very hard. The issue concerned the choice of a few individuals to fill vacancies on the executive committee of the KANU Parliamentary party. Odinga thought he had bribed enough back-bench members to ensure the election of candidates who would support him, and who would secure a majority for his views in that crucially important body. Suddenly Kenyatta came out in opposition to them, gave his blessing to rival nominees, and gained their election. The political war continued, but a battle had been won which turned the tide in the fighting. From that moment the Prime Minister asserted his authority with no wavering. Often he acted with patience and subtlety, and invariably with well calculated timing – and all Odinga's rearguard actions failed to avert his ultimate humiliating defeat.

*

A certain element in Kenyatta's personality always interested me. How much was his thinking on political matters influenced by his contact with British ideas during the fourteen years that he lived in England? Fundamentally he was of course an African who reacted to events in ways native to the African temperament. Thus, the strong touch of personal authoritarianism in his leadership sprang from deep roots originating in the traditional powers of tribal chiefs. At the same time his inclination to base all his important actions on popular opinion was also an indigenous African instinct, growing from the custom in many tribes to hold *barazas* for the discussion of significant affairs. Those *barazas* were gatherings of the whole adult male population of a tribe at which their elders presented problems to them for collective consideration before final decisions on policy were taken. The subsequent discussion often lasted several days, every individual being free to express his views at any length without inhibition. The elders' ultimate decision was then based on a consensus of tribal opinion.

Yet I think that the democratic tendency in Kenyatta's attitude – including his faith in cabinet and parliamentary rule – owed something also to British political liberalism. He had spent many years of his life in England, working among farm labourers in the fields, gossiping with villagers in pubs, and exchanging opinions with fellow students at the London School of Economics. During that period he admired and partly imbibed various British habits of mind. In discussing propositions with him I often felt that his approach was partially un-African, influenced by notions with which he became familiar in England (as well, perhaps, as during his earlier missionary schooling in his native Kikuyu-land). Yet the trait was of secondary importance in his make-up. Fundamentally he was an African in general and a Kikuyu in particular, and on all vital questions his mental and emotional reactions were profoundly African.

This mixture was illustrated by his marital arrangements. Among the Kikuyu as well as other tribes in East Africa polygamy was universally accepted, and Kenyatta had married several successive and still living wives who all bore him children. But whereas most of his colleagues who practised polygamy cohabited simultaneously with two or more spouses, he lived with only his latest one. The others were his acknowledged wives, and he supported them in their different homes; but they were, so to speak, parts of the earlier history of his life, not of his contemporary activities.

One of those wives was an English school teacher whom he married during his years in England. The pair had a highly intelligent son who, in the early 1960s, was an undergraduate at Cambridge. He and his mother both came to the Independence celebrations in Nairobi in 1963 as Kenyatta's special guests. It was charming to see the affectionate relationship which existed not only between the Prime Minister and the English Mrs Kenyatta, but also between her and his latest, much younger black wife named Mama Ngina. In all the ceremonies Mama Ngina appeared as the Premier's consort, the first lady in the land after Audrey, who occupied that position *ex officio* as the Governor-General's partner. Kenyatta's English wife never intruded into that eminent position; but she always sat in a place of honour among the principal guests, and was received cordially as one of his still undivorced wives in accordance with Kikuyu custom.

*

Kenyatta's proud African nature was illustrated by an incident which occurred just before the inauguration of the Republic, when I was about to move out of State House as Governor-General and he was due to move into it as President. For some time I had been transforming much of the interior furnishings of the great mansion. When I arrived there as Governor two years earlier it had appeared like the home of some English aristocrat situated in London's Mayfair. The tables and chairs, sofas, pictures, *objets d'art* and other contents arranged through its rooms were all British or European. Except for a couple of Zanzibar chests in a back corridor, there was no touch of Africa anywhere. Yet this was supposed to be the official residence of the Head of State of Kenya, an abode which should be redolent of the Kenyan soil and expressive of Kenyan character and culture.

So I began to Africanise much of it. Naturally a lot of the furniture could not be banished, but I took down the English landscape paintings adorning its entrance hall and replaced them by decorative Kikuyu, Luo and other tribal shields and spears; removed specimens of European porcelain, silver and similar wares from mantelpieces and cabinets in the State rooms, and substituted fine examples of Wakamba wood carvings, Kisii soap-stone figurines and other Kenyan handicrafts; and hung paintings and batiks by talented contemporary Kenyan artists (both African and European) on the walls in the most important rooms. I also introduced additional African creations like Congolese masks, Nigerian sculptures and Ghanaian stools into the place.

I thought it would be excellent to adorn some of the public corridors and smaller rooms with a number of Joy Adamson's water-colour portraits of Kenyan tribal types. Mrs Adamson's genius is many-sided; besides being the introducer of the famous lioness Elsa to the world, she is (I am told) a pianist of high concert standard, and (I know) a gifted artist. Her numerous fine paintings of East African wild flowers are exhibited in the National Museum in Nairobi, and that institution also owns a few hundred sketches made by her of men, women and children belonging to various Kenyan tribes dressed in the traditional costumes which they wore on ceremonial occasions – and which have now become mostly extinct because of the spread of modern, more Westernised fashions in dress. Some of these colourful pictures were displayed in one of the museum's galleries, but I found many others stored away in cupboards there.

I thought a selection of them would look splendid hanging in State House, and so I proposed to show them to Kenyatta to seek his opinion. Some of my European advisers warned me against this, fearing that he would feel offended and indeed insulted at the suggestion that rooms in the Presidential palace-to-be should be adorned with representations of his simple, illiterate fellow-countrymen clad in primitive costumes – or in some cases virtual lack of costumes. He would think I was adopting a patronising attitude towards those folks, exhibiting portraits of them as 'savage' natives to be displayed as museum specimens.

Needless to say, this was not my attitude. In my judgment their portraits were not only historically important but also aesthetically pleasing, and brilliantly illustrative of the characterful past of various Kenyan tribes. I realised, however, that my counsellors' concern about Kenyatta's reaction might be justified; so I was rather non-committal when I broached the subject to him. I told him that I had an idea about the interior decoration of his future official residence which he might think good or he might think bad, and that I would like to show him some samples of it for his consideration.

When he came to State House to view them he brought with him his colleague Joe Murumbi, who had considerable knowledge and good taste in artistic matters. In preparation for their arrival I laid on a table in my study a dozen specimens of Joy Adamson's works. As soon as the two visitors set eyes on them they became very excited, starting at once to examine every detail of the head-dresses, facial pigmentations, ear ornaments, necklaces and clothing, commenting on the accuracy of various items of adornment, and remarking regretfully how this or that traditional piece of decoration was no longer used. For a long time they studied and re-studied every portrait with enthusiasm and admiration. Kenyatta welcomed the idea of having about seventy of them framed and hung in State House, feeling proud of the vivid impression they would preserve of his compatriots in their ancient native garbs.

And there the water-colour sketches have hung ever since, adding distinction to the rooms of the great mansion.

*

Naturally, not all Kenyatta's characteristics are praiseworthy. He himself would be the first to admit that, like all human beings, he has his faults as well as his virtues, his weaknesses as well as his strengths – although I doubt whether he would agree with some of my judgments on what those weaknesses are!

To start with an example in light-hearted vein, I do not think he is a good architect. He may be a great nation builder, but he is a poor house builder. Among other creations he conceived the new dwelling which is his family home on his farm at Gatundu. With characteristic self assurance he sketched a plan of the residence-to-be, and ordered the workmen to construct it accordingly. But that was not all. As it gradually rose from its foundations he kept changing his mind about this or that detail, and instructed the brick-layers to alter what they were doing. Quite often those revisions affected bits of the place already built, and involved pulling down a stretch of wall, a half-finished staircase, a doorway, or some other feature which he had previously favoured. The concoction was therefore ever changeable, remaining of uncertain design until the final tile was at last laid on its roof. I cannot say that I think the result is a gem of architecture.

Many people outside Kenya criticise Kenyatta and his Ministers for their treatment of sections of its Asian population; and I agree that they are partly responsible for the unfortunate situation in which those people find themselves. But the blame must be shared also by British governments which for a long time refused to negotiate the sensible settlement of the problem which the Kenyan authorities were ready to conclude. However, the main fault lies with many of the Asians themselves, because they did not show loyalty to independent Kenya, sometimes sought to break its laws, and continuously treated black Africans as inferiors. Large numbers of local Asians who have behaved properly are welcomed by the government as citizens of their multi-tribal and multi-racial nation.

One of Kenyatta's most serious errors is his tacit assent to the acquisitiveness of some of his Ministers and civil servants. Soon after attaining power they began to buy (sometimes with money gained by dubious means) large houses, farms, motor cars and other possessions. This development not only tainted his administration with a reputation for corruption, but also produced a wide economic division between governors and governed, the former becoming rich 'Haves' whilst many of the others remained poor 'Have-nots'. Large sections of the humbler citizens in Kenya did gain materially from 'Uhuru', enjoying a higher or more secure standard of living than they had known hitherto; but others received no such benefit. Naturally Ministers and civil servants were entitled to all the normal privileges of their posts, in which they performed fine services for the nation; but some of their rewards far exceeded what they earned.

In many newly independent nations, both inside and outside Africa, similar conduct by politicians has become more or less accepted practice, just as such behaviour marked British, European and American societies in comparable stages of their political development – and, indeed, still persists among them in certain forms. It is also true that in numerous other African countries corruption and nepotism have thrived on a much larger scale than in Kenya. Nevertheless, it would have been more prudent as well as moral if Kenyatta had enforced on his colleagues and subordinates a stricter code of conduct, preventing them from becoming such a conspicuously privileged class. Widespread criticism of the present situation has shaken confidence in the regime, and this may have prejudicial results on national unity and stability when Kenyatta's powerful presence disappears from the scene.

Incidentally, President Nyerere in neighbouring Tanzania

has asserted his authority in a courageous attempt to establish greater integrity among Ministers and civil servants. Whether he will succeed in maintaining this at present somewhat un-African policy remains to be seen. Nyerere is an immensely gifted African leader who may well become another Titan among contemporary men.

*

In 1966 my diplomatic duties were extended to include various other lands throughout Africa in addition to Kenya, and from then onwards I spent comparatively little time in Nairobi. So I lost intimate touch with Kenyan affairs. But whenever I stayed there for a while I enjoyed talks with the President, and was always cheered to find how much of his abilities and authority he preserved in spite of his approach to the age of four-score years.

Long live Mzee Jomo Kenyatta!

Index

Index

Adamson, Joy, 276–7
Agung, Tjokorda, Balinese prince, 148
Amery, Rt. Hon. Leopold, politician, 1873–1955, 94–5
Amulree, Lord, 41
Anderson, Sir John, politician, 1882–1958, 95, 102
Athlone, Alexander, Earl of, Gov. Gen. of Canada, 1874–1957, 115, 116
Attlee, Clement, Earl, politician, 1883–1967, 122

Baldwin, Stanley, politician, 1867–1947, 56, 59, 62, 63, 66, 69, 75, 89
Balfour declaration, 1917, 90
Bali, Isle of, 147–9
Beaverbrook, Max Aitken, Lord, politician, 1879–1964, 95, 106–107
Bebel, Ferdinand, German socialist, 1840–1913, 19
Besant, Annie, philosopher, 1847–1933, 25
Bevin, Ernest, politician, 1881–1951, 110
Bibesco, Princess Marthe, 52
Bondfield, Rt. Hon. Margaret, politician, 1873–1953, 25
Bonnet, Roger, painter, 148
Burns, Rt. Hon. John, politician, 1858–1943, 26
Butler, R. A., politician, 91

Cambodia: border disputes, 189–190, 195–7; constitution, 177–8; foreign policy, 185–6, 187, 191; 194–6; independence, 169–173 and India, 131; royal court, 160–5; reforms in, 179–181, republicanism, 170–1
Canada, 106–7
Chamberlain, A. Neville, politician, 1869–1940, 61–2, 75–6, 80, 82, 92, 99
Chou En-lai, premier of China, 153, 215, 229, 230
Churchill, Sir Winston L. S., politician, 1874–1965; in Canada, 115–18; critics of, 109; election defeat, 121; his funeral, 125; his humour, 93, 104, 116; and Ireland, 78, 85; as leader of Opposition, 122–4; and Palestine, 91–9; as Prime Minister, 82, 93; militarism, 97–8, 112, 121; personality, 92, 99, 100–1, 117, 124; and Roosevelt, 112, 114; his writings, 89, 120
Civil Defence, 102, 103
Clarke, Arthur, diplomat, 223, 225
Cohen, Harriet, pianist, 52
Commonwealth, 66–8, 71–2, 81; *see also* independence
Communism, 31, 32, 194–5, 197
Conservative Party; and Ireland, 57, 59, 60–2, 73, 78; and Ramsay MacDonald, 13; also 29, 33, 36, 37, 44, 119
Cooper, Alfred Duff, politician 1890–1954, 105
Co-operative societies, 30

Craigavon, Lord, Irish politician, 78
Cripps, Rt. Hon. Sir Stafford, politician, 1881–1959, 109–10
Crookes, Will, 25
Cunliffe-Lister, Philip, 105

Dawson, Lord, 35–6
De Valera, Eamon, President of Eire: blindness, 56; and Conservatives, 57, 60–2; and Irish unity, 64, 70, 74, 76, 84; nationalism, 56, 65, 83; and prisons, 79–80; republicanism, 56, 66–8; personality, 65, 73–4, 75–7, 86
Depression, 1929, 37–9
Dulanty, John, diplomat, 56, 57, 63
Dulles, J. Foster, U.S. Sec. for State, 1888–1959, 187, 222
Dunkirk, 95

East Indies, Netherlands, 131; *see also* Indonesia
Eden, Sir Anthony (Earl of Avon), politician, 95, 223, 224
Edward VIII, King, 66–8, 103

Fabian Society, 24

Gandhi, Indira, Indian politician, 206, 210, 214
Gandhi, Mahatma, 1869–1948, 131, 169, 210, 218–19
General election: 1906, 24; 1918, 28; 1922, 29, 32; 1923, 33; 1924, 36; 1945, 121–2
George V, King, 35, 40, 56
George VI, King, 68, 103, 121
Gichuru, James, Kenyan politician, 244, 268
Gladstone, Margaret Ethel (later MacDonald), 16
Gladstone, William Ewart, politician, 16
Glazier, Bruce, journalist, 25

Hailsham, Viscount (later Hogg, Quintin), politician, 60
Halifax, Edward, Lord, 1881–1959, 91, 101, 105, 107, 120, 122–3
Hamilton, Mary Agnes, writer, 52
Hankey, Maurice, politician, 47
Hardie, Keir, politician, 1856–1915, 24–5, 27
Henderson, Rt. Hon. Arthur, politician, 1864–1937, 25, 38, 41, 42
Hertzog, Gen. James, South African politician, 1866–1942; 66, 71
Hinduism, 216, 227, 228
Hitler, Adolf, 1889–1945, 47, 80, 92
Ho Chi Minh, 169
Hoare, Sir Samuel, diplomat, 79
Hodge, Rt. Hon. John, politician, 25
Hopkins, Harry, Presidential aide, 1890–1946, 117–18

Imperial Conference, 1926, 69
Independence of colonies; in Africa, 72, 208, 240, 241, 249; in Asia, 72, 131–9, 143, 165–9
India: independence, 45, 72, 131, 208; problems in, 216; reforms in, 217–18; Round Table conference, 1930, 46; *see also* Hinduism, Nehru
Indonesia, 135–9
Ireland, 55–85
Irian, West, *see* New Guinea
Irish Agreement, 75–9, 82
Ismay, Lord (General 'Pug'), 1887–1965, 111

Jaurès, Jean, French politician, 1884–1963, 19

Kashmir, 227–9
Kennedy, John, President of U.S.A., 1960-1963, 222
Kenya: Asians, 278; constitution, 243–251; elections in, 247–51; independence, 243, 249, 260; reforms in, 267–8; as republic, 269; tribes, 243, 248, 255
Kenyatta, Jomo, Kenyan President; personality, 241, 253, 256–7, 260–2, 263–5, 274–5, 278–9; as President, 270–80; as Prime Minister, 252–69; as reformer, 267–8; temperance, 242, 244, 245, 260; vigour, 253, 259; wisdom, 247; also 153
Kikuyu, *see* Kenya, tribes
King, Rt. Hon. W. L. Mackenzie, Prime Minister of Canada, 1874–1950, 106, 112, 116–17
Kruschev, Nikita, Soviet politician, 1894–1971, 215

Labour League, Women's, 20
Labour Party; divisions in, 38–41; early years, 24, 26, 31; in government, 33–4, 36, 37; opinions of, 34–5, 36; also 119
Labour Representation Committee, 1900, 19, 24
Land annuities, 56
Lausanne Conference, 1932, 46
Leakey, Louis S. B., anthropologist, 263–4
Lemass, Sean, 58
Liberal Party, 13, 24, 29, 34, 36, 59
Litvinov, Soviet socialist, 33
Londonderry, Marchioness of, 52
Lyttelton, Oliver (Lord Chandos), politician, 106
MacDonald, Alister Ramsay, 22
MacDonald, Audrey, 213, 242, 269, 275
MacDonald, Ishbel R., 22
MacDonald, James Ramsay, politician, 1866–1937: birth, 15; as Foreign Sec., 37; home life, 16–23, 30–1; and India, 45–6; as leader of Labour Party, 24, 26, 29; as leader of Opposition, 29, 37; as Lord President of Council, 48; pacifism, 26–8; personality, 48–52; philosophy, 26–7, 30–3, 47; as Prime Minister, 37, 41–4; public image, 13–14, 27–8, 32, 37–8, 48; religion, 21; as Sec. of Labour Rep. Committee, 24; writings, 31, 32, 52
MacDonald, Malcolm: and abdication of Edward VIII, 66–72; in Africa, 125, 239–280; in Asia, 46, 122, 124, 121–235; in Canada, 106–18; childhood, 17–23, 30–1; and Ireland, 57–65; as M.P., 38, 40, 42, 45, 48, 82–3, 94; as Sec. of State for Colonies, 90, 93; as Sec. of State for Dominion Affairs, 55, 66, 70
MacDonald, Margaret Ethel Ramsay, 16–23, 52
Mackenzie, Bruce, politician, 257–8
Macmillan, Rt. Hon. Harold, politician, 106
Malaya, 132
Malinowski, Prof. Bronislaw, anthropologist, 1884–1942, 263
Mao Tse-tung, Chinese politician, 153
Marxism, 29–30, *see also* Communism
Mboya, Tom, Kenyan politician, 1930–1969, 244, 268

Monarchy, 66–72
Morley, Lord, politician, 1838–1923, 26
Morrison, Herbert, politician, 1888–1965, 43, 44, 102
Mountbatten, Lord Louis, 203
Munich Agreement, 1938, 80, 81, 92
Murumbi, Joseph, Kenyan politician, 277

National Government, 1931, 13, 32, 38, 41–4
Navy, British, 56, 82–3
Nehru, Pandit Jawaharlal, Indian politician, 1889–1964: aggression, 226; artistic taste, 213–14; and British, 207–8; and China, 229–31; energy of, 211, 232; foreign policy, 229–31; and Kashmir, 227–9; personality, 205–12; as politician, 217–22; popularity, 212, 234; and Suez, 223–6; and U.S.S.R., 231; and yoga, 204
Netherlands in Asia, 131, 135, 139, 142
New Guinea, Dutch, 142, 154
Ngala, Ronald, Kenyan politician, 242, 251, 254
Nyerere, Julius Kambarage, President of Tanzania, 279–80

Odinga, Oginga, Kenyan politician, 125–6

Palestine, 90–9
Panch Shila, 226, 229
Patel, Sardar, Indian politician, 217
Pearl Harbour, 108
Prasad, Rajendra, Indian politician, 1884–1963, 215

Ramsay, Annie, d. 1910, 15, 23
Roosevelt, Franklin Delano, President of U.S.A., 1882–1943, 107–8, 112, 114, 116–17
Russian revolution, 29, 31

Sandys, Rt. Hon. Duncan, politician, 239, 250–1
Sankey, Lord, politician, 1866–1948, 41, 42
Sharjir, Dr., Indonesian politician, 133–5
Shaw, George Bernard, writer, 1856–1950, 25
Sihanouk, Prince of Cambodia: abdication, 178; exile, 198, 200; hobbies, 161, 163–4, 167–8, 180, 183–4; personality, 160, 162–3, 167–9, 192–3; as politician, 168–173, 174, 185–6, 187, 191, 199; popularity, 175–177, 182–3, 199, *see also* Cambodia
Sikorski, Gen. Wladyslaw, Polish leader, 1881–1943, 105
Simon, John, politician, 1881–1951, 66
Simpson, Mrs., 69
Snowden, Philip, Viscount, politician, 1864–1937, 25, 38, 39, 41, 44
Socialism, 25, 29–30, 31
Suez crisis, 223–6
Sukarno, Achmad, Indonesian politician, 1901–1970; artistic taste, 141; and Great Britain, 135, 143; personality, 135–8, 145, 149–50, 151–2, 153; as politician, 152–5; popularity, 150; promiscuity, 145–6; religion, 144; also, 169

Taoiseach, *see* De Valera
Thomas, Rt. Hon. James, politician, 1874–1949, 41, 55
Tibet, invasion of, 230

Tobruk, 103, 109
Trade unions, 30, 39
Trotsky, Leon, 1879–1940, 33

Ulster, 56, 64, 78, 84
Unemployment benefits, 39, 40
United Nations Organisation, 114–15

Vandervelde, socialist, 19

Versailles Treaty, 29, 37
Vietnam, 165–6, 171–2, 186

War, First World, 26–8
War, Second World, 93–121
Webb, Beatrice, socialist, 1858–1943, 25
Webb, Sidney, socialist, 1859–1947, 25
Wilkinson, Ellen, 95